A Lady's Peninsular War Experiences

ELIZABETH, LADY HOLLAND IN THE EARLY DAYS OF HER
MARRIED LIFE WITH SIR GODFREY WEBSTER. SHE HERE
APPEARS IN FANCY DRESS AS A 'VIRGIN OF THE SUN.'

A Lady's Peninsular War Experiences

The Spanish Journal of
Elizabeth, Lady Holland 1808–1809

Elizabeth, Lady Holland

LEONAUR

A Lady's Peninsular War Experiences
The Spanish Journal of Elizabeth, Lady Holland 1808-1809
by Elizabeth, Lady Holland

FIRST EDITION

Leonaur is an imprint
of Oakpast Ltd

ISBN: 978-1-78282-471-8 (hardcover)
ISBN: 978-1-78282-472-5 (softcover)

http://www.leonaur.com

Publisher's Notes

Contents

Preface

This *Journal* deals almost exclusively with the incidents of the early part of the Peninsular War. Lord Holland's name was well known in Spain, and his sympathy with the cause was apparent to many outside his own circle of friends. Thus he was in a position to obtain much information which would not have been vouchsafed to the ordinary traveller.

It was Lady Holland's daily habit to jot down the reports which were received from the front and the information which she collected from Spanish sources. Her narrative is, therefore, often disjointed, and I have endeavoured, by means of brief notes, to compare her version with the various histories of the war now at our disposal. Especially to Mr. Oman's invaluable work am I indebted for much of the information which has enabled me to link together the incidents which she records.

During the stay of the Hollands in Seville they were in close communication with many members of the Central *Junta*. Naturally, their views on the situation carried much weight, and Lady Holland's remarks are frequently tinged with a thoroughly Spanish flavour. This is especially noticeable in her comments on Moore and his campaign. Frere was at her elbow, despatches were continually arriving from La Romana the two men who had considered themselves slighted by the British general; and it was as yet too early for the inhabitants of the South to realise the debt of gratitude which in reality they owed to Moore for his strategic retreat.

It is curious to note in contemporary records of the war the complete spirit of self-satisfaction in which the Spanish leaders were accustomed to pencil their despatches, whatever was the nature of their contents. Defeat was often described on paper as victory, and the truth of a report was sometimes only to be judged in the light of subsequent events.

It can be no matter of surprise that on the spot it was difficult to differentiate between fact and fancy. Even in dealing with letters from British commanders a remarkable divergence of opinion is manifest. This is well illustrated by those from Lord Paget and Sir Robert Wilson, which are included in the Appendix.

Though operating only a few hundred miles apart, their ideas of the Spanish character and disposition will be found to be entirely different. The one mistrusted every action, report, or emissary of the Spaniards; the other praised their perseverance and their ardour in the cause of liberty. The *Journal* is thus valuable as a sidelight upon the history of the war, and as evidence of the contradictory rumours and petty jealousies which were so common at the time. I have taken the opportunity of inserting a number of unpublished letters in the Appendix, which may be of some interest to students of these early campaigns.

It should be clearly stated that Lord Holland was travelling entirely for his own pleasure. He had no official position of any kind in 1808-09, though it appears from the Buckingham Memoirs that some hope of the offer of an Ambassadorship to Spain was held out to him in 1811, as a bait to gain his support for the government. Indeed, in a letter enclosing passports, dated October 1808 (Holland House MSS.), Canning definitely requested him to be careful to make it clear to the Spaniards that his communications with them were in no way authorised by the British Government.

He even warned him that he held himself at liberty, if necessary, to take steps to prevent such misapprehensions. Lord Holland was not at one with his party on the subject of Spain. He was throughout an ardent supporter of the war and was always convinced that, with outside assistance, the patriotic spirit of the Spaniards would in time prevail against their oppressors.

From a recently discovered paper I am also now able to give further and more correct details of the early pedigree of the Vassall family. It appears from the account I have before me, entitled '1588 to 1831' that one Samuel Vassall died, leaving a son, John, who married Anna Lewis. Four sons were born of this marriage, John, William, Henry, Leonard. William, the second son, married Miss Mills, and left Bathsheba (who died unmarried) and Florentius, Lady Holland's grandfather.

The original spelling and punctuation of the *Journal* has not been retained. In the case of proper names especially, where confusion

might easily arise, alteration has been made, and the more usually recognised Spanish version, taken from *Arteche* and *Toreno*, &c., has been
substituted. A map of Spain and Portugal has been added, showing the
principal places mentioned in the text.

Ilchester.

August 1910.

Lady Holland's Journal 1808-1809

During the three years which had passed since the Hollands left Spain in 1805, many events of importance had taken place in that country and in Portugal. War had broken out between England and Spain early in 1805, but Napoleon's hopes of a naval supremacy had been dashed to the ground by the defeat of the joint fleets of France and Spain at Trafalgar. Godoy himself, though nominally in alliance with France, was casting about for means of escape from the thraldom of the emperor; while Ferdinand the heir-apparent was openly desirous of peace, and looked to ah alliance with England as the only means of saving his country. For Napoleon's plans for bringing the whole of the Peninsula under his sway had gradually been maturing. Portugal had been occupied by Junot in 1807 with a large force of French troops, and the Royal family had been forced to take refuge across the seas in far distant Brazil. Nominally for that purpose troops had been massed in Spain, but it ere long became plain to all observers that the yoke of France was soon to be extended over her so-called ally. Events played into the emperor's hands, and dissentions between Charles IV and Ferdinand made it easy for him to entice them both across the frontier to Bayonne, there to submit to whatever terms he chose to dictate.

The folly and instability of the rulers of Spain was easily overcome, but not so the people themselves. The rising in Madrid of the 'Dos de Mayo' was but a signal for similar riots and insurrections in every part of the country. Emissaries were sent early in May (1808) from the Northern provinces to England to ask for aid. The government was sufficiently impressed by their patriotic spirit and earnestness of purpose to decide upon affording immediate assistance. Money and arms in large quantities were sent out; while agents, both military and civil, were dispatched to the various provinces to confer with the Spanish leaders. At the same time a force collected for other employment was diverted to Portugal. They were landed in July, and under Wellesley defeated Junot at Vimiero. The Convention of Cintra followed, and secured the evacuation of Portugal by the French.

After the abdication of the Spanish Bourbons Napoleon had given the crown to his brother Joseph, whose entry into his capital in July took place at an inauspicious moment. Throughout the summer the Spanish armies had more than held their own: but within ten days of his arrival came the news of Dupont's capitulation at Baylen, and the new king was forced again to retire behind the Ebro.

It was at this period that the Hollands embarked on their second visit to the Peninsula. Their decision to undertake the journey was probably made some months previously, and it is likely that Lord John Russell was induced to join their party when the Hollands were staying at Woburn in July. He accompanied them throughout the expedition, and also kept a journal of their movements, which is quoted by Sir Spencer Walpole in his Life. Lord Holland was in close touch with the Spanish emissaries during their stay in England. The glowing accounts of the enthusiasm and successes of their compatriots would have eradicated any fears which might have arisen, regarding the advisability of attempting the journey at such a time and the probable difficulties of travel. It was not then known that Napoleon was straining every nerve to revenge the recent checks sustained by his arms in the Peninsula, and many months had elapsed before the real numbers of the French troops in Spain were even suspected in England.

The Hollands left London for Falmouth on Oct. 9, but it was not until the first days of November that they landed at Coruña. The complexion of affairs in Spain had assumed a more serious aspect during those weeks of waiting, owing to the increased activity of the French. Sir John Moore had taken over, early in October, the command in Portugal of the British troops destined for an advance to Madrid and the Ebro. The intelligence as to the best routes for his troops to follow was lamentably scarce, and neither the Spanish nor Portuguese authorities seemed able to give him any information as to the state of the roads. What little knowledge Moore could obtain was faulty, and he was thereby induced to send his cavalry and artillery under Hope by the circuitous route of Elvas and Escorial to join at Salamanca the rest of his force, which was moving by the direct routes to that city. Of necessity a long delay occurred in this way, which completely altered the character of the campaign. To co-operate in the North with

Moore and effect a junction with him as soon as practicable, a force of over 12,000 troops under Sir David Baird were shipped from England to Coruña. The first transports arrived there on Oct. 13, but owing to the action of the Spanish authorities, no troops were landed until Oct. 26. The disembarkation of the infantry was only concluded on Nov. 4, the date upon which Lady Holland again takes up her pen.

On Sunday, 9th October, we set off to Falmouth in hopes of being able to get there in time to embark with the expedition to Spain. Our party consisted of ourselves Mr. Allen, Chester, and Ld. John Russell (who overtook us near Andover), 2 maids, and five men; two carriages only, being resolved to take as few persons and encumbrances as possible. On the road near Bridport, we heard of the departure of the expedition, but nevertheless continued hastening on to Falmouth in hopes some lagging transports might remain for a convoy. Reached Falmouth early on Thursday; pleasantly lodged in a house at the skirts of the town. We had obtained Ld. Mulgrave's, (Lord Mulgrave was First Lord of the Admiralty from 1807 till 1810), permission to go in any king's ship, so our only difficulty was to get an accommodating captain. Fortunately Edward Young received Admiralty orders to send round from Plymouth the *Amazon* to convoy four transports which had arrived, like ourselves, too late. The commander, Capt. Parker, offered us a passage.

★★★★★★

Sir William Parker (1781-1866), Admiral of the Fleet, who was in command of the *Amazon* for eleven years. He was created a Baronet in 1844 for his services in the Chinese War.) Mr. Ward in a letter to Mrs. Stewart (*Letters to Ivy*), dated Falmouth, Oct. 21, says, 'Lady H. has resolved to force herself on board it (the *Amazon*), in spite of the evident reluctance of poor Captain Parker, who has some friends of his own going with him.' Ward was, however, no friend of Lady Holland's, from expressions of his own in the same letter and a tirade against her badness of heart. His feelings were evidently fully reciprocated.

★★★★★★

At length after waiting upwards of a fortnight, on Sunday, the 30th, we embarked on board the *Amazon*, After a delightful passage of five days, we reached Coruña. I never thought it could have been possible to have felt regret at leaving a ship, but Capt. Parker's was so pleasant that longer stay *even* on board would not have been irksome. He is a nephew of Ld. St. Vincent's, and he has the reputation of being

13

worthy of his relationship. To those who only know the interior of a man-of-war from *Roderick Random* the difference between the reality and the description is striking. The order, civility, discipline, and cleanliness is astonishing. We admired Capt. Parker's manner on deck; without losing his dignity towards his officers and men, they approach him with respect and friendship, not terror. Mr. Tennant, (William Tennant, Esq., of Aston Hall), a Staffordshire gentleman, a friend and countryman of Capt. P. was on board; he is married to a daughter of Ld. Yarborough's.

We were delayed by the convoy, otherwise we should have made our passage in less than 50 hours. Once or twice I was alarmed by the report of strange sails and the bustle in consequence of pursuing them, but they were only our own cruisers. The French are sending out corvettes to the Islands, and now and then they hazard a pair of frigates. By daybreak we lay before Coruña, and entered the harbour early. Appearance of the town, castle, and fortifications very pleasing. The shores are rocky and barren, and the waves of the Bay of Biscay strike against them with great fury, and produce very constantly a good deal of surf. A high building, called the Tower of Hercules, is the lighthouse. The Galicians complain of their poverty, and make that an excuse for not lighting it.

Admiral de Courcy came on board to make a visit to Ld. Hd. He seems to be a very excellent, goodhearted man: he is the commander on this station. He confirmed the stories we had heard of the unwillingness of the Spaniards to receive our troops. It appears that the arrived without having obtained permission from the Central *Junta* (at Madrid) to disembark; at length when leave was procured the expedition quartermasters, commissioners, &c., &c., had been so negligent or ignorant, that the troops were many of them 36 hours without food.

★★★★★★

Lady Holland mentions later in these pages that Saavedra told Lord Holland that Santander was actually decided upon as the landing place for Baird's troops, and attributed the subsequent disasters in the Asturias to this change of plan. No allusion to such an arrangement is made by Arteche or Toreno. The British government considered that ports like Gijon and Santander were too small for the disembarkation of so large a force, and that Galicia would be best able to victual the army. Napier states that the Galician *Junta* tried to drive them to another port in order to save themselves trouble. No answer was received from the Central *Junta* for thirteen days.

★★★★★★

Great difficulties also arose from want of money. Several Spaniards came out to offer us their services in their own names and those of the ladies. We dined on board, and in the evening landed and found, to my very great dismay, two coaches full of ladies who had been waiting near two hours to receive me on my landing and to conduct me to my house. One was the wife of Sangro, the Galician deputy, the others, Madame Mosquera, Marquesa de Vianze (*sic*) , &c. (Sangro was one of the five Spanish deputies sent over to England during the summer of 1808 to implore aid against the French.)

The house which they had procured for us was thoroughly in the Spanish fashion, spacious, but *totally* void of furniture. Afterwards we went to a *tertulia* at Mde. Mosquera's. The Duque de Veragua, a *grandee* and descendant of Columbus, told us he had received accounts from Astorga informing him that Romana, who had set off *en pasta* from hence to Madrid, had there received orders to proceed directly to the army, without going to the Central *Junta* for instructions.

★★★★★★

At the time of the first risings in Spain La Romana was in command of a Spanish force in French service stationed in Denmark. These troops he contrived to embark in transports lent him by the English, and landed them at Santander on Oct. 11. He himself visited England on his way, and arrived at Coruña on Oct. 20, by the same ship which brought Frere. He went at once to Madrid, but was sent after the Battle of Zornosa to supersede Blake.

★★★★★★

They describe the reception given to Romana by the people as being touching; they drew the carriage, an honour never bestowed upon any person in Spain before, dragged him along the principal streets, and were only interrupted by acclamations of '*Viva, Viva!*' He was quite overcome, and sobbed aloud; as soon as he could speak he addressed them and said these testimonies of their attachment were gratifying, but they were not due to him, that the praise belonged to the army, for he only felt in common with them, and shared an impulse which their own generous character had excited.

The Freres proceeded straight to Madrid. (John Hookham Frere had again been appointed Minister to Spain, and arrived at Coruña, accompanied by his brother, on Oct. 20).

15

On Friday we dined at Mde. Sangro's; Capt. Parker and Mr. Tennant were there, and the rest of the party was composed of Spaniards. An offensive old *debauchée*, who is the Governor of Coruña, prevented me from deriving any pleasure whatever from the society; he is the author of a maritime dictionary, his name is Alcedo, Don Antonio de Alcedo, a Spanish American, and author of a dictionary of America and the West Indies, published 1786-1789); he becomes nearly frantic after drinking punch, and descants on topics that are rarely discussed before women. Went in the evening to the theatre; very tolerable exhibition, in the midst of which, unfortunately, I was seized with a sudden illness, and fell down in a fainting fit which lasted me some time, the consequence probably, of the sea voyage, where those who are not sick on board suffer afterwards for that exemption.

Saturday.—Capt. Parker, Mr. Tennant, and Ward dined with us; we could not boast of our comforts yet. Went to the play, and with great regret took leave of our shipmates. The *Amazon* was ordered off Ushant.

★★★★★★

Hon. John William Ward (1781-1833), first Earl of Dudley, eldest son of William, third Viscount Dudley. He had left Falmouth on Oct. 22 in a packet bound for Coruña, but was back in the former port on the 25th, owing to adverse winds and bad weather. He appears, from a subsequent letter from Captain Parker to Lord Holland, to have returned to England about Dec. 1.

★★★★★★

10th November, Coruña.—Walked with Mr. Allen to the lighthouse about a mile and three-quarters from the town. The view of the town and harbour, now filled with shipping, is very magnificent. We saw some Spanish recruits exercising; they were healthy, well-looking young men, clothed rudely, but did not appear the less military. It is a glorious sight to behold the population of a country turning out with zeal in a fresh cause and against such an enemy. The English cavalry were landing in small detachments from the transports; though not very well conducted for want of proper preparations to facilitate their disembarking, few horses perished. Met many acquaintances in the streets; Frederick Howard, Clifford, Baron Robeck, &c. Mr. Lemon on his way to Cadiz; a Capt. Gordon, recommended by Sydney Smith; Ld. Paget, uncommonly obliging and pleasing. The Spaniards very much struck with his beauty; they call him an '*arrogante mozo y muy bizarre,*' (a haughty young man and very gallant).

******

Major the Hon. Frederick Howard, third son of Frederick, fifth Earl of Carlisle, an officer in the 10th Hussars. Born in 1785: killed at Waterloo. John Michael Henry Fock, Baron de Robeck (1790-1856), a cornet in the 7th Hussars. His mother was a niece of John, first Earl of Upper Ossory. Henry William, Lord Paget (1768-1854), afterwards Earl of Uxbridge and Marquess of Anglesey. He reached the rank of lieutenant-general in April 1808, and was given command of Sir David Baird's cavalry division.

******

The dress of the officers excites more wonder than admiration; they observe that it is not warm for winter, nor cool for summer, and utterly inconvenient in a campaign. The height and size of the Englishmen surprises them; the physical difference is very apparent. The ladies praise the complexion, blue eyes, and height of the men, but complain of want of expression in their countenances, and delicacy in the shape of the limbs, especially about the knees; they add that they are in general '*muy frios!*' (very cold).

Freire, Admiral de Courcy, and Fred. Howard dined with us. (Manoel Freire (1765-1834), Spanish general, who served with distinction throughout the war.)

In the evening the ball, which had properly been put off on account of the bad news from Blake's army, was, with more civility to me than discretion with respect to the public feeling, fixed for this evening at Mosquera's.

******

The Battle of Zornosa on Oct. 31, in which Blake made but a feeble resistance, but was able to draw oft his forces without serious loss. Joachim Blake (1759-1827) was member of an Irish family settled in Spain. He was colonel of a Spanish regiment when appointed Captain-General of Galicia at the commencement of the war, and had no experience whatever of handling troops. He was superseded by the *Junta* after the Battle of Zornosa, and the command given to La Romana. The intelligence, however, never reached him till after his second defeat at Espinosa. La Romana joined him at Renedo on Nov. 15, but did not actually take over the management of the scattered remnants of the army until they had reached the neighbourhood of Leon. Blake obtained further employment in Catalonia and Valencia. He was taken prisoner in 1812, and sent to France.

★★★★★★

I called for Ld. Paget, and took him and F. Howard. The ladies were sitting, according to the Spanish custom, all round the room on chairs close to the wall. I had to run the gauntlet along a whole range of them, till La Mosquera seated me on the couch. The middle of the room was occupied entirely by men, chiefly English officers. The dancing was bad, and the women, out of their own costume of the *basquiña* and *mantilla*, awkward and ill-dressed. A gavotte was danced by Mde. Sangro, and a few national dances at my request. A Spanish general arrived from Oporto during the ball. The absence of the young men who are at the army, and the decorous behaviour of their wives, mistresses, &c., who abstained from appearing in public under these circumstances, deprived the ball of much gaiety; however, it went off very tolerably well.

The reports of Blake's death at Zornosa are so various and contradictory, that one hardly knows how much to give credit to. The only information which is avowed is contained in his letter to the Central *Junta*, which was published here, and a letter to his wife, whom he of course encourages by giving hopes of future success. Some persons are dissatisfied that he should be superseded in the command by Romana. Blake is the idol of this province, and was lately chosen their Capt.- General, a preference which is supposed to have contributed greatly towards increasing the animosity already subsisting between him and Cuesta.

★★★★★★

Don Gregorio Garcia de la Cuesta (1740-1812), Capt.-General of Old Castile, commander of the Spanish armies in the Talavera campaign: He resigned his command in 1809, and retired to Majorca, where he died.

★★★★★★

11th Nov.—Mde. Sangro accompanied me to return some of the innumerable visits which the ladies had quite overcome me with. We found several at home. We had to dinner Col. Kennedy, Mr. Ward, Mr. Bruce, and Baron Robeck.

★★★★★★

Captain Kennedy, a British military agent stationed at Coruña by Colonel Doyle, who obtained for him in Madrid the local rank of lieut.-colonel.

★★★★★★

In the evening to the theatre, where there were rumours founded upon obscure letters from Madrid of Castaños having met with a check, of the French crossing the Ebro at Logroño, of their being masters of Burgos, and other stories equally unpleasant. Ld. Paget thought it not impossible that the French might make a push to prevent the junction of our armies, *i.e.* that of Sir John Moore's from Salamanca with Sir David Baird's from Astorga. He apprehends much for the cavalry, their want of forage, &c. Upon the whole all he says appears to proceed from good sense and observation.

★★★★★★

Don Francisco Xavier de Castaños, Duque de Baylen (1756–1852), commander of the Spanish troops in Andalusia, and leader of the Spaniards at Baylen (July 1808). He sustained a severe reverse on the Tudela late in November, and was only employed by the *Junta* in subordinate positions during the remainder of the war.

There was foundation for both these rumours. Pignatelli, who was removed from his command, was forced by Ney to abandon the bridge at Logroño, without even firing a mine in it, and retired on Castaños' force near Tudela. Napoleon himself routed Belvedere at Gamonal on the 10th, and entered Burgos.

★★★★★★

The packet from Falmouth arrived; all well at home. No public event of any importance, except a declaration made at Erfurt by Napoleon that he intends taking the command of his armies in order to place the crown of Spain on the head of his brother, Don Josef (*sic*) Napoleon, and to plant his eagles on the towers of Lisbon.

The jokes against Mr. Ward for his want of nerves, proved by his desire of returning instantly to England, have reached his ears, and to show his courage he is resolved to wait a little time longer at Coruña. His courage is like Falstaff's, who thought discretion the best part of valour! His fickleness and selfish caprice is astonishing; he is a living proof of the misfortune of being an only child and heir to immense wealth. He is whimsical and discontented.

12th Nov. 1808.—Upon hearing that a letter had arrived from Mr. Stuart to D. Baird, Adl. de Courcy was good enough to go and make enquiries. He read the letter dated 3rd, from Aranjuez. It mentions the passage of 13,000 or 17,000 men through Madrid to Burgos; his silence about the army of Castaños is a sort of negative proof that the story circulated here is unfounded, as any disaster which might have taken place at Logroño on the 28th Oct. most have been known by the 3rd.

******

Charles Stuart (1779-1845), afterwards created Lord Stuart de Rothesay. He was *chargé d'affaires* in Madrid until Frere's arrival.

******

Set out for Santiago at 2. In consequence of the doubtful state of the news resolved to return by Coruña for one night, in order to ascertain the truth, and, if very bad, shape our future plans accordingly. The English cavalry barracks just out of the gates made a very cheerful object, the country *très riant*; villages and scattered houses all along the sides of the hills, apparently very populous. The road greatly animated; carts drawn by oxen, full of commodities for the market now so abundantly supplied, in consequence of the great demand.

Arrived at Santiago at about 5 o'clock. Much diverted by meeting on the road two pieces of English artillery *surmounted* by two fat Franciscan friars, sitting astride the cannon; a strong proof of the close alliance between the nations. Entered one of the city gates; narrow streets, well paved, houses built upon arcades within which people walk, and the shops display their contents. Greeted and molested by a concourse of persons crying out '*Viva, Viva*,' in honour of the Alliance. The front of the cathedral is richly but heavily ornamented. We were shown the *relicario*, and went to the treasure; at the latter we were joined by the archbishop, and his attendants. He is a stout, hearty man, nearly sixty years of age. In showing the treasure we were told that Godoy (for now he is never called by any other name) had plundered them upon the pretext of the exigencies of the State.

The archbishop made us walk with him in a sort of procession. He was preceded by a priest carrying the crosier; he took us to a nunnery, which being under his jurisdiction he had the power of granting us permission to visit throughout. The nuns are of the order of St. Francis de Sales; they receive pensioners to educate, and also girls from the town who come during the day. They were delighted at seeing us, chattered away briskly. The archbishop seemed to like patting his young flock under the chin, and giving them little caresses. After seeing everything in *detail*, and the cells of the nuns which are very spacious and airy, we sat in the *salon de recreacion*, where some of the pensioners danced to the thrumming of an old nun upon an instrument between a spinet and virginal; one danced a hornpipe. The good sisters gave me a heap of little articles of their own workmanship, and would have given all their worldly goods.

One nun is a hearty, cheerful woman, a sister of Mosquera's. We returned home to a very early dinner, in order to get out in the *tarde*, (evening), to see with the Archbishop other churches, &c. At three he sent us a present of sweet things, and we went to meet him at San Martin's Convent. He flattered himself that his applying to the Superior would enable me to enter the cloisters, but he met with a positive refusal. It was evident that the man's vanity was gratified in having an opportunity of denying the archbishop's request. San Martin is a rich Benedictine convent, and they told me the monks were better informed than in the other communities. After a very fatiguing day, not the less so from the oppressive importunity of the archbishop, who wanted us to stay another day in order to dine with him, we finally took leave of him at our *posada* door at 6 o'clock.

The archbishop's name is Muzquiz, (D. Rafael de Muzquiz y Aldimate). He was formerly Bishop of Avila until 1801 when he came to Santiago, and three years Confessor to the queen, (he died in 1821). Supposed to have been devoted to Godoy whilst he was powerful. He was the person who instituted that famous suit against the Cuestas, two canons of Valencia, who subscribed to the tenets of a Pastoral letter written by the B. of Palencia, which was supposed to contain some Jansenist doctrines. They were imprisoned and persecuted for several years; one contrived to make his escape into France, the other was in the prisons of the Inquisition whilst we were at Valladolid in 1804.

In the evening we were serenaded by a concert sent from the public authorities—the musicians of the Cathedral. During the intervals between the music, fireworks were displayed, accompanied by acclamations of '*Viva*,' of '*Inglaterra*,' '*Jorge III y Fernando VII*.' At every shout we went out upon the balcony to answer their *Viva*, by *Vivas*, for '*España*,' and '*Fernando*.' The musicians proposed coming upstairs, and they sang some good Italian music. A civil *canonigo*, and Sr. Don Josef Juan Caamaño, now Conde de Maceda in right of his wife, and a member of the *Junta*, came up with them; they were very civil, obliging persons.

★★★★★★

D. Juan José Caamaño y Pardo, Señor de Romelle, married Da.

Ramona Escolástica Pardo de Figuera, VIII Condesa de Maceda, who died in 1838. Her cousin from whom she succeeded to the titles was killed at the Battle of Rioseco in 1808.

★★★★★★

Returned to Coruña, 16th. Pizuela received letters from Valladolid of the date of the 10th. Burgos had been alarmed by the sight of some French troops, several leagues off, but they withdrew, and on the 7th and 8th 13,000 troops belonging to the Army of Estremadura had reached Burgos.

★★★★★★

These were Galluzzo's three divisions, now under the command of the Conde de Belvedere, which were defeated by Napoleon at Gamonal on the 10th. Galluzzo had been superseded on Nov. 2, and recalled to answer certain charges brought against him by the Central *Junta*.

★★★★★★

This intelligence seems so well authenticated, that we feel the utmost confidence of getting securely on our journey. Letters came from Sir J. Moore from Ciudad Rodrigo of the date of the 12th. He was advancing then without his army: that unfortunately was considerably in the rear.

★★★★★★

The first British troops reached Salamanca on Nov. 13, and the whole of Moore's 15,000 infantry were assembled there by the 23rd.

★★★★★★

A letter from Sr. Robt. Wilson mentions great sickness in that army, even specifying that it was to the amount of 2000 men. They were proceeding without sufficient camp equipage to protect them from the rigor of the season, or rather the severe rains.

Five hundred of the volunteers of Cadiz belonging to the army of Castaños were surrounded at Lerin and made prisoners. Castaños preferred losing them by not attempting a rescue, which might have brought on a general action; in the course of a day 220 made their escape and returned to him.

General Pignatelli, the uncle of Ct. Fuentes, has been suspected of a treasonable correspondence with the French; a spy was posted at his quarters, and his orders were so contradictory and his conduct so suspicious that he is removed.

17th Nov.—Admiral de Courcy again and again repeated his kind and friendly offers of the *Tonnant* being at our service in case we should be compelled to make our *retreat* through Coruña.

18th.—Left Betanzos at ¼ past 10. At about a league before Guitiriz we met a Scotch officer riding past, whom we stopped to ask news. He belonged to Gen. Mackenzie's, and brought a disagreeable report of Blake having been again defeated, and of the French advancing to prevent the junction of the two English armies; of Burgos being in the possession of the French.

★★★★★★

Blake was defeated by Victor At Espinosa on the 10th and 11th. His troops made a creditable show, but suffered severe losses, including San Roman, second-in-command of the troops who had just returned from the Baltic. Blake reached Reinosa on the 12th, where he collected about 12,000 men, about half his original force. He was not allowed a moment, however, as Soult was close at hand. Striking into the mountains with about 7000 troops he evaded his pursuers, and reached Leon on the 16th.

★★★★★★

The *venta* at Guitiriz large, and for Ld. Paget and his staff; he had secured us the best part. He and his brother, Major Paget, and Baron Tripp' dined with us. Ld. P. thinks ill of the business.

19th.—We did not set off until Ld. Paget had mustered his men: they rode off with regularity, preceded by the band playing. We met a Spanish gentleman riding past, and stopped him to enquire the news. He confirmed the report of Blake's second defeat. At Lugo it seems Sr. D. Baird received a messenger from his own commissary at Leon, containing the account of the defeat of Blake on the 10th, but the gentleman added that from Sr. David's pronunciation of the proper names in Spanish, he could not understand where the action happened. Also that he received news from his advanced guard at Astorga and a messenger from Salamanca.

The result was his taking the resolution of setting off in haste with his staff to Astorga. His conduct is surprising. He has not communicated a syllable to Ld. Paget, a general officer commanding the cavalry, and I believe 3rd in command of the whole army. One should think in such a moment as this is likely to become, that it would be advisable to have as many opinions in council; not only for the good of the cause, but for his own character, either to have the sanction or escape the censure of Ld. P. Ld. P. and his men remained at Baimonde. Great losses amongst the cavalry. The horses, after 7 weeks confinement on a ship and then plunged into the sea to be swum on shore in a state of fever, have of course suffered severely, especially in their feet; besides the change of food from oats and hay to chopped straw and maize has affected their health. Seventeen were left at Betanzos. Three young men died, and on the road we saw several horses lying dead, and others who had fallen but could not rise. Soon after our arrival at Lugo, the two cousins, *las primas* (cousins), *de la Sangro,* came to visit and offer their services. Da. Maria de Prado. They invited us to dinner on the following day, and sent us presents of live turkeys and hares.

20th—At breakfast we received a visit from the Prior of the place, a friend of Quintana's, D. Manuel Fernandez Vanela, a very sensible, clever, well-informed man. The bishop soon after came; an Asturian, very ignorant and *grossier*, quite the manners of a *fraile*. He owed his elevation to the favour of Campomanes in his quality of countryman. The ladies came in a carriage to fetch me to go into the town to see the cathedral, &c.

Ld. Paget arrived from Baimonde at about 2. He argues well from Baird's silence, for if the news were true to the extent reported, he thinks it would have been impossible that he should not have received a messenger.

We dined at the house of Prado, all the five *primas* of Mde. Sangro, her stepmother, and various other persons; fortunately for me, our sensible acquaintance the Prior in the evening. Followed a dreadfully formal *tertulia*. Among the guests we had an *oidor*, (auditor), of Valladolid and his family. He fled from thence on the arrival of the French, and he again fled from the persecution of Cuesta, who threatened to arrest him for having gone to Lugo as a deputy from Villafranca del Vierzo, (see letter from Mr. Charles Vaughan in Appendix F.) We had a boisterous canon, a native of Africa, who to show his zeal and adoption of English customs, drank bumpers of wine and roared out toasts—the usual ones of *Ferdinando* and *Jorge*, the union of the two countries, and compts. to Ld. Hd. He owed his place to the favour of Mallo, the queen's lover, who was banished to Astorga. The bishop had invited me to a *refresco*, but on discovering that I was likely to be the only woman, when the time came to go I declined the visit. Ld. Hd. went with Ld. Paget.

Just afterwards, Monroe, the messenger bringing dispatches from

Aranjuez, brought letters from Baird to Ld. P. The 1st, dated the 18th Nov., desires him to halt his cavalry at Lugo in consequence of the disastrous news from Blake's army, and the State of Burgos being in possession of the enemy. The 2nd, 19th, bids him cancel all the orders about halting the cavalry, because, from a letter of Sir John Moore's, he finds the French have never been in any great force at Valladolid. In this letter he omits one very important point, which is from whence Moore writes, and it is only by hearsay that it is supposed his army had reached Salamanca. He urges Ld. P. to take the post and join him, as he wants his advice in the very critical position of affairs.

Blake appears to have been, after more fighting and great exertions on his part, completely beaten, and driven with the fragment of his army into Santander. Romana is there going to take the command of the scattered troops. Blake was attempting to join Baird at Leon, but a body of French intercepted him, and it is said that at Sahagun he lost his whole park of artillery. This news overset the whole *tertulia*. I went to Ld. P., and wrote by the messenger whom he stopped to take his letters.

21st Nov., Lugo.—Early this morning Ld. Paget and his two *aide-de-camps* set off *en posta* for Astorga. B. Frere writes from Aranjuez, 15th: advises us not to advance until something decisive is seen from the armies; complains of the insalubrity of Aranjuez at this season. They live in our old house belonging to the Marquis de Santiago. We have resolved upon returning for *the present* to Coruña, but shall spend the day here in order to write letters, &c., &c. This is Ld. Hd.'s birthday, on which he completes his 35 years.

Drove in the bishop's carriage, with four mules and two postilions in cocked hats, round the city walls. *El Prior*, Don Manuel Fernandez Vanela, dined with us and passed the evening. He told us a great many interesting anecdotes regarding the affair of the Escorial, the *motin*, (mutiny), at Aranjuez, and the disturbance at Madrid of the 2nd May, etc.; P. of P., on sounding some of the military whom he had raised to high stations, on being refused complained that he had the misfortune to make ungrateful followers not friends. The prior is full of humour and wit; told us several stories admirably. One of the Irish colonel whom he had clothed when wet, fed, and lodged, who just before he set off fell upon his knees and, meaning to ask his benediction, in bad Latin, said, '*Redde benificium tuum*': for that, 'No,' said the prior. His benefice is worth about 1000 *pr. ann.* He has lived a great deal at

Madrid and has a quick conception of ridicule; he made apologies for the provincial and boisterous behaviour of the gentlemen *Gallegos* at dinner yesterday.

22nd Nov.—This day as foggy and damp as that of yesterday. We left Lugo late, 11 o'clock. The English troops concerned at our leaving them; they were told we were only making an excursion for a few days, and should rejoin them on the road. Met Gen. Slade and young FitzClarence. He said the ammunition and artillery were behind, complained of the want of assistance from the *Juntas* who had not furnished them with cattle or guides. 36 waggons containing artillery left on the road for want of means to come on.

******

General Sir John Slade (1762-1859), commanding the Hussar brigade and FitzClarence eldest son of William IV and Mrs. Jordan, created Earl of Monster in 1830. He was a cornet in the 10th Hussars, and was only fifteen at that time.

******

The road very fine, but the country a moor and swamp bounded by distant mts. The 15th regt. Dragoons passed us; they appear to be in much better condition than either the 7th or 10th. (These regiments later were termed Hussars. They still, however, appeared in the army list of 1809, and for some years after, as Light Dragoons). They were on board ship only eleven days; the first was on board upwards of seven weeks. It is very vexatious to feel it indispensable to retrogade; it really is an act of self-denial not to proceed. I am persuaded one's courage rises in proportion as one approaches the scene of danger, and at Astorga I should have felt less terror than I did in apprehension at Hd. House.

Reached Guitiriz at 6 in evening. In Galicia one may always find milk, eggs, and potatoes; the first is supplied abundantly from numerous herds of goats, whose white coating mingles well in the distant views with the black, shaggy flocks of sheep. The eggs they owe to their poultry, of which there is a vast quantity, especially about Lugo; the capons are very fat. Their method of fattening them is by giving a walnut with the shell every day, increasing the number to forty, at which time they are reckoned to be in a state of perfection, and are then killed. The culture of potatoes has been introduced from England; they are much used. On the roadside the countrywomen bring them ready boiled to sell to the troops as they pass. The mutton is nauseous, beef excellent; pork in every shape famous all over Europe. Fish very good; the eels and trout of the Mino are reckoned exquisite. Fruits, from the specimen which was given of them when prepared, delicious. Bread, except at Santiago, quite execrable.

At Coruña and all the way to Lugo it is gritty from a mixture of sand and filth, heavy and brown. The common wine very palatable, light, and wholesome. The salt brown and foul; the Spaniards scarcely eat any. They consider it as very pernicious, although they eat great quantities of salted meat, ham, pork, sausages, pigs' faces, feet, lard, &c. Water excellent, it is generally brought along open aqueducts, both at Coruña, Lugo, and, I believe, at Santiago. Candles are in common use, not lamps as in the other parts of Spain. The floors are of wood; not brick or stone pavements like those I have seen in Spain. The houses are not large, nor are they built round a court or *patio*. The *ventas* or *posadas*, though far from being good, yet furnish more articles than many do in the south of Spain, such as chairs, sheets, mattresses, and plates.

23rd.—Awoke in the night by a strong smell of fire, and found the room full of smoke. There not being a chimney in the house but that of the kitchen, which I knew had been long extinguished, and know-ing that in and about the house there were 36 waggons laden with ammunition, I thought it might be advisable to make some enquiry. It was 3 o'clock. Upon examination it appeared that in the stable under the room in which I slept, the muleteers had wanted a light, so not having anything conveniently at hand they made straw torches. The only *outlet* to the smoke was through the crevices of my floor.

On the road we passed several divisions of the 15th in excellent condition. The last of the cavalry leave Coruña *today*, They march in 9 divisions, and the first ought by this time to be at Nogales, but if the French are assembling at Benavente, the cavalry can be of little use, as perhaps all the English Army have to look to is to defend themselves and protect the frontier of Galicia, and on those heights cavalry are of no service whatever. Sr. D. Baird has about 10,000 infantry 'forward,' but whether that means at Astorga, or on their way hither, I know not.

A large train of artillery is waiting here (Betanzos) for the want of horses to convey it on forward; a commissary has been employed above a month to procure the means. From all I can observe, the serv-ice would be greatly benefited by the dismissal of the whole *commis-*

sariat; the artillery lags behind, and the men are distressed frequently for want of provisions. No army can less endure privation from food and no one is more liable to it than the English, entirely from the ignorance and unskilful management of the commissaries. Between Coruña and Lugo a number of men were 36 hours totally unprovided with food, and for two days another division had not received their ratio of wine. Nothing could be more true than a brother or relation of Ld. Rosslyn's saying, when being appointed commissary to an army, that he was going out to cheat the King and starve the troops.

Two companies of the 60th composed of foreigners; it is well managed keeping them here upon duty of guarding artillery, &c., as they would find some difficulty in deserting, if they should become so inclined.

24th Nov., Coruña.—Arrived at 2 o'clock. We have taken up our residence in a small house occupied formerly by Sr. David Baird; it was the only one to be procured. Received English letters and papers to the 8th Nov, Dined at Mr. Barrie's, the merchant's. Met Mr. Stuart, the *aide-de-camp* of Gen. Mackenzie, the same person who gave us the bad news on the road to Guitiriz. An army of reserve is forming at Pontevedra; Mosquera is gone thither to take command of his regt. A person has been sent to the Supreme *Junta* to complain of the proceedings of the one here, and to recommend that a military officer of distinction should be sent here with full powers to supersede the *Junta* and take measures necessary for the defence of the kingdom, for which purpose they have shown themselves totally incapable and unfit.

25th.—Adl. de Courcy came early. Under the strictest seal of secrecy he revealed some very unpleasant circumstances to us. He received orders from Sr. D. Baird directing him to choose a safe and proper place from whence troops might embark with safety, and the vessels remain at anchorage out of reach of batteries. This order was so precise that he leaves it to be acted upon without any further reference to himself. Accordingly as the Bay of Coruña is commanded by forts, the fire of which would if in the enemy's possession render the embarkation unsafe, de Courcy has fixed upon Vigo, and has already taken measures accordingly. Under the pretext of sending to England the empty transports, he has ordered the *Endymion* to convey them to Vigo. As he knew we were to return here he very kindly gave orders to the *Champion* to be ready, and kept her 24 hours longer on our account, to send her home to demand of the Admiralty ships of the line and frigates to protect the transports in case there should be a necessity of their returning with the army. He intends to follow shortly with the *Tonnant*. As we were resolved upon attempting the road into Portugal, we have declined his offer of the *Champion*, and he has accordingly dispatched a small sloop instead, as he will require all his force.

Sr. D. Baird seems to have been alarmed almost unjustifiably, though the junction of the two armies is still a very doubtful point, and all that is known for certain of Sr. John Moore is that on the 24th Nov. (yesterday) he could not have with him at Salamanca more than 16,000 men, but without artillery or cavalry. Baird is at Astorga with about 10,000, *quite* without cavalry, little artillery, and less ammunition. The first division of the 7th Light Dragoons will not be able to join him till the 26th, and the rear of the cavalry will not get up before the 2nd December. Tonight Lt. Laroche, an officer of the 15th, brought on a dispatch from Lugo, forwarded from Astorga, containing merely a repetition of those orders to the admiral. He brought a verbal report that the 15th have been ordered to halt and fall back upon Baimonde. Notwithstanding these symptoms of a speedy retreat, no bad news seems to have arrived. The Madrid post arrived at the regular time, a proof that the French did not, or could not intercept them at Benavente on the 22nd.

Letters from Gijon of the 19th are free from alarm as to the approach of the French, but in a letter from Sr. D. Baird to Ld. Hd., it appears that they made an attack upon San Vicente de la Barquera, a place situated about 3 leagues on this side of Santander. Romana, who is at Santander, is said to be greatly cast down by these disasters; the guns of the batteries that command the harbour have been spiked by his orders on the 12th, and many thrown over into the sea, and casks of stores and ammunition.

★★★★★★

Soult entered Santander on Nov. 16, and captured a quantity of heavy stores. He again dispersed the remains of Blake's Asturian division at San Vicente; but advanced no farther, and struck southwards to Saldaña, where he regained touch with Lefebvre.

★★★★★★

26th.—Adl. de Courcy brought and introduced to us a cousin, Capt. Digby, of the *Cossack*. He arrived yesterday from Santander; he left Romana there on the 13th, who was just setting off *en posta* with his *aide-de-camps* and 5 hundred 1000 *duros* to *find* Blake, who was *supposed* to be at Reinosa. Romana had 5000 of his dismounted cavalry, who were armed with new English muskets supplied from the *Cossack*. The fugitives from Blake's army were numerous; they represented their sufferings as having been great.

Capt. Birch, who was wounded in one of the engagements, admitted that the army had been reduced to the greatest straights. For 5 days they had no supplies, and their food was just such as they could find— wild goats and animals they could catch in the mountains; many perished from hunger and fatigue, and the want of provisions contributed as much as the superior force of the enemy to disband and disperse the army. Romana's famous Catalan regt. were in an advanced post; on the 31st they were surprised by daybreak by the French, who opened three fires upon them in the most furious manner. They refused to surrender, and were to a man destroyed, (this was at Durango on Oct. 31, one of the actions which preceded Blake's defeat at Espinosa).

At Bilbao 2 Spanish soldiers were left sick in the hospital, and when the French arrived were given up as prisoners. Merlin, a genl. of division, ordered them to be carried to the *plaza* and shot as rebels. It is reported that he has been since mortally wounded in some of those battles with Blake.

★★★★★★

The sack of Bilbao by General Merlin took place at a much earlier date (September) than the period with which Lady Holland is now concerned. It was the result of a premature rising which was easily kept in check by Marshal Bessières' 2nd Corps. Christophe Antoine, Comte Merlin (1771-1839) received the rank of general in 1805.

★★★★★★

Captain Digby, who has been all the summer and autumn stationed off the coast, says that the French did not receive reinforcements to the number of 5000 men from the beginning of July to the end of Sept., but it is said that lately 60,000 have passed Bayonne. Joseph went to Madrid escorted by not more than 2500 men, but by sending forward parties of Dragoons to order rations for 5 times the number of men they have, they spread an alarm in the villages through which they pass of the vastness of their numbers. Capt. Birch, of the artillery, is come in the *Cossack* wounded; he was with Blake in three actions. He blames the plan of campaign of the Spanish generals. It was planned by Castaños and Palafox, a confidential officer of Blake's assisting in order to carry back to Blake their determination. Blake was much against the plan of his advancing into Biscay, but the Supreme *Junta* compelled him; they were dissatisfied at him for delay. The soldiers behaved with great courage and firmness in these actions, but some of the officers conducted themselves infamously. Romana ordered that all the officers who should be found without a passport should be put under arrest. Fortunately 3 victuallers put into Santander and fed the starving army.

Two Spanish frigates came in at the same time with the *Cossack* from Santander. The Conde de San Roman, 2nd-in-command in Blake's army, died of his wounds on board; they threw his body over board. He was an excellent officer and much esteemed by the army. All seem to agree that cavalry ought to have been sent to Galicia in July; if even the present forces had reached Spain 3 months ago the face of Spain would have been very difft. Junot's army was by its position *hors de combat*. Capt. Digby dined with us.

The *Minerva* and two brigs are come in from Gijon; the former brings accts. of the French having entered Santander on the 15th. They saw the dragoons riding down into the town. The town was nearly deserted by its inhabitants. The bishop came in the *Minerva* and was landed at Luarca. The Spaniards fled shamefully from San Vincente de Barquera from 1800 French. In one of the brigs are Mr. and Mrs. Hunter and daughter, (Mr. Hunter was the British agent at Gijon); they left Gijon on the 24th. Late at night, Mills, an English messenger from Madrid, brought letters from Astorga, one from Ld. P. to Ld. Hd.

★★★★★★

See Appendix A, Nov. 24. Napoleon had no idea of the dose proximity of the British, and halted at Aranda de Duero from Nov. 23 to 28, with his mind fixed on the capture of Madrid. Hence the French advance from Valladolid towards Salamanca, which Moore expected, never took place.

★★★★★★

Worse accounts than ever from the army urges us without loss of time to quit Spain. Romana is at Leon without troops; the French are running over Asturias, and their cavalry scouring over Castile. They have concentrated a force of 14,000 men at Rioseco, but none have advanced as yet to Benavente. On the 21st *probably* Sr. J. Moore would fall back upon Ciudad Rodrigo, and he has ordered D. Baird to look

31

to the supply of his troops and re-embark as speedily as he can. The cavalry are to go on to cover the retreat of the infantry. The *Cossack* is to sail tomorrow, *nominally* for Lisbon, but in fact for Vigo with transports.

27th Nov., Coruña.—Dispatches from Sr. David Baird from Astorga. In consequence of Sr. John Moore's orders that he would do well to consult the safety of the forces under his command and look to speedy embarkation, he has reiterated his demands for transports. It appears that Romana transmitted the acct. of Blake's army being cut up, that the French were in possession of San Vicente de la Barquera and of Colombres, and that the Asturias could not be defended. Sr. D.'s dispatch to Ld. Castlereagh states that by a dispatch from Moore, dated 21st, Salamanca, that general apprised him that as soon as he should hear that the French *had left* Valladolid, he should fall back upon Ciudad Rodrigo, and that, in that case, Baird ought to retreat with a view to embark at Vigo, and if possible transport his cavalry to Portugal over the Mino; this however he left to the judgment of Baird.

Reports that Blake has saved his artillery, and that it is at Leon. The battering train of artillery which Blake took from Ferrol (perhaps to bombard Pampeluna) is returned in the Spanish frigates which arrived yesterday.

In a confidential letter from Ld. P. to Ld. Hd., (see Appendix A, Nov. 24), among other things, it seems apprehensions are entertained that the French may penetrate into Galicia by the way of Orense, so as to harass the English on their retreat to Vigo.

A report that General Vives, after a severe engagement with the French in Cataluña, had approached close under Barcelona, (he was besieging Duhesme in Barcelona).

Mr. Hunter and Sr. Thomas Dyer describe the public feeling in Oviedo as being much more enthusiastic than it is amongst the *Gallegos.*

★★★★★★

Sir Thomas Dyer, who succeeded his father as seventh Baronet in 1801. He became lieut.-general, and died in 1838. He was one of the military agents in the Asturias.

★★★★★★

All these alarms have induced us to renounce our journey to Vigo by land; we were upon the point of setting off, the mules were actually tinkling their bells at the door. The worthy admiral assures us of a retreat in the *Tonnant*, and an earlier one in the *Champion*, but the orders are so urgent for the detention of every vessel, that none can now be sent out either to Vigo or to England.

28th.—Gen. Broderick has received a letter from Col. Bathurst, the quarter master at Astorga, containing more favourable accounts.

(Hon. John Brodrick (1765-1842), sixth son of George, third Viscount Midleton; military agent in Galicia. (*Napier*, Bk. III. ch. i.)

Blake has brought part of his army to Leon, and many of the fugitives are collecting together, which will form in the course of 8 or 10 days a force of 20,000. His artillery are arrived, and a junction of his army with Sr. D. Baird is supposed to be practicable and likely to be effected. Broderick's expression is that, '*Safety and honour go together.*'

★★★★★★

La Romana had nearly 26,000 men near Leon on Dec. 4, but they were badly equipped and short of clothing; and 23,000 were collected there ten days later (Oman), He did not actually move from there till much later, but wrote to Moore on Nov. 30, saying that he hoped soon to be able to do so.

★★★★★★

Broderick thinks the junction between Blake and Baird as good as done, whatever orders to fall back may have been given previously. Capt. Crauford of *Champion*, has lately been at Cadiz. Dupont was very turbulent and troublesome. Morla confined him and his staff in lighthouse. In his baggage was found an immense quantity of plate from churches, and spoons, forks, and even buckles beat down into a mass. His mistress stole at Cordova cambric to make herself three hundred shifts. Reports of disturbances against the English at Oporto. Sr. Robt. Wilson is there raising a legion of 5000 men.

★★★★★★

General Dupont, the commander of the French army which capitulated to Castaños at Baylen. He and his staff were sent back to France soon after this.

★★★★★★

29th.—Blake's army at Leon is said to be 18,000 strong. It begins to transpire here among the merchants that preparations are making to embark at Vigo.

30th.—Bissett, a King's messenger, arrived in the eve., with dispatches from Sr. J. Moore; private letter from Ld. P. to Ld. Hd., (see Appendix A). Moore was at Salamanca on the 28th with 18,000 men, no sickness prevailed in his army. Infantry of Baird had fallen back. By the letters from Astorga the opinion entertained there is that the French have no infantry or very few, and that their whole force consists in cavalry; they are supposed to be pushing their force towards Navarre in order to demolish Castaños and Palafox. Ld. P. writes in the highest spirits, it having been decided upon that the junction of the armies is to be attempted; the cavalry will begin the operations on the 3rd, the infantry will follow on the 4th or 5th.

Romana, who is at Leon with his army, is disposed to join the English armies, but Ld. P. rather wishes him to retrograde on Asturias to intercept the retreat of the French who are advancing to Oviedo; this last fact however, does not appear to be quite certain. Ld. P. says the marquis might make a *joli coup*. The people here discredit the report of the French having as yet got into the Asturias, and that at headquarters they have been deceived. A French corps pushing through the Asturias might easily surprise Ferrol, which is entirely stripped of troops. At Ferrol there are 7 ships of the line, three of which are 100 guns. General Müller, a naval architect and engineer, came over yesterday from Ferrol, and he considers it as impracticable for the French to pass through the Asturias.

The Hunters dined here, and gave the following account from Mr. Hay, an *aide-de-camp*, of Genl. Leith's report. He was sent by Frere with dispatches from Madrid to Santander, but was compelled by the progress of the French armies to go to Gijon. 'Nov. 10th, French attacked the 1st division of Estremadura army at Burgos, defeated and took from it 10 or 12 pieces of cannon. Entered Burgos in the evening.'

★★★★★

Andrew Leith Hay (1785-1862), *aide-de-camp* to his uncle General Sir James Leith. He wrote *A Narrative of the Peninsular War*, (also reprinted by Leonaur), and other works.

★★★★★★

Dec. 1st.—All hope has vanished, and orders are given for retreating: orders dated, 29th, at night, from Sr. D. Baird to repeat the necessity of the transports and all being '*ready to sail at a start (?).*' He has received positive orders from Sir J. Moore to begin his march towards the shipping without delay. Sr. J. Moore is determined to fall back upon Ciudad Rodrigo. The cause of this sudden determination on the part of Moore he rests upon the defeat of Castaños.'

★★★★★★

Castaños and Palafox met the French under Marshal Lannes at Tudela on Nov. 23, and were utterly routed. Castaños' own troops retreated on Madrid, while the remainder found their way to Zaragoza. The news of this disaster reached Sir John Moore on the 28th, being brought him by Vaughan, Charles Stuart's secretary, who was actually present at the battle. The dismal tidings were sufficient to cause him to decide on retreat, and orders to that effect were dispatched forthwith to Baird and Hope. Moore himself remained, however, where he was, on the chance of picking up the latter's force; and these few days put a new complexion on the face of affairs which enabled him to pursue a very different line of action.

★★★★★★

Neither the date, nor place where this disaster happened are known, but the circumstances are said to be similar to those of Blake. Ld. Paget went to Leon and saw Romana; he does not think much of the *quartier-général*. In the dispatch to Ld. Castlereagh, Baird encloses Ld. P.'s report of the conversation he had with Romana on the 26th. Romana complains that he has been deceived and not communicated with by his govt.; that he was appointed to the command of an army which does not exist. As to spies, he can get no information, although he has great reason to believe the French are well supplied with information about all that is doing in his army. His men are half-naked, and starving, and unless equipped they cannot be kept together. He was confident of having in 8 days 20,000 men collected; he has only 12 pieces of cannon. Nothing but the most *precise* and peremptory orders can justify Moore in acting as he is going to do. It is too mortifying.

Dec. 2nd.—Baird hears from Moore that the Supreme *Junta* are going to move to Toledo, in consequence of the news of Castaños's defeat. At Vigo there are 140 transports under convoy of *Endymion, Cossack, Minerva*; here about 32 under the *Tonnant* and *Champion*. Upon the whole we think it safest to hasten to Vigo and there embark, for if the French should pursue hotly and seize the batteries, it may be a very serious state of commotion here.

At eleven at night, to our great surprise, our old friend Mr. Vaughan arrived *en posta* from Madrid, having carried dispatches from thence to Moore at Salamanca, and so on through Astorga, where he saw Baird.

★★★★★★

Sir Charles Richard Vaughan (1774-1849), the well-known

traveller and diplomatist, for many years Minister to the United States (1825-1835). He accompanied Charles Stuart to Spain in 1808, though in no official capacity, and was present at the first siege of Zaragoza with Col. Doyle. He was again in Spain 1810-1816 as Secretary of Legation and *chargé d'affaires*. See Appendix F, for his letters previous to this date.

★★★★★★

He brings the account of the defeat of Castaños, with whom, I regret to find, there was a large body of Palafox's army. Castaños escaped with 3000 men to Calatayud. On the arrival of the intelligence, Mr. Stuart dispatched Vaughan with it to Lord Castlereagh in a dispatch from Col. Doyle.

★★★★★★

Afterwards Sir Charles William Doyle (1770-1842), employed in military and political duties in Galicia and later in Catalonia. He was at this time assisting in the direction of affairs at headquarters.

★★★★★★

At Villacastin Vaughan met with Gen. Hope's division, 21 leagues from Salamanca, 7000, chiefly of cavalry, and a large train of heavy artillery, which was on its march to join Moore. At Salamanca he found Moore very much out of humour, abusing the poor Spaniards, and dissatisfied with the service on which he was employed. Moore told him that if the junction had been formed he would then 'throw himself into Spain,' but as Baird could not advance before the 4th, he should not attempt it. At Benavente he found some English dragoons, and was told that French patrols had been at the bridge the night before. At Astorga he found Sr. Dd. Baird more out of humour with the Spaniards even than Moore, saying they had no enthusiasm, no order, and wanting nothing but our money, &c. 7th Dragoons at Astorga; 10th at Cacabelos, and some of the 15th at Villafranca. Artillery returning to Betanzos.

People of the country ignorant of this *glorious* retreat; they suppose the English are falling back in order to oppose the French who are marching through the Asturias. A French *aide-de-camp* was stabbed by his guide whilst passing a ford, and the letters of which he was the bearer betrayed a scheme being in contemplation of getting along the coast through the Asturias. Ld. Paget believes they have actually 12,000 men in that principality; confidentially mentions that our going to Lisbon will not secure us quiet, as Moore has applied for transports to the Tagus, apprehending that Portugal is not to be defended, and that whoever is the master of Spain must be also of Portugal.

★★★★★★

This was quite incorrect. Soult having forced the remnants of Blake's force over the mountains to Leon, never went farther west than Columbres, but turned south through the mountains to Saldaña and Carrion.

★★★★★★

At Madrid they are preparing for a similar resistance to that made by the inhabitants of Saragossa against the French. Morla and Castelar, are at the head of the military force, (Marquis de Castelar, Captain-General of New Castile). From intercepted letters it appears that the French intend to enter that city and wreak a dreadful vengeance. Vaughan describes great enthusiasm to prevail in Aragon, Catalonia, and New Castile; in Old Castile and Leon the affair of Cuesta has done harm.

★★★★★★

In Aug. 1808, soon after the Battle of Rioseco— the scene of Cuesta's defeat and consequent loss of prestige, the revolutionary *Juntas* of Leon and Castile were joined by that of Galicia and constituted themselves a joint assembly under the Presidency of Valdes. Cuesta, however, as Captain-General of Castile, considered himself the supreme authority in those parts and refused to recognise them. In order to constitute a central authority to prosecute the war a Supreme *Junta* of 35 members, deputies from the various *Juntas*, was appointed to assemble at Aranjuez in September. While proceeding thither the deputies from Leon, Valdes, and the Vizconde de Quintanilla were arrested by Cuesta and thrown into the castle of Segovia, there to be court-martialed for disobedience to his orders. They were at once released by the command of the Supreme *Junta*, and Cuesta was deprived of his command for his presumption.

★★★★★★

A considerable Spanish force on the Somosierra; 20,000 Spanish soldiers excellent, officers indifft., ignorant, and great want of military knowledge in the generals. Palafox is indefatigable, but without any knowledge of the military art, or indeed of any kind. Montijo he rates low. Romana was appointed to the command of Castaños's army just before the Battle of Tudela.

★★★★★★

37

José de Palafox y Melchi (1776-1847), the most distinguished of three brothers, of whom the eldest was Marqués de Lazan, the youngest Francisco de Palafox. He accompanied Ferdinand to Bayonne, but returned to Zaragoza when he saw the impossibility of the latter's escape from the clutches of Napoleon. He was there proclaimed Captain-General of Aragon, though he had no knowledge of military matters. He at once proclaimed war against the French, and held the command in both the sieges of Zaragoza.

★★★★★★

When Palafox declared war against France he had only 250 regular troops in Aragon, and 2000 *reals* in the public treasure. Palafox is the author of the proclamations which appear in his name. He has a chaplain of the name of Tas, who distinguished himself during the siege. He himself is so much beloved by the Aragonese, and next to Our Lady of Pilar is the person who enjoys most of their confidence, (a very ancient wooden figure of the Virgin preserved in the Cathedral of Zaragoza). V. saw the heroine who defended a battery after all the men were killed, and defeated a French column who were advancing to take possession of the battery by firing off a 24-pounder. She is a pretty, modest-looking woman, and ascribes her mighty deeds to an inspiration from Our Lady del Pilar.

★★★★★★

Agostina Zaragoza, who in battle snatched the lighted match out of her dying lover's hand and applied it to the gun. The Spanish soldiers shamed by this heroic deed returned and beat off the French column, Palafox made her a sub-lieutenant of artillery. (*Oman.*)

★★★★★★

3rd December.—Sr. Dd. Baird continues sending dispatches to repeat the urgency of the retirement. He has ordered all ships of war to be detained, as in case of a hot pursuit all must take troops on board. He has desired de Courcy to inform the *Junta* of the retreat of the army, but that he may assure them the English will never abandon the Spanish cause! What a jest! To insult and deride them at the moment we are abandoning them thus disgracefully. I thought it friendly to hint the danger to Mrs. Hunter. Mr. Arbuthnot, her brother, is here; he arrived by the last packet, meaning to pass a few months with her quietly in the Asturias.

4th December.—Mr. Vaughan set off in the *Snapper* schooner laden with letters, &c., for England. We are hastening to Vigo, and shall set off in an hour. A variety of delays owing to the difficulty of getting mules and conveyances. The Governt. have laid an embargo upon all mules and horses in order to facilitate the departure of the artillery and stores to Leon. In consequence of Ld. Hd's application to the *Junta* we have one *tiro*, (team), released. We are obliged to use a *calesin* and mules of burthen.

Beautiful evening, very light the moon being nearly full; reached Herbes, a wretched *venta*, for the third time in which we slept at it. The Madrid post has not arrived; the *correo*, (mail), only came from Benavente, a clear proof that the enemy have intercepted the road. Ld. Hd. received a very kind and friendly letter from the D. of Infantado. Also a present from Jovellanos of a new edition, handsomely bound with Ld. Hd.'s name and his own on the cover, of the *Siete Partidas*, the code of laws instituted by Alonzo el Sabio.

5th December was one of the most delicious days I ever felt; the sun was very powerful, and yet there was a gentle air to temper its ardour. The usual occupations of the peasants made some pretty scenes; sowing, ploughing, and harrowing in the same open space. The road less good than when we passed before, partly from the heavy rains, and partly from the passage of artillery. The recollection of our late reception at Santiago made me feel a dread of encountering similar and now undeserved expressions of kindness to the English nation. I dreaded entering amidst acclamations of '*Viva*,' '*Viva*,' knowing how soon, and justly, those friendly expressions must be changed to contempt and aversion.

6th December.—Received by the post a letter from Adl. de Courcy, in which he mentions the arrival of the *Lavinia*, Ld. Wm. Stuart, and enclosing a handsome letter in which Ld. Wm. offers, considering our forlorn condition, to look into Vigo purposely to take us up and convey us on to Lisbon and further if we choose. As it is a stretch of power to do this, he urges us to be ready to meet him. He was to sail on the eve of the 6th, and might get there in 24 hours. He has brought Matarrosa, &c., &c., and Gen. Cradock, who is going to take the command at Lisbon.

★★★★★★

José Maria Queipo de Llano Ruiz de Saravia, Vizconde de Matarrosa, and afterwards Conde de Toreno (1786-1843), a member of one of the leading families of the Asturias. He had been to England as one of the deputies sent by the Northern *Juntas* to seek assistance against the French. He was the author of the well-known history of the insurrection in Spain.

Sir John Cradock (1762-1839), created Lord Howden in 1819. He was sent out to take command of the troops left by Moore in Portugal, but was superseded by Wellesley in April 1809, and sent to Gibraltar as Governor. He was appointed Governor of the Cape of Good Hope in 1811.

★★★★★★

7th.—As we ascended the hill looking down upon Vigo, we saw the beautiful but melancholy sight of 140 transports and three ships of war! The harbour is very spacious; it is reckoned one of the finest in Spain. The English Consul, Melendez, had procured a very tolerable house for us upon the beach. In the evening Capts. Capel and Digby came to see us; they were very obliging and friendly in their offers of service. The former commands the *Endymion*, a fine, large frigate, but of course his motions are uncertain, as he must superintend the embarkation of the troops, and as yet no acct. is come of their progress. The wind fair for the *Lavinia*. Agreed with Capt. Capel upon his signal in case she should arrive at night. (Captain Capel afterwards Admiral Sir Thomas Bladen Capel (1776-1853), youngest son of William, fourth Earl of Essex).

9th.—A fleet of transports were entering about 5 o'clock under the convoy of the *Orestes*. The admiral writes from Coruña that he sends round by desire of Sr. D. Baird all the headquarter ships; and that Sr. D. was at Villafranca on the 4th, and the whole army falling back.

10th.—Just after breakfast Capt. Capel and the capt. of the *Orestes* came to announce the dismal news of the *Lavinia* having sailed from Coruña the day before the *Orestes*, and that without doubt from the fairness of the wind she had passed this port in the night of the 7th, and was already at Lisbon! It was a sad *contretemps*; but we must prepare for a land journey, first because we wish to avoid the painful sight of witnessing the embarkation of our fugitive army, and secondly because the delay may be very great, and we may be detained for the *Endymion* above a fortnight.

11th.—The first news this morning was as disastrous as surprising—the loss of the *Jupiter*, 50-gun ship, almost in the harbour! They think against a rock. The heavy guns are overboard; the crew, it is certain, are all saved. I am going to hear some particulars. The guns we heard were signals of distress; Capt. Capel was out all night with her. The fault was entirely owing to the ignorance and presumption of the capt. He had only an old chart, drawn a century ago, and he refused the pilot who went out to offer his assistance; the guns were thrown overboard.

12th.—Col. Long, a staff officer belonging to the 15th Dragoons came from Coruña; he read the orders to the commanding officer at Santiago, the purport of which was that the troop was not to proceed to Vigo, but to wait there till further orders for their proceeding *forward* again.

★★★★★★

Colonel, afterwards Lieut.-General Robert Ballard Long (1771–1825), a colonel on the staff of Spain. It is stated in the *Dictionary of National Biography* that he only landed in that country the day before the Battle of Coruña.

★★★★★★

Thus there is great reason to hope Sir John Moore has decided upon advancing. The women at Santiago, when our soldiers entered the town, called out to them that they were not taking the right road to meet the French, and pointed to the one they had left as the fittest for them to go. Such expressions and marks of contempt must be expected.

13th.—Soon after we were in bed we were roused by the arrival of a messenger from Coruña, who brought us an immense packet of old English letters. The messenger was Col. Kennedy's servant, and his verbal acct. was highly gratifying. He represented his master as being in great joy at the news from headquarters, orders being issued for the advance of the army once more to Astorga.

★★★★★★

Baird's force was the only one which actually commenced a retrograde movement, and they received a new set of orders from Moore at Villafranca on Dec. 6.

A variety of reasons had caused Moore's change of mind during those days of waiting at Salamanca, though the 'great exertions making by the Spaniards' was an invention of Frere's fertile brain. Hope had reached him with the cavalry and artillery, his own force was full of discontent at the thoughts of retreat, and La Romana seemed stronger than he had supposed. Above

41

all he had discovered that there were no French troops near enough to hinder his junction with Baird, and that Napoleon's real point of objective was Madrid. A blow dealt on the flank of the French he rightly conjectured would draw them upon him in force, and thus ease the pressure upon the capital. He little knew that Madrid had fallen several days before he commenced his hazardous advance, and that the enemies' forces totalled not 80,000, as he supposed, but three times that number. Yet his enterprise was even more successful than he can have imagined or lived to realise, for by that dash on to the Carrion he undoubtedly saved Spain.

★★★★★★

In the morning a confirmation of all the good reports in a letter from Admiral de Courcy to Capt. Capel. Sir John Moore, in consequence of the great exertions making by the Spaniards and the general appearance of affairs on the 5th Dec, took his determination of doing what he *never* ought to have abandoned, *viz.* proceeding from Salamanca to the junction with Baird. Orders are issued for all officers to proceed immediately to headquarters, and all preparations for fitting up the transports for the reception of cavalry to cease; indeed it is even hinted that the transports may perhaps be sent back to England immediately. It is most natural to infer from this resolution of Moore's, that Gen. Hope effected his junction successfully, and made so just and fair a report of the state of the public feeling and determination sooner to perish than yield to Napoleon in Castile, that he has convinced Moore not only of the practicability but of the *moral* necessity of advancing to succour the Spaniards.

By letters from the Asturias it seems the alarm of the French was greatly exaggerated, and the few who entered that principality were already withdrawn. 7th Dec. was the last date from Oviedo. The transition from sullen discontent to frank joy at this place is very striking. Great exertions are making everywhere to recruit the Spanish armies. 250 volunteers are now under arms at this little place, who are to be sent to join the army of rescue. Romana is said to have removed, in other words disgraced, many of the officers. Madrid post has failed. Capt. Capel dined.

14th.—We were woke again in the night by the arrival of an express. Col. Long stopped a messenger from Sr. Robt. Wilson to Broderick, which contained a passport for us and an extract of a letter from

Gen. Anstruther, at Almeida, dated 7th:—

I am happy to say that three battalions from Oporto are ordered forward to Salamanca with all speed, and I am sanguine that things may yet go well. The Spaniards are making a desperate effort at Madrid; God grant it may be successful. (Of these one battalion only, the 82nd, reached Moore in time. The other two were too far behind, and returned to Portugal.)

★★★★★★

Brigadier-General Robert Anstruther (1768-1809) took part in the Vimiero campaign and commanded a brigade under Edward Paget in his advance from Portugal to join Moore at Salamanca, His brigade protected Moore's retreat to Coruña, but the magnificent services he performed were too much for his strength and he died of exhaustion the day before the battle.

★★★★★★

12th.—Oporto, from Sr. Robt. Wilson:—

I march on Wednesday morning. All in high spirits. Capt. Peacock with a British detachment has entered Bragança. We suppose this to be Sr. D. Baird's military chest. Pray tell Ld. Holland this intelligence.'

15th.—Began our laborious and hazardous journey by land on mules and in litters to Lisbon.

20th December, Tuesday, Oporto.—Mr. Butter communicated the sad and melancholy news of the capitulation of Madrid; the enemy were repulsed three times, and it must have been about the 10th that the event took place. (Madrid surrendered at 8 o'clock on the 4th, after holding out for one day). The Supreme *Junta* had removed to Truxillo, and were on their road to Seville; the Freres were with them. The particulars are not known. Col. Trant was sent over to England in the *Lavinia*, the bearer of this intelligence. It came from Lisbon in a private letter from an *aide-de-camp* of Col. Cradock's to his uncle. Moore had made the junction with Hope, and was in hopes of effecting that with Baird. Sr. Robt. Wilson has set off from hence with his Lusitanian legion, consisting at present of 800 men.

★★★★★★

Sir Robert Wilson had raised his 'Lusitanian Legion' around Oporto, and in time it amounted to about 1300 men. Napier says the project was originated by Souca, the Portuguese Min-

43

ister in London, with a view really to dominate the situation in Oporto which was seething with faction. Wilson, however, had different views and moved off his available force (Napier says, by Sir J, Cradock's advice) to other quarters as soon as he was able to do so.

★★★★★★

This undertaking does not meet with the hearty support of the Regency, who do not confirm his military appointments or furnish supplies either for the equipment or pay of the troops; he is very anxious to get on to Spain where their *solde* will be at the expense of our Govert. The re-establishment of the *Regency* has been a most unpopular measure in this country.

★★★★★★

After the evacuation of Portugal by the French, the original Regency, appointed by Dom John when leaving for Brazil nine months before, was reconstituted by the proclamation of Sir Hew Dalrymple, the English general. Those members however were omitted who had sided with the French, and the Bishop of Oporto was added, making in all seven members. The *Junta* of Oporto, who had borne the brunt of the fray, considered it should have received more recognition, and the fact that the Constitution was settled through the agency of the English did not tend to increase its popularity with the Portuguese.

★★★★★★

The persons in high offices are suspected of being strongly addicted to the French cause. Mr. Villiers, 'handsome with the flaxen hair,' is arrived at Lisbon as envoy; his sagacity will hardly mend matters. Bernardino Freire, the Captain-General and Commander-in-chief of the Portuguese forces, called. He appears disposed to be very serviceable and obliging. His manner is formal and extremely ceremonious.

★★★★★★

The Hon. John Charles Villiers (1757-1838), who succeeded his brother as third Earl of Clarendon in 1824. He was envoy to the Court of Portugal from 1808 till 1810. Lady Holland's quotation is from the *Rolliad*.

Bernardino Freire de Andrada, a cousin of the general in the French army: born about 1764. He took a leading part in the insurrection in 1808 against the French, and was present at the Battle of Vimiero. During Soult's invasion of Portugal in the following year he fell a victim to an outburst of frenzy on the part of his soldiers, who accused him of treachery and murdered him.

★★★★★★

We removed from our wretched *posada* to the inn built in the Factory House for the accommodation of the English travellers; spacious, clean, and possessing the comforts of fireplaces. Sr. Robt. Wilson had prepared a house for our reception, one formerly belonging to the English Consul; we only heard of it after we had settled to come here. In the eve. Mr. Butter, Mr. Noble, and Capt. Stanhope. The latter came in two days from Vigo; he left England on the 11th. The alarm there was so great in consequence of the dispatches from Sr. D. Baird, that all the troops, cavalry, and infantry which were embarked at Portsmouth were ordered immediately to disembark, and the empty shipping sent to Vigo to bring away our army.

Mr. Noble dined with us. In the evening the worthy Bishop of Oporto came to see me. (Dom Antonio de San José de Castro, President of the 'Supreme *Junta*' of Oporto, and a member of the Regency of Portugal.) I was very sorry, as he had been confined to his bed for five days; he looks sick and dying. He is greatly beloved by the people, and his presence alone keeps them from committing acts of violence. Went to the opera; had offers of several boxes, Bernardino Freire sent his *aide-de-camp* offering *Madame's*. I went into Sr. Robt. Wilson's. The theatre is very large and handsome. The troop good, much better than that of the Haymarket without Catalani. The 1st *basson*, Scamarelli, is engaged at a high salary for the Haymarket. Bernardino Freire and his wife made me a visit: very obliging. He offered, if we chose, to send forward and order the monks of Grijo to prepare for our reception. We accepted.

Dec. 30th, Marinha Grande.—Met Ld. Ebrington, who was riding past with Gen. Cameron from Lisbon to Almeida in order to join Sr. John Moore. He gave a confused acct. of public affairs; could scarcely collect a single fact from his statements.

★★★★★★

Hugh, Viscount Ebrington (1783-1861), who succeeded his father as second Earl Fortescue in 1841. He went out to Spain as a volunteer, acted as *aide-de-camp* to Wellesley at Vimiero, and was sent back to England on Oct. 18 as the bearer of a despatch. He must have returned almost immediately to Portugal. He was later attached to Venegas, and was present at the Battle of

45

Almonacid.

General Sir Alan Cameron (1753-1828), who was left in command of the troops at Lisbon by Moore when he moved forward to Salamanca. On Cradock's arrival, however, he advanced to join Moore, but hearing at Almeida of the tatter's retreat, he remained there and occupied himself with collecting the stragglers.

★★★★★★

It appears certain that Madrid is in possession of the French, as he had seen the capitulation, but he did not know the date, nor the stipulations whether the Spanish Army had surrendered, &c. Ld. Hd. got a hurried note from Sr. Robt. Wilson at Lamego, 23rd, in which he refers him to a Portuguese officer for particulars of news, but said officer is not forthcoming. Met other travellers who said the reports were very contradictory.

3rd Jan., 1809.—Remembered the road: it was so rough that I was obliged to ride almost into Lisbon. Met about 3000 Portuguese troops marching to the frontiers. Very tolerably lodged owing to the kind civility of Mr. Bulkeley. He and Mr. Bell called. Gen. Cradock sent his *aide-de-camp* to offer his services.

4th Jan., Lisbon.—Ld. Hd. went yesterday to Mr. Villiers who was inclined to be very civil. This morning he breakfasted with Sr. John Cradock, the commander-in-chief of the forces in Portugal. He was very communicative and even confidential to Ld. Hd. It appears that the French, who were as far as Merida on the 26th, and had levied contributions in Truxillo, afterwards retreated and rather suddenly re-crossed the bridge of Almaraz, and, it is said, directed their course to Plasencia.

★★★★★★

With a view to discover the whereabouts of the English, and also ultimately to act as an advance guard for his descent on Seville and Lisbon, Napoleon had pushed Lasalle's cavalry far south to Plasencia on Dec. 17. But as soon as Moore's real position became known, on the 21st, the emperor collected all the troops he could lay hands on to overwhelm him, leaving only part of Victor's 1st corps, and Lefebvre's (Duke of Dantzig) 4th corps, to protect Madrid. The latter had orders to dislodge, with the aid of Lasalle, the remains of the Spanish armies defeated at Gamonal and the Somosierra from the bridge over the Tagus at Almaraz, where they had collected under the command of Galluzzo. This Lefebvre effected without difficulty on Dec. 24, and after pushing forward to the south a few parties of cavalry, he withdrew, not as Lady Holland says (just as does Napier) to Plasencia and Talavera but right over the Guadarrama to Avila, where he appeared on Jan. 5. This act of disobedience disarranged all Napoleon's plan, and cost Lefebvre his command. Galluzzo was relieved of his command by the Supreme *Junta* after his retirement from Almaraz, and his troops were handed over to Cuesta.

★★★★★★

It seems that a French column is *at Salamanca and Ciudad Rodrigo*, and that the communication of Sr. J. Moore with Portugal is of course intercepted. The junction of Romana, Moore, and Baird it is certainly believed was effected on the 22nd, Moore having fallen back from Toro for that purpose.

★★★★★★

The junction between Baird and Moore was effected at Mayorga on Dec. 20, and La Romana joined them at Astorga on the 30th, much to Moore's annoyance. The latter had requested him to retire through the Asturias if forced to evacuate Leon, and leave Galicia for the British. Moore commenced his retreat from Sahagun on Dec. 24.

★★★★★★

From the letters found upon a French courier whom the Spanish postilion had murdered (the 3rd within these two months) Moore knew that the army of Soult, who is opposed to him, was stronger than he expected, and dispatches of importance with regard to the plans of the French Army are in his possession. Cuesta is at the head of the forces in Estremadura; he was proclaimed almost by acclamation their chief, and his nomination has been confirmed by the Supreme *Junta*, Galluzzo, the former general of that army, having lost the confidence of that province by his loss of the bridge of Almaraz. One English regt. and some Portuguese are at Elvas. Col. Kemmis, who commands, writes that he is prepared to hold out in Fort la Lippe to the last extremity. There is a very small English garrison at Almeida. Portuguese troops are collecting at Thomar and at Guimaranes, but excepting these there seems *nothing* to prevent the French from penetrating when they choose to Lisbon.

★★★★★★

Cradock found thirteen battalions of infantry, besides cavalry and artillery, at his disposal upon his arrival in Portugal. Of these, one battalion, the 40th, was at Elvas, garrisoning the citadel. Fort la Lippe; four at Almeida, two of which had been sent back by Moore, and two had started too late to reach him. The rest were at Abrantes and Lisbon.

Considering these too few for the defence of Portugal Cradock, early in February, withdrew all but the battalion at Elvas to the neighbourhood of Lisbon, and commenced to dismantle the forts on the Tagus in case of the necessity of an evacuation of the town. This in itself was perfectly correct, as they were useless for defence against a land force, but the result showed the proceeding to be both unfortunate and inopportune. The populace at once began to suspect that they were to be deserted by the British, and serious riots were only obviated at the end of January by the presence of the soldiers.

The Portuguese troops at the end of 1808 were practically a negligible quantity. With the exception of five or six battalions near Lisbon, they were scattered all over the country, and having no transport available were not in a position to take the field.

★★★★★★

Mr. Villiers has already given an intimation to the factory that they must be ready to depart at a moment's warning, as it may be necessary for them to do so, and measures. Sir J. Cradock told Ld. Hd., were taking already to render the fortresses on the Tagus unserviceable; it seems they are defenceless towards the land. In short the inhabitants of Lisbon are rather *dans un très mauvais pas*, and our journey through Badajoz and Seville is not quite so safe an undertaking as we had expected to find it. Mr. Bell and Mr. Bulkeley dined with us.

★★★★★★

Lord Holland notes of Mr. Bell in *Further Memoirs of the Whig Party,* 'An English merchant, whose talents and intrepidity during the French occupation of Portugal should have entitled him to the place of Consul in 1809.'

Mr. Bulkeley is perhaps the same mentioned by Lord Broughton (Reminiscences, vol. ii) as having 'charged us 13 *per cent* for changing money.'

★★★★★

Sir John Cradock called: great offers of service. Mr. Villiers, the

48

same. He is not a Solomon from his manner. Sent key of his box at San Carlos. Lugo, the Spanish Consul-general, Don Pasqual ———, the Spanish *chargé d'affaires*, called. The latter is suspected of being a Frenchman in his opinions. Went to the Opera. The singing is not so good as at Oporto; the dancing better. Slender audience. *5th Jan., Lisbon.*—Went with Ld. Hd. who made some visits; the town full as dirty as formerly. The houses bear evident marks of decay from being shut up, neglected, and uninhabited. Mr. Bell dined with us. Great alarm amongst the merchants, many of whom are already dispatching their property on board of ships. Went to the National Theatre, where complimentary songs to the English and Portuguese were sung.

Sr. J. Cradock went to place his men this morning at Sacavem, *now* the only military post between us and the force of Napoleon; he has about 3000 men. He was awoke in the night by the news brought by an officer who says the French column from Plasencia have entered Coria, and some already pushed into Castello Branco. If this is so, this place must fall immediately. All the ships of war were hastened off to Vigo, and we have only a Commodore and two frigates. The forts being dismantled on the Tagus has contributed to spread the alarm amongst the merchants. Many French spies are suspected to be about under the disguise of friars and priests. An English packet in 13 days from Falmouth; no letters later than 16th, newspapers down to 21st. The Court of Inquiry is over; but the result is not public, as it has not been laid before the king. (The Court of Inquiry on the terms of the Convention of Cintra commenced its sitting on Nov. 14 under the presidency of Sir David Dundas. Its report was issued on Dec. 22).

Lord Liverpool is dead. The Spanish *chargé d'affaires* told Ld. Hd. that he had heard from Badajoz of the death of Count Florida Blanca at Seville—(he died of bronchitis, the result of a chill caught during the hurried journey of the *Junta* from Madrid to Seville)—and that he was succeeded in the Presidentship Altamira, (Conde de Altamira and Marqués de Astorga), Cevallos Vice-President, and Garay Secy, of State, (Don Martin Garay (1760(?)-1822), Secretary to the Cortes, and Minister of Finance under Ferdinand VII from 1814 till 1818). Much afraid that our Badajoz expedition will not be safe to attempt.

6th.—Dined at Sr. John Cradock's, where our party consisted of Generals Mackenzie and Cotton, Mr. Wellesley, Ld. Ipswich, Commodore Halket, Mr. Wynne, Capt. Francis, Mr. Fremantle, and Baron Quintilla the owner of the house, which is a noble palace.

★★★★★★

General Sir Stapleton Cotton (1773-1865) who was created Lord Combermere in 1814. He was sent to Vigo in August with a cavalry brigade, but its destination was changed to Lisbon. *The Golden Lion*, the early life and military career of Stapleton Cotton by Mary Combermere, W. W. Knollys & Alexander Innes Shand is also published by Leonaur.

Lord Ipswich, Henry, afterwards Earl of Euston, and fifth Duke of Grafton (1790-1863). He was an officer in the 7th Light Dragoons.

Commodore Halket succeeded Admiral Cotton as commander of the naval force on the station, and is highly spoken of by Napier.

★★★★★★

During the French tyranny Junot was quartered upon him; all the expenses of living were at his cost, and even the *fêtes*, to many of which the Baron was not even invited. The lowest sum at which this was estimated to have cost Quintilla is £40,000.

The story of the French being already at Castello Branco is not credited; it came from the Portuguese Regency. No news from Moore. Genl. Cameron is at Almeida, and Ld. Ebrington, who was knocked up by the journey and had remained at Coimbra, has resumed his intention of proceeding. Mr. Wellesley appears to be very pleasing and intelligent. (Perhaps one of Lord Wellesley's two illegitimate sons, born before his marriage in 1793 or 1794 with their mother Hyacinthe Gabrielle, daughter of Pierre Roland).

8th.—Bad news from Catalonia; Rosas is taken and Gerona is invested.

★★★★★★

The capture of the fortress of Rosas was effected by St. Cyr's force early in December. In the meanwhile, however, the relief of Barcelona had become an urgent necessity, and the French commander was unable to undertake the reduction of Gerona until May.

★★★★★★

I had a letter from Bartholomew, dated, 4th, Seville. Florida Blanca is certainly dead; he attended his funeral.

★★★★★★

He was buried in great state: the function lasted four hours. He lay in state yesterday evening, and was carried to the Cathedral upon an open bier, with his hat, uniform, cordon, and cane in his hand; and though I was shocked at the idea of seeing him in this way, when he passed by there was so little difference between the face of the corpse and his face when alive that I could hardly believe but that he was asleep.—B. Frere to Lady Holland.

★★★★★★

Capmany is safe at Seville; he escaped from Madrid on the 4th. Quintana left Madrid before it was taken. Capmany is as full of energy as ever; he says his mind has not suffered, and that instead of getting weaker as it grows older, as other peoples' do, it is like the arm of a blacksmith that the more it works the more nervous it grows. Sir John Moore was to leave Carrion de los Condes on the 23rd, in order to attack Soult, who was at Saldana. (This is incorrect: Moore was never at Carrion. He had arranged to attack Soult there at dawn on the 24th, but received the all-important news on the 23rd of Napoleon's advance in force from Escorial and Madrid, which was to be his signal for immediate retreat).

On the same day Napoleon left the Escorial, and an army of 30,000 men marched to attack Moore. Letters from Elvas and Badajoz. The French have abandoned the bridge of Almaraz. Letter from Col. Peacock, who is entrusted with a large sum of money, under an escort of 500 men, to join Moore, dated the 30th Dec, Miranda del Duero. He had received a letter from an English officer. Col. Harvey, at Zamora, dated 28th, from which it is clear that the French had never been at Salamanca as was believed here at headquarters. Some of the patrols had been at Toro. (Lapisse's force which was detailed to deal with this district was still at Benavente on Jan. 1. Moving south immediately he stormed Toro, and Zamora only fell after a determined resistance on Jan. 10.)

The 7th and 18th Dragoons had an action in which they had greatly the advantage of the French. Col. Peacock, was advised, however, not to proceed by Zamora but to go round by Bragança. Letters from Salamanca of the 28th, from which it is certain the French had not been there.

Cuesta has scarcely any troops at Badajoz; he is not over and above satisfied with our commander for refusing him aid, which considering the smallness of the force here could not be granted. There have been popular commotions, excesses, and murders at Badajoz. Dined at Mr.

Villiers's.

9th.—The French who entered Plasencia advanced on the 1st in the direction of Salamanca and Ciudad Rodrigo. This corps is said to be 8000 strong. Cevallos is appointed Ambassador to the Court of London. Cuesta has advanced from Badajoz to reoccupy the bridge of Almaraz. A heap of good news from Sr. Robt. Wilson, but not sufficiently authenticated to justify great confidence in them. It appeared to be the determination yesterday at head-quarters to make a great effort to assist Moore, *viz.* to send forward all the troops here. The policy at present is to bring from the country all the magazines which had been collecting at Vizeu, Lamego, &c.; but Sr. Robt. Wilson has, upon his own judgment, proceeded on to Ciudad Rodrigo with his Lusitanians, and taken with him provisions and ammunition, which, as he will most likely be taken prisoner, will fall into the hands of the enemy and be of infinite service to them.

★★★★★★

Wilson remained near Almeida in order to observe Lapisse's force which had now taken up its quarters at Salamanca. With a force varying from 1500 to 3000 men, he managed most skilfully to keep in check the French corps of 9000 men from January till April, and for some weeks actually interrupted their communications with Madrid.

★★★★★★

Junot, in his march from the frontier, lost 600 men from fatigue and hunger. Went to the Opera in evening.

10th.—Accounts of cruel excesses having been committed in many parts of Spain. Many officers murdered by their soldiers from suspicion of treachery. Cuesta is gone forward with troops to the bridge of Almaraz, and is organizing the army. I walked in Quintilla's garden. Mr. Setaro—called in the evening and gave some interesting particulars respecting the departure of the prince regent, and confirmed what we had already heard that Lord Strangford, far from being instrumental in inducing the prince to take the resolution of going to Rio Janeiro, was not aware of his determination till after he had embarked full 24 hours.

★★★★★★

Mr. Setaro was a Portuguese merchant, in whose charge was the victualling of the British fleet at Lisbon.

Lord Holland gives a full account of the Strangford controversy in his *Further Memoirs of the Whig Party.*

★★★★★★

11th.—The Regency received news from an officer in whom they have the greatest confidence, date, 4th, Zamora. He had been at the headquarters of Sr. John Moore at *Villafranca* on the 31st. He sends accts. of various actions both before and after the 31st, all of which appear to have terminated to the advantage of the English, and in one subsequent he reports Lefebvre to have been taken prisoner. (General Count Charles Lefebvre-Desnouettes (1773-1822) was captured by the British at Castro Gonzalo, near Benavente, on Dec. 29. The 18th Light Dragoons and the 10th Hussars were the chief troops engaged in the action. Lefebvre was sent to England, but escaped in 1811 by breaking his parole).

Gen. Cameron has left Almeida with 2 regts. in order to penetrate Tras os Montes to Moore's army. The 14th regt. of cavalry, (these had only arrived at Lisbon from England in December), which are embarked, were to have been sent round to Vigo by sea without delay, but the news of Moore's retreat will probably suspend their departure. The P. Government are out of spirits and depressed at the departure of our troops. From Badajoz they write confidently of Infantado's being at the head of a considerable army with which he is advancing against Madrid. (This was Infantado's 'Army of the Centre,' which was established at Cuenca in New Castile—about 21,000 men in all. The operations miscarried owing to the incapacity of the commander, and resulted in a disaster at Ucles. Infantado fled to Murcia, and was deprived by the *Junta* of his command, which was given to Cartaojal.)

Not above 8000 French are left to garrison Madrid. We are taking measures to go to Seville by the way of Ayamonte.

12th.—Gen. Cameron left Almeida on 5th; his line of march was through Torre de Moncorvo, Mirandella, and Bragança. Major Roche and Ld. Ebrington came from Pinhel. The magazines collected at Almeida are moving back to Oporto, and the officer who has charge of them has orders to destroy them in case of the approach of the enemy. The French have not been nearer than 12 leagues to Salamanca. Roche is quite a partisan of Cuesta's, and takes his part in that unfortunate dispute with Blake. (Major Roche had originally been sent to the Asturias, as a military agent under Sir Thomas Dyer, and was attached to Cuesta's headquarters—*Napier.*) The 14th are embarking, and Gen. Mackenzie with 2 regts. of infantry are to go with them to Vigo.

Upon a strict investigation of the Portuguese account from Zamora, it seems that the officer saw the English Army at Manzanal on the 31st, fortifying a place called Cevadon and cantoned in Ponferrada, Villafranca, and Viana de Belo.

13th.—We received a heap of letters from Coruña, Vigo, and Oporto. One from Ld. Paget, of the 23rd, at Sahagun, (see Appendix A). He mentions three brilliant affairs in which the cavalry distinguished themselves; in one my son, and Capt. Jones at the head of thirty dragoons charged 100 of the enemy, killed 20 and took five prisoners. (Sir Godfrey Vassall Webster—1789-1836—was Lady Holland's eldest son by her first husband. He was gazetted to the 20th Light Dragoons on Jan. 3, but was soon afterwards transferred back to the 18th, which was the regiment here engaged. This skirmish took place on Dec 23).

Complains of the apathy of the Spaniards, and rallies Ld. Hd. upon his *misconceptions* in their favour, adding that they are a *people not worth saving*. He adds in a postscript, 'We march to attack Soult tomorrow,' and seemed confident of success. Unfortunately this bright hope was betrayed, as Adl. de Courcy, in his letter to me of the 1st Jan. from Coruña, mentions that the meditated attack on Soult was not made on account of the great reinforcements from Madrid on their way to join him.

★★★★★★

Compare a letter in the Record Office. Sir John Cradock to Edward Cooke (Under Secretary, War Office), Feb. 26, 1809:

> I saw a letter today from those shocking people Lord and Lady Holland (I always put them together) at Seville. His Lordship says the French never had so large a force in Spain as was represented in England, and, what is worse they (the French) made our army believe it. Was not his Lordship content with the loss we sustained? (In the retreat to Coruña) I believe he would give the lives of ten English to save one Spaniard.

★★★★★★

The English have fallen back on the mts. of Galicia. Mr. Noble mentions the action near Castro Gonzalo, in which Lefebvre was made prisoner. Capt. Capel tired to death of Vigo, and is superseded by Sr. S. Hood. Gen. Broderick writes to Sir J. Cradock at Moore's desire to apprise him that the army is falling back to re-embark, and that transports for at least 14,000 men are wanting, and desires empty ones may be sent round to Vigo. This is dated the 3rd Jan., Coruña. (Capt. Capel wrote on Jan. 1 from Vigo: 'We have now 11 sail of the line here with 200 sail of transports, the whole of which force will, I conclude, remain here until the fate of Spain is fixed.'—*Holland House MSS.*)

An English officer writes from Puebla de Sanabria that the English headquarters are at Lugo. From an intercepted correspondence of Berthier's and Josef (*sic*) Bonaparte, it appears that Napoleon was at Astorga on the 31st Dec., (he reached that place on the evening of Jan. 1.—*Balagny*), and from an expression of reassurance it would seem that the great Napoleon himself had been alarmed, as Berthier says, surely, *assurément*, the emperor must be at his ease as he has 5 regts. of cavalry and 4 of infantry, a force quite sufficient.

He complains of Lefebvre (the D. of Dantzic), for sending a force from Avila to Plasencia, (Lady Holland was mistaken, the movement was really in the opposite direction, *i.e.* from Plasencia to Avila), a movement he says which disconcerted an operation of the emperor's; he adds, 'But one is not surprised at his obstinacy and stupidity, after his indecision in the *place d'Aranjuez*.' (This alludes to an affair of which, of course, we are ignorant.) The troops which were at Plasencia are gone to Bejar, and not to Ciudad Rodrigo.

14th Jan., 1809.—Everything prepared for our departure to Aldea Gallega. Carriages and mules already there, packages in the boats, and *all* ready. *I* was seized with a dreadful panic at the state of the public mind at Badajoz, and the journey to Seville by land is put off *sine die*. We dined at Mr. Villiers's.

Seville *Gazette* of the 6th, containing the capitulation of Madrid and that precious villain Morla's letter to the *Junta*.

From Vigo it appears that the advanced guard of the army was expected the next day; the soldiers march at the rate of 7 and even 8 leagues a day. Adl. Berkeley arrived with his family in the *Conqueror*; he of course supersedes the commodore. The ophthalmia rages in his ship.

★★★★★★

Admiral the Hon. George Cranfield Berkeley (1753-1818), son of Augustus, fourth Earl of Berkeley. He held the post of Commander of the Portuguese station until May 1812. He married, in 1784, Emily Charlotte, daughter of Lord George Lennox, and sister of Charles, fourth Duke of Richmond.

★★★★★★

16th.—Orders had been received at Vigo to send round the transports to Betanzos Bay, as Moore intended to embark his army there. On account of the swell and overflow of the Duero, ships cannot pass the bar, nor can they receive their lading. The consternation here is very great, every effort is making by the merchants to embark their property on board of the ships in the river.

★★★★★★

Robert Crawfurd and Alten's German brigade (3500 men) left the main body of Moore's troops at Astorga and retreated on Vigo, where they re-embarked without molestation. As to the rest, Moore did not finally make up his mind until he reached Lugo, which harbour he would use. In fact the transports only reached Coruña after arrival of most of his force, and it was only by good fortune that they arrived then. Lord Holland relates (*Further Memoirs of the Whig Party*) that the order to move the transports from Vigo miscarried, and it was only through a private letter to Captain Capel that Moore's intended line of retreat was made known to the British admiral.

★★★★★★

The Portuguese begin to murmur and complain of the English for coming among them to expel the French, and then abandoning them to their rage. Common people and clergy good, and ready to make any exertion and sacrifice. The Regency frightened. Freire begins to be insolent.

17th.—A perfect deluge of rain, and a westerly wind. Bar impassable.

18th.—Hazy weather, wind S.W., bar rough, and all matters very blank. Two letters from Col. Kemmis at Elvas, of the date of 16th. He complains of the want of accurate information of the force and position of the enemy; surprised at Gen. Cuesta's want of intelligence. Kemmis expected us, and sent a courier to meet us at Evora on 15th. Lt. Ellis writes from Truxillo, 12th, he saw a Spanish officer who had escaped from Madrid, and upon the strength of his report he went to Talavera la Reina. No French troops nearer than Madrid (and there not above 7000); in Toledo not more than 4,000 or 5,000. Bridge of Almaraz *impregnable with common perseverance*, but the Spaniards fled without firing a shot. (On Dec. 24, before the Duke of Dantzig's attack—it was his incomprehensible march to Avila which thus exposed Madrid). League and a half south the Puerto de Mirabete, the only one for nine leagues on either side and might easily be defended by a few hundred men.

This day being the queen's birthday, we dined at Mr. Villiers's, all from headquarters and the heads of the navy. Admiral and Lady Emily Berkeley; she is a very pleasing, handsome person. Many expressions, and I believe sincere ones, of good will and readiness to serve us from the admiral, but stated the utter impossibility of his being able to part with any force during the actual state of affairs, indeed that nothing could stir until they knew what Moore's destination was to be in future. One officer goes tomorrow with money to Col. Kemmis at Elvas to enable him to march from thence to Seville. (Col. Kemmis had orders to hand over Elvas to the Portuguese, and march his regiment, the 40th, to Seville. He was there to place himself under Mr. Frere's orders). This, coupled with the difficulty of getting a vessel, has induced us to resume our project of going by land, and accepting the opportunity of marching with the English garrison as an *escort*.

19th Jan., 1809, Lisbon.—Blew a heavy gale all night, the passage to Aldea Gallega too rough to cross; the bar is roaring audibly, consequently no ships could hazard to cross it in its present state. Called upon Ly. Emily Berkeley; she has a delightful house at Buenos Ayres. A messenger last night from Sr. Robt. Wilson; he is still between Almeida and Ciudad Rodrigo. He says he intends to *cover* the frontier of Portugal, or fall upon *Seville* if the enemy approaches. He has about 800 Lusitanians! An incomprehensible kind of letter from the Vice-Consul of Viana to Mr. Villiers; he transmits the copy of a letter from the *Junta* of Orense to the Govr. of Viana, with date of the 8th Jan., in which mention is made of the arrival of a corps of 4000 English. A postscript of the 10th adds, '5000 more English have entered, and Romana is expected, but his artillery came another route, a proof the French are not near.' (La Romana took the same line of retreat from Astorga as Crawfurd's force, and collected near Orense the remnants of his force, which had been severely handled by Franceschi on Jan. 2.).

Also that a *posta* had come with a letter for Romana, upon not finding him at the English headquarters at Lugo, and that Blake had taken it not knowing where he was. Sr. John Cradock is greatly alarmed at the position of Moore's army, and expects daily to hear of capitulation or convention. God forbid affairs should be in such a desperate state.

This day we were employed in taking measures for our journey, which is to commence tomorrow. Gen. Mackenzie, his *aide-de-camp*

Mr. Stuart, and Mr. Rawlins, Commissary-General, dined. The former is very restless at his detention here; he is pressing to get employed in S. Spain, and was almost embarked to go, but Mr. V. was frightened and did not think he could venture upon his instruction to send him away. This, under the strictest promise of secrecy, he told me. He is a man of an excellent, sound understanding, remarkably well informed in his profession, and very correct in his judgment. He laments the division of the English forces, wants them to concentrate in Spain. Catalonia would have been the best point; but Cadiz at present is the only one. Mr. Rawlins very obliging about mules, carts, &c., &c.; delayed the departure of Major Stuart with the money for Elvas to give us the certainty of reaching Elvas before the departure of the whole garrison. General Cameron is safe at Lamego with his 2 regts. Cypriano Freire complained to Ld. Hd. today of the sudden alarm which the English had taken, and the fluctuation of their plans. Spanish *chargé d'affaires* wants all troops to go to the Algarves.

Castaños is safe at Seville, and is to undergo his trial. (Ridiculous accusations were brought against Castaños and other generals of treachery and secret communications with Napoleon). The Supreme *Junta* are sending all the force they can collect to Infantado, who commands an army at Yepes, where he has had some advantage over a corps of French cavalry. They are allowed officers to raise companies consisting of one hundred horsemen, and each horseman has a man on foot; these companies are to harass the French, and to keep for themselves whatever they may plunder. When these armed bands are roving about, it will sometimes be a matter of fine distinction betwixt a friend and a foe.

21st.—One of the stormiest days we have seen this year. *En dépit du mauvais* temps we *embarked* at two o'clock on board an excellent boat belonging to the Govt. The waves ran high and the wind burst upon us in sudden and violent squalls; I scarcely know the inducement which could tempt me to encounter another such voyage! The boatmen were very skilful; we had engaged that they should only row, but such was the violence of the current that they could hardly stem its violence. We came in 2½ hours, the longest of my life! Reached Aldea Gallega by ¼ past five. A courier from Seville, who is charged with a letter to Romana, which he must deliver whenever he can find him. The commissioners, who had been sent by the Regency to examine into the sufferings of the people at Evora from the French, returned and arrived here this evening.

******

Evora was attacked by the French under Loison in July 1808, and was sacked by them. It was one of the seats of the Portuguese insurrectionary *Juntas*. Foy puts the numbers of Spaniards and Portuguese killed at 2000, while another historian speaks of four times that number. Lady Holland mentions 800 later in this book.

******

23rd, Arrayolos.—Lt. Ellis arrived from Lisbon during the night; he brought a letter from Sr. John Cradock to Ld. Hd., which he would not deliver to any person. He breakfasted with us. He is active, zealous, and seems intelligent. The enemy quitted Talavera on the 8th, but returned on 14th. (The 4th corps had been hurried forward from Avila, and with further reinforcements Joseph and Jourdan were able to again take up the positions allotted by Napoleon for the various bodies of troops south of the capital).

The column which crossed the Tagus was entirely composed of Poles; the cavalry keep with the infantry, and all march in a compact and numerous body; they are aware that all stragglers are cut off. Lt. Ellis was instrumental in saving the lives of 29 whom the peasantry had taken. They pretended not to understand French; he thought they were in reality foreigners, Poles. Had the Spaniards maintained themselves in Mirabete, and kept the bridge at Almaraz and Galluzzo advanced against the two regts. which forded the river, they must have been cut off, as the flood swelled the stream and they could not cross the ford. Cuesta has sent that general to take his trial at Seville.

He praised Cuesta for his activity and great abilities; already he is at the head of eleven thousand men, whom he has clothed in a uniform which gives them a more military appearance, and makes them forget that they are peasantry. He told us of 700 horse at Merida, an excellent, well-conditioned troop. He is the bearer of a letter to counter-order the departure of the garrison from Elvas, in case they should not have marched; if they have, they are to continue their route.

We met a Spanish messenger from Seville, which he left on the 22nd. He reports that the D. of Infantado had been compelled to fall *back* upon Cuenca in consequence of the affair at Tarancon, where the division of his army under Venegas was not supported as it ought to have been by M. del Palacio.

This evening Mr. Fletcher of Elvas came to see us; he is on his way

59

to Lisbon. Cuesta left Badajoz for the frontier of the Tagus on the 22nd. He thinks the road by Badajoz and Seville perfectly safe for us. He remained at Elvas while the French were in Portugal, being specially protected by Junot, who had lodged at his house and received civilities from him during his embassy. They did not suffer much from the French at Elvas. Terrible cruelties at Villa Viçosa and Evora; at the latter, persons of all ages and sexes were murdered in cold blood, two fine young men of Mr. Fletcher's acquaintance. Mr. F. knew one who was massacred in his own house and in the arms of his mother by a party who broke into the house and plundered it. The *cotton* which was taken by some English dragoons and Spaniards is now at Badajoz; Mr. Fletcher purchased it, and advanced 10 thousand crowns to the *Junta* upon it.

Elvas, 25th.—No certain information of the position of the enemy upon the Tagus. General Cuesta left Badajoz suddenly on 22nd. Part of his army had preceded him several days. His headquarters were at Merida, but although there are many stories, such as his movements being combined with those of Infantado, yet nothing is known for certain. He is said to be a person who consults with no one, and never imparts his plans. It is said that the French are at the bridge of Almaraz. Mr. Trabassos related some atrocities which the French had committed at Villa Viçosa. (During the occupation of Portugal by Junot. It was plundered by Avril at the end of June 1808).

Several persons were seized and brought to Fort la Lippe and shot without any process or form even of trial. One priest having been twice fired at and did not fall; the soldiers cried out he was sorcerer, and running at him with their bayonets, hacked, and mangled him shockingly. The people at Elvas, as they did not resist, smarted only in exorbitant contributions. Trabassos intends, if possible, to escape, and get away to *Brésil*. Ld. Hd. gave him letters to Adl. Berkeley and Mr. Villiers, in order if possible to facilitate his scheme. Col. Kemmis obliging, an Irishman; very pompous, and not to all appearance very wise. The garrison of Elvas are to march tomorrow to Seville—our road. The convalescents and cavalry return to Lisbon.

26th.—Left Elvas at 9. General Moretti, an Italian in Spanish service, met us on the Spanish ground with Col. Kemmis; Ld. Hd. rode on with them. I felt very happy to be once again on Spanish ground. Peasants scampering about on horseback in the true *Andaluz* style. Entered Badajoz under one of the arches of the bridge, which we afterwards went upon to cross the Guadiana. Crowds of people were assembled to view the troops; pretty sight. Rejoiced to see the *basquiña* and *mantilla*. We went to refresh at the house belonging to the Conde de Torre Fresno, murdered a few months ago by the people; he was the nephew of the P. of the Peace. His widow resides in the house, and came up to me and offered all sorts of civilities. (The Conde de la Torre del Fresno, Captain-General of Estremadura, was killed by the mob in Badajoz on May 30, because he was unwilling to give his support to their demonstrations against the invaders of their country).

We were visited by the bishop, the ex-capt.-general, the governor, &c., and by one of the inquisitors, who remembered us at Valladolid. An English officer, Mr. L'Estrange, came post from Sr. Robt. Wilson on his way to Seville; he left him at Ciudad Rodrigo on 24th, where he had assured the people he would remain and defend it to the last. The town is surrounded by an old wall, and is safe from a *coup de main*. There are heavy cannon which the French might employ in the reduction of Almeida. Salamanca yielded without striking a blow to 1800 Frenchmen. The Bishop went out at the head of some inhabitants, displaying a banner on which '*Vive Napoleon*' was inscribed.

He, Sr. Robt. Wilson, attacked an outpost and took a few dragoons, but had an English officer made prisoner. He contrives to keep the enemy at bay by spreading exaggerated reports of his strength and the approach of reinforcements. The common people thereabouts well-disposed, but the higher sort very frigid. A person of the name of Marshall introduced himself to Ld. Hd. as an acquaintance of Petty's. He states himself to have served with the Spaniards, and to have been made prisoner at Somosierra; examined by Napoleon himself, who was sitting before his tent at a fire an hour before sunrise, surrounded by his French. There is something *louche* in his story, the being prisoner and then assisting, after his escape from Madrid, in the assault of the *Buen Retiro*.

28th, Fuente.—Reached Los Santos at ½ past four. Baron A——, who commands a division of Romana's dismounted cavalry, called: his position is very distressing. (The four cavalry regiments which La Romana brought from Denmark did not Join Blake, having no horses, but marched into Estremadura to obtain them—*Oman*.)

The Supreme *Junta* are much to blame for negligence in not mounting these men, and securing them from falling into the hands of the French in their present defenceless state. He complained that he was detained by Monsieur Cuesta. When on their way to the Supreme *Junta* he undertook to mount them, but they say the horses of this province are incapable of sustaining the duty of a cavalry horse. They left Romana at Leon on the 3rd and 4th, and performed their journey by that identical route which our generals deemed unsafe to attempt their junction upon. When at Salamanca the *Junta* applied to them to assist in defending their walls in case of an attack; this they declined, as they were unarmed and unused to the use of artillery. The baron was too Frenchified for a Spaniard; he grumbled, and though he has much to make him complain, yet I did not like his series of grievances.

Lt. Ellis came whilst we dined. One of the deputies from the provincial *Junta* at Seville, who had been at Lisbon, and was just returned from Badajoz, having left it at 11 last night, brought an acct. from thence, *viz.* that the advanced guard of Cuesta's army had had an affair with the French, whom they had compelled to retreat and recross the Tagus at Almaraz. (Cuesta occupied the bridge at Almaraz on the 29th, and broke the central arch). Cuesta's headquarters were said to be Jaraicejo.

Arrived at Fuente de Cantos at ½ past one. Ourselves and maids were lodged in the house of a priest, the secretary of the Prior of Santiago. The priest could not comprehend who and what we were, when we assured him that we were not military, ambassadors, or merchants. I remember the last time we were in Spain persons were equally puzzled; they then satisfied themselves by asserting that Ld. Hd. was a *grandee* exiled from England.

Jan. 20th.—Arrived at Seville. The inn, in consequence of the fugitives from Madrid, is excessively full, and we were compelled to be contented with a very indifferent house. Dined at Mr. Frere's. Capmany was rejoiced at seeing us; he escaped from Madrid, and found his way here on foot, after experiencing some very severe hardships. Duchess of Osuna came to see me; she recounted, with great energy, her disasters. She fled from Madrid in the night upon the news of the French having broken the Spanish line at Somosierra, her three daughters, 9 grandchildren, and the wife of Gen. Pena and other friends, with no change of clothes. Her plate, &c., &c., all left to the mercy of the enemy. Quintana delighted at seeing us; he got away on the 4th from Madrid. I omitted an incident which occurred. About two leagues from Seville in the mts., we met a terrified friar on horseback, who had been attacked by robbers about a quarter of an hour before, and fired at as he made his escape. He seemed much concerned at the fate of his companions:—two *propios*, (messengers) of the Govt, he feared had fallen into their hands, and the robbers had drawn them off the high road into the wood. We left him encompassed with *tropas*, (soldiers).

31st.—Quintana and Rodenas came to see us, as did the Duquesa de Hijar and the Marquesa de Ariza; also Jovellanos, who had a very long conversation with Ld. Hd. We dined at Frere's, and in the evening I went to see the Dss. of Osuna.

An account from Mazarredo of the state of the English Army at Coruña; he left them on 13th. He draws a most disgraceful and lamentable picture of their retreat. They had not had any action of importance with the French, but had been fortunate in all the skirmishes. They lost in the retreat their baggage, their artillery, and even a portion of their money, and from the forced marches and state of exhaustion in which they arrived at Coruña, he is convinced many must have been left to perish on the road. They were so worn by hunger, want of rest, and disfigured by dirt, that they were scarcely to be recognised; the inhabitants scarcely could credit that they were the same men who set forth a few weeks before in all the pride and pomp of health and confidence.

They were employed in killing their horses, from an apprehension that there would not be sufficient number of horse transports. (The horses were in a shocking state, and over 2000 were slaughtered in this way). He describes having seen a number of dead bodies of horses floating in the bay. The French pursued them hotly, and from on board the *Tonnant*, he saw a party of French capture, on the opposite side of the bay, some sailors who were employed in dismantling a fort. The Duque de Veragua and Mde. Blake and her daughters were on board the *Tonnant*. Mde. Sangro in endeavouring to quit the town some days before had been stopped by the populace. *He says* Admiral de Courcy told him that when the order for retreating was communicated at Benavente to the soldiers, it was received with universal discontent, and the murmur was so great that they even refused to obey at first. Romana marched from Leon after the English had begun to retreat, and at Astorga he lost 2 battalions in an action with the French.

★★★★★★

La Romana lost 1500 men at the bridge of Mansilla on Dec. 30, the day on which he evacuated Leon and marched to join

Moore at Astorga. Lady Holland, however, more probably refers to an action on Jan. 2 near the pass of Foncebadon when Francheschi caught up the Spanish rearguard and took 1500 prisoners and two standards.

★★★★★★

1st Feb., Seville.—I called upon Madame d'Ariza; she had through Mr. Stuart's means complied with my wish of allowing me to occupy her house during her absence. The house is spacious, and has a fine garden; we move out tomorrow. (At time of publication the present residence in Seville of the Duque de Alba in the Calle de las Dueñas). Poor woman! She fled with her sister and son, the young Duke of Berwick, very precipitately, without taking even common necessaries; many of her jewels and all her plate is left.

2nd Feb.—Dined very early and moved in evening to this magnificent Casa Liria, a fine palace belonging to the Duke of Berwick, inherited from the family of Alba. In the evening Mde. d'Ariza, her son, Messrs. Arbuthnot and Wynne.

4th Feb.—Went to see the books at Casa Aguila; the library has been sold, and the best books purchased before we came. The house belonged to the Conde de Aguila, who was the first victim to the Spanish cause.

★★★★★★

The Conde de Aguila was shot in the streets of Seville on May 27, 1808, by the populace, though accused of no crime. Napier suggests that the assassination was instigated by a personal enemy of the Count. The early months of the rising against the French are full of these atrocities, for which the ungovernable fury of the mob was responsible.

★★★★★★

Mde. Santa Cruz called in evening. She is in great beauty, having preserved her looks much unimpaired. Rodenas, Major Roche, and Quintana dined with us. People called in the evening.

5th Feb., Seville.—Went to Santi Ponce to see the remains of Italica. On our way we stopped at the Hieronymite convent where General Castaños undergoes a sort of confinement, not being permitted by the Supreme *Junta* to enter Seville, though allowed to walk about the environs and see whom he chooses. Ld. Hd. made him a visit, and he came to see me in the sacristy. His manner is a good deal constrained, and he appears, from the size of his clothes, to have fallen away in bulk. He spoke of Gen. Fox with esteem, lamented that the *Junta* had not mounted Romana's cavalry in preference to the raw recruits; observed that on this day three months Napoleon had just entered Spain; sneered at the *grandees* (especially Osuna) for their want of zeal and military spirit; praised Perico Giron; expressed a wish to see Ld. Hd. another time. Went afterwards to see the remains of the amphitheatre, which is in a state of great decay. Dss. Osuna, Mde. de Sta. Cruz, Manuelita, Jovellanos, Capmany, Mariscal de Castilla dined. Some persons called evening.

6th Feb.—Went in the morning to see the Hospital de San Bernardo, called commonly Los Venerables. In the church a picture by Murillo, in which he imitates the manner of Ribera or Españolito, 'San Pedro'; 'the Concepcion,' a beautiful figure full of grace and dignity, the groups of angels airy and light, something about the mouth of the Virgin which betrays the manliness which he is accused of giving too much to his female figures. In the Refectory is the deservedly famous picture of 'the Infant Jesus giving bread to the old and infirm priests,' alluding to the foundation of the Charity.

★★★★★★

These three pictures were all removed to Paris by Soult. The Conception is now in the Louvre: the Distribution of Bread in the Gallery at Buda Pesth, the whereabouts of the St. Peter weeping is unknown.
The portrait of a *Canonigo* is that of Murillo's friend Don Justino Neve, the founder of the Hospital. It now belongs to Lord Lansdowne, at Bowood.
Of the Caridad pictures, the *Distribution of the Loaves and Fishes, Moses sinking the Rock*, and the *St. Juan de Dios* still remain in their original places. *Sta. Isabel (Elisabeth)* of Hungary is in the Prado Gallery, Madrid; *The Angel releasing St. Peter* at St. Petersburg (Hermitage); *Christ raising the Paralytic* belongs to Capt. Pretyman, at Orwell Park; and the other two are at Stafford House.

★★★★★★

Santa Cruz, where we expected to find the Tomb of Murillo, but the priests knew not where he lay. This church contains a 'Descent from the Cross' by Pedro Campana, which it is said was much studied by Murillo.
Caridad contains the famous collection of Murillo. 'Sta. Isabel of Hungary washing the sores of the lame and sick.' 'The angel releasing

St. Peter' (the worst picture). 'Christ raising the paralytic man.' 'The Distribution of the loaves and fishes.' 'Moses striking the rock.' 'The return of the Prodigal Son.' 'Angels visiting Abraham,' and 'San Juan de Dios embracing a sick man.' A few small altar-pieces of single figures. A 'Virgin and Child' near the high altar. The altar-piece is carved by Roldan and assisted in the perspective by painting and *basso relievo*. The founder is buried under the altar with an ostentatious show of humility, calling himself in his epitaph '*el peor hombre en el mimdo*.' The weather was delicious.

English forces under Gen. Mackenzie are arrived at Cadiz. An officer from Romana's army was an eyewitness to the embarkation of the British Army on the 18th from Coruña. On the 16th, 17th, a heavy fire of cannons was heard, which ceased suddenly, and upwards of 200 sail of transports was seen going out of Coruña, but they were soon becalmed, and their course could not be ascertained. The French were on the glacis before the embarkation was completed. Romana, in the gentlest terms, ascribes the ruin and dispersion of his army to Sir John Moore having deceived him; he promised to defend the pass of Villafranca, and Romana accordingly made his movements with that object, but in this he was disappointed, and lost on the 30th 2 battalions. Romana is making his way through the North of Portugal. Saavedra, the Minister, told Ld. Hd. that Sir D. Baird's army, it had been settled at Madrid, should be landed at Santander, in consequence of which preparations were made at that place for their reception. It was to the strange change of destination of the army that the difficulty arose at Coruña about their landing, and the subsequent delay of getting them forward.

★★★★★★

Any idea conceived by the British Government of landing Baird's troops at Gijon or Santander was given up owing to the smallness of those ports and the probable difficulties of finding supplies in the surrounding country.—Oman.

★★★★★★

Whilst Moore was at Salamanca, Escalante and another officer of high rank were sent to him from the *Junta* in order to urge him to advance; they remained with him some days. He was cold, repulsive, scarcely civil to them, and not in the least disposed towards the cause he was employed in serving.

★★★★★★

Don Ventura Escalante, Captain-General of Granada, and General Augustin Bueno reached Moore's headquarters early in December. That their reception by the British commander was not cordial is clear from his letter to Frere, dated Dec. 6. But perhaps it is hardly to be wondered at, for their glowing accounts of the condition of the various Spanish armies corresponded but slightly with those Moore was receiving from Stuart and Lord William Bentinck. Before their departure also he was able to introduce to them Col. Graham, who had just returned with an account of the action at Somosierra and the French advance upon Madrid.

★★★★★★

Ardelberg, Col. Duff called evening. There is a *poste* from Cuesta, in which he states having repulsed the French from an attack upon the bridge of Almaraz. Strong rumours of the French armies retreating into France, and of Napoleon's retiring to Vitoria. Successes also in Saragossa. (James Duff—1776-1857—afterwards fourth Earl of Fife, He took service with the Spaniards in 1808, and was made a major-general in their service. He became Lord Macduff in 1809; was severely wounded at Talavera, but continued in Spain till his father's death in 1811, when he succeeded to the titles, and returned home).

7th Feb.—Jovellanos dined and gave us some very interesting particulars respecting the present and past state of affairs. The D. of Infantado is removed from the command of the army, and the command is conferred upon Urbina, Conde de Cartaojal, a man who distinguished himself at the Battle of Baylen. The action at Ucles, Jovellanos thinks, has been the severest blow to their cause. The vanguard of their army, which was entirely cut to pieces, had been placed nine leagues in advance *sin apoyo ningun*, (without any support). Palafox is shut up in Saragossa with 25,000 men, troops of the line, besides the citizens; he is reduced to straights for want of provisions. (He had 32,000 trained fighting men shut up in the town. Lazan had moved his force of 4000 men from Catalonia to the neighbourhood of Zaragoza as soon as the investment commenced, but his force was insufficient to give efficient aid to the besieged).

His brother Lazan has written to Jovellanos for reinforcements, as 5000 men carrying in supplies had been cut off. Orders are sent to furnish what relief may be afforded, but as Reding writes from Cataluña that he occupies a very favourable position for destroying the French, he will not move. They reckon upon having 40,000 men in

Cataluña. Romana, with what he calls his *noyau d'armée*, is at Oimbra, near Chaves, in Portugal.

★★★★★★

After parting from Moore at Astorga, La Romana gained time to collect his scattered and disorganised force at Orense. There he remained till the middle of January, when the approach of a portion of Ney's force drove him to take shelter in the mountains on the frontier near Monterey. He was able to collect and reorganise a force of 9000 men, but was constantly obliged to move about owing to lack of provisions.

★★★★★★

His letters are 28th and 30th. He lost some of his best troops in consequence of co-operating as he expected with Moore, but Moore disregarded the combination and left him to shift as he could; and in consequence of Hope's division marching upon Vigo just before him, he had a corps consuming provisions in his front and a harassing enemy in his rear. (Hope himself was present at Coruña and took command after Moore's fall. Crawfurd's brigade was a part of his division). He writes that the French general had solicited an interview with him. He reports that Moore was killed whilst covering the embarkation of his men, that the French were on the glacis, and that they took possession upon capitulation of Coruña. He adds that Moore would have done better to have made the attack they had agreed upon on the 24th upon Soult at Sahagun than fallen thus.

Jovellanos is a good deal annoyed at the urgent manner in which the English press to be admitted at Cadiz.

★★★★★★

This was Mackenzie's brigade, which had been sent by Cradock from Lisbon on Feb. 2, at Sir George Smith's urgent request, to garrison the town in case of a French invasion of Andalusia. Smith, who was one of the many military agents, had neglected to consult the Home or Spanish authorities before taking this step, and Frere himself seems to have been unaware of what was taking place until he had sounded the *Junta* on the same subject and had met with an unqualified refusal. The *Junta*, disturbed by rumours of a British evacuation of Portugal, remained firm in their refusal to allow the troops to land. During the month which the transports spent in the harbour, riots, due entirely to internal causes, took place in the town. Sir George Smith died of fever about the middle of February, and the troops returned to Lisbon soon afterwards.

★★★★★★

The *Junta* are afraid of the suspicions which it will excite among the people, nor are they free from entertaining some apprehensions themselves of the views of the English Govt, in demanding that permission. A certain Sir G. Smith, a confidential friend of Ld. Mulgrave's, an *aide-de-camp* of the king's, and a man closely connected with Worontzow, pretends to be endowed with powers to call for any number of troops he may choose. He offered some to the Govt, of Cadiz. From the proceeding the *Junta* naturally infer that, as the English Govt. employs agents independent of their accredited envoy, designs are in agitation which are kept secret from him.

This, combined with the arrival of Mackenzie's small corps accompanied by the news of the retreat of the English from Galicia and a general belief that they are gone home, has naturally enough excited very strong alarm that the English may think their cause desperate and wish to pillage their arsenals, shipping, &c. Mr. Frere is very ready to insist upon the troops quitting Cadiz two days after they are landed, but he makes a sort of point of honour that they should be admitted there and not, as proposed, at Puerto Sta. Maria, as that would show in a marked manner distrust on the part of the Spaniards, and give a confirmation to Morla's insinuations.

8th.—Capmany dined with us. During the dinner. Padre Gil called. He is an incessant talker, full of himself and all he did; his loud voice and disgusting vanity displeased me so much that I fled for refuge speedily into my own room. He saved Andalusia certainly by his courage and presence of mind, but he is a man of such a turbulent nature that he is likely to lose it from mere restlessness and vanity. He is still a member of the *Junta* of Seville; he is discontented with the Supreme *Junta* for having usurped authority over them, and they in return are displeased with him and are going to dispatch him to Sicily to get him out of the way.

★★★★★★

A Franciscan and native of Andalusia, born in 1747. He was appointed Royal historian, but fell under the ban of the Prince of the Peace. He reissued from his monastery in 1808, and took a leading part in the resistance to the French, especially in the organisation of guerilla warfare, becoming Secretary to the *Junta* of Seville. He died in 1815.

★★★★★★

Poor Infantado is universally blamed for the loss of the army at Ucles. They say the French were really preparing to evacuate Madrid. The French have fallen back from Madridejos towards Toledo. The cause of this retrograde movement is not known. (Victor withdrew his main force to Almaraz, in accordance with Napoleon's orders that he should be ready to assist Soult's invasion when required, by a diversion in the direction of Badajoz. A screen of cavalry were left at Madridejos and Ocaña).

Napoleon has certainly quitted Spain and taken the road towards Toulouse. Rumours of war with Austria. *Oxala*!

9th Feb.—Two English ships of war arrived at Cadiz; they met the convoy *returning* from Coruña to England. Moore was killed; he remained to the last with a light corps whilst his men were embarking. Baird has lost an arm, and two other generals severely wounded. No mention is made of horses or artillery. The officer who spoke to them estimates the loss of the English at 3000. A corps of French which had reached Betanzos before them was cut to pieces on the 15th.

★★★★★★

The total loss at the Battle of Coruña of British troops was estimated by Hope, who took command after the fall of his superiors, as between 700 and 800. Mr. Oman considers this was probably an overstatement of the facts of the case. Soult's losses were perhaps about double.

★★★★★★

The *Junta*, by permission of the French in possession of Coruña, has received an official acct. of the capitulation of that place and of Ferrol, which surrendered on the 26th. Moore has closed the mouths of his accusers, and sought the only exculpation left to him.

Jovellanos and his nephews dined here. One is the Canonigo Cienfuegos, a member of the Seville provincial *Junta*, a cheerful, agreeable man, half-brother to the Asturian, Conde de Peñalva. The other —— was employed in the *bureau* of *Gracia y Justicia*; he is a remarkably unpleasant and even offensive person in his manners.

10th Feb.—There is a letter from Col. Whittingham to Mr. Frere, in which he represents the army of Palacio as being in a most flourishing condition.

★★★★★★

Colonel afterwards Sir Samuel Ford Whittingham (1772-1841).

While on his way to take up a staff appointment in Sicily, he got leave to join Castaños as a volunteer, and was instructed from home to remain with him. He took part in the Battle of Baylen and was made colonel of Spanish cavalry for his services. He was sent away by Infantado, and went to Seville, where he was subsequently employed under Albuquerque and Cuesta. He remained in the Peninsula throughout the war, and received honourable notice by Wellington in his dispatches.

Infantado had 12,000 men left after Ucles, and these added to 6000 or more with del Palacio and some new regiments from Granada make up the number. Cartaojal had taken over the whole at La Carolina on Jan. 24.

★★★★★★

The infantry amounts to 22,000, and 1700 cavalry, very fine men and all well accoutred, besides 10,000 men ready but wanting musquets. The Spaniards say they stand not in need of men, money, cannon, nor horses; saddles, musquets, and ammunition are all they require. Garay told us that great exertions had been made both in and out of Spain to procure *monturas*, (accoutrements), and that persons were employed in Sweden, Lisbon, and Constantinople even, to make them, and that a supply is expected from England. All the workmen in the province are *embargoed*—put into requisition. Infantado's army is in a wretched plight; they are at Sta. Cruz. Rodenas, who is in Garay's office, told me confidentially that it is in agitation that as soon as the army is well collected together under Urbina they are to advance towards Toledo in order to form a junction with Cuesta and attack the French on the N. side of the river.

Went by appointment to see the *Alcazar* with Jovellanos and his *agreeable* nephew. The lower apartment is occupied by the provincial *Junta*. The large halls, built by Charles V, are filled with modern pictures and the fragments of Roman antiquities found at Italica. The Central *Junta* hold their sittings above; adjoining to the room in which they deliberate Florida Blanca died. Jovellanos gave an affecting and philosophical description of his death; he was not aware of the approach of his dissolution, his memory flagged, and the whole moral system sank from the mere exhaustion of his physical powers. He was nearly 90. A pedantic physician termed his death *hydropesia senil.*

There were models of pikes and *crows' feet* (to injure the cavalry) lying about the tables of the room; they had been submitted to their inspection. Jovellanos presented to us his colleague from the Asturias,

71

the Conde de Campo Sagrado, (deputy from Asturias to the Central *Junta*): he is the 2nd in the *bureau* of War. He appeared active and zealous. Caught a glimpse of the man who seized the Viceroy of Mexico in his bed and compelled him to return to Europe, which he did and is now under confinement at Cadiz.

★★★★★★

José de Iturrigaray was Viceroy from 1803 until Sept. 1808. The Mexicans firmly refused to recognise the decrees of Joseph sent out to them from Spain, and had them publicly burnt. At the same time the viceroy was unwilling to receive representations from the *Juntas*, and gave the impression to many that he was about to usurp for himself plenary powers. To frustrate this a plot was set on foot, and the conspirators surprising him one night as he slept, formally deposed him. He was sent to Spain, where he lingered for some years in prison.

★★★★★★

Visited Garay in his office; he was busily employed, and surrounded by his secretaries.

The Spanish prisoners have the alternative offered them of being sent into France, or of taking the oath and serving Joseph; many to avoid the *agony* of being driven like a flock of animals have taken the latter part, doubtless with a mental reservation and strong feeling that what is done by compulsion is not binding in any court of conscience. King Joseph has issued a *bando*, announcing to his beloved *Madrileños* that he is going to quit them upon a military expedition, and requests them not to show demonstrations of attachment by delaying him; that that might ultimately be prejudicial to the general good. Persons from Madrid declare that it was generally considered there to be quite a matter of certainty that Austria had declared war against Napoleon, and that offensive operations in the Tyrol had been actually begun. (Austria declared war against Bavaria, an ally of France, on April 9; and the people of the Tyrol, who had been placed under the dominion of Bavaria, rose at the same time).

The Govt, are vigilant about the persons who come from thence with this sort of news, as they are probably spies disguised in the garb of friends and fugitives. It is rumoured that the titles of some of the *grandees* are already, with their estates, bestowed upon a number of French generals, Infantado, Osuna, Santa Cruz, Belliard, Bessières, Victor. Escaño, the Minister of Marine, is named to the Govt, of Mexico, but he is unwilling to abandon the *Junta* at this moment of peril. Since the occupation of Madrid by the French those ladies of distinction who have remained in it have never appeared in the streets, and to communicate with each other they have broken doors through the walls of houses, and can by that means maintain any intercourse they may choose to have together. The whole length of two streets and across the Plazuela in one place, and a singular mode of meeting in another part of the town has been opened.

11th Feb. 1809, Seville.—Kearney, an Irish English language master came from Carthagena, where he describes the slow state of preparation of 6 ships of the line.

We went to the Geronymite convent of La Bella (*sic*) Vista. A beautiful small picture by Murillo of the 'Concepcion'; a statue of San Jerome by Torregiano. It is highly esteemed; it represents the Saint on his knees before a book of devotion, with a crucifix in one hand, in the other a large stone with which he inflicts blows upon his heart. The material is of clay, and it is coloured. (At time of first publication these are now in the Picture Gallery). In the sacristy some pictures by Louis de Vargas. The architecture of the courts is in very excellent style, and a staircase, which being in the interior of the convent I was not permitted to see. Received some old letters from England, a very entertaining and well written one from L., (Lauderdale), with some good hits at Mr. Canning.

Col. Kemmis and Major Thornton to dinner. Great alarm prevails about Cuesta; the *Junta* are pressing Mr. Frere to make the troops advance from Cadiz.

★★★★★★

Napier relates that the *Junta* made four proposals regarding the disposition of the British troops: that they should land at Puerto Santa Maria and be quartered there; that they should be sent up to help Cuesta; that they should be sent to Catalonia; that they should be divided up among the Spanish armies. Frere suggested that part should join Cuesta and the rest garrison Cadiz, but no one considered this a satisfactory solution of the difficulty. Mackenzie contended that it would be exceeding his orders, and that re-embarkation after an advance towards the French would attach a stigma to his troops: while the *Junta* remained resolute that the force should not enter Cadiz.

★★★★★★

They show their adherence to official forms by requesting in the public note that he will order round the English Army from Galicia, whilst in fact they have received the official terms of the capitulation of Coruña and Ferrol after the departure of the English. Cuesta, in the *poste* of today, says the enemy are at Talavera making great preparations to cross the river and attack him.

The French at Madrid are said to be very crestfallen and dejected, and that even among the soldiery, especially the German and Poles, strong symptoms of discontent are manifested. Many desert to Cuesta. Mr. F. is desirous of making Gen. Mackenzie march on, and told Ld. Hd. that he had thought of employing him to go over and urge this measure. There are many letters from Galicia complaining of the atrocities committed by the English, and in one there is this expression, '*Terror enfurecido de nuestros aliados*,' (Fear spreads of our allies), who ravaged towns and villages and even surpassed the French in some of their excesses.

The substance of Jovellanos's conversation with me, when he spoke in the most open and frank manner possible, was as follows:—

1. An application was made to the English Govt, to furnish military support to Gen. Blake. Through Mr. Stuart, a promise of 10,000 men was made to them, who were to be landed at Santander to co-operate with Blake, then at Reinosa. Orders accordingly were issued by the Minister of War that every preparation should be made for the reception of this force. To the great astonishment of the Supreme *Junta*, the Governor of Coruña announced the arrival of the English Army in that harbour demanding cantonments about Ferrol, which request the governor did not think was consistent with his duty to comply with until he knew what were the intentions of his Govt, with respect to that armament.

★★★★★★

La Romana's force from Denmark, 10,000 in number, was first sent to Coruña: but orders were there received from England to send them on to Santander. Lord Castlereagh's dispatch to Lord William Bentinck, Sept. 30, 1808, states clearly the attitude of the British Government. 'It would have been more satisfactory, had our army been equipped for service, to have disembarked it at St. Andero, or some point nearer the enemy; but as it is of equal importance to the Spaniards, as it is to us, that the army should not be partially committed or brought into contact with the enemy, till the means of moving and following up an advantage is secured; and as the navigation on the coast becomes extremely precarious towards the close of the year, it was the decided opinion of all military men and of none more than the Marqués de la Romana, whose sentiments on the subject are stated in the accompanying memorandum, and will be expressed on his arrival in Spain as fully approving the decision that has been taken, to make Coruña our principal *depôt* and operate from thence.'

******

2. They have received from Apodaca, (the Spanish Ambassador in England), *las quejas* or griefs which the Eng. Govt, has against them. I could only collect three, but rather think there is a fourth which has escaped my memory, 1st, the delay in allowing Baird's army to land and the want of alacrity to supply and further them on their march. 2ndly, the reserve and want of confidence in the Spanish. 3rdly, their requiring the English generals to be subordinate to the Spanish generals.

The *Junta* set forth in reply and vindication that the disembarkation having been adjusted for Santander, there could be no complaint at their not being prepared for the reception of any army at Coruña. For in the place agreed upon between the *Junta*, Stuart, and perhaps Ld. Wm. Bentinck, the English were to act as auxiliaries to Blake; the plan of a junction with Moore having been quite a secret and subsequent project, it never having been understood by the *Junta* that the English were to act as a separate and distinct army.

******

Lord William Cavendish-Bentinck (1774-1839), second son of William Henry, third Duke of Portland. He was raised to the rank of major-general in 1808 for his services in India and was sent on a mission to the Supreme *Junta* in Spain. He joined Sir John Moore after Mr. Frere's arrival at Madrid, and took part in the battle of Coruña. He was sent to Sicily as Envoy in 1811. He was subsequently Governor-General of Bengal, and the first Governor-General of India.

******

To the accusation of reserve, Jovellanos says that the English Minister has access to the *Junta* during its deliberations, and gives an opinion upon the change of generals, movements of armies, &c., &c.

3. They have copies of Romana's notes to Sr. John Moore, in which

he offers to serve in any way, with or under any English general whom he may approve, only requesting Sr. John Moore to employ and dispose of him and his army in the manner he may deem most advisable for the general cause.

He complained of Moore's whole conduct, and his offensive treatment of the persons sent from the *Junta*. Escalante, when the first retreat was known, was deputed, and found him sulky and repulsive at Salamanca. In reply to the arguments urged to induce him to advance, he made no reply further than that, '*Mon parti est pris, mon parti est pris*; Romana has only 5000 men. I have ordered rations at Ciudad Rodrigo for the 10th of Dec, and *mon parti est pris*.' Escalante, disgusted at his reserve and haughtiness of manner, quitted him, finding it hopeless to attempt to make any impression upon such an obdurate character.

On his return towards Madrid, he met Don Juan de Texada, the Gov. of Ferrol, who was just come from Romana, and in great spirits at having been surrounded by an army already composed of 17,000 men, and which was daily increasing. This intelligence induced Escalante to return to Moore with Texada in order that he might hear a distinct account from an eye-witness, but Moore was contemptuous and incredulous, and they departed in despair of shaking his resolution. Mr. Stuart went from Truxillo in company with Caro, a deputy from the *Junta*, (and they were more successful, for after an interview with them Moore determined upon advancing.

★★★★★★

Don Francisco Xavier Caro, a professor of the University of Salamanca, and brother of La Romana. One of the deputies for Old Castile.

Stuart and Caro saw Sir John Moore at Toro on Dec. 16. They certainly had no hand in influencing the latter's decision to advance, for that was taken at Salamanca on Dec. 5, and the infantry actually commenced their march on the 11th. Moore's remark about Escalante being an old woman was repeated in a letter to Frere.

★★★★★★

(Moore told Stuart Escalante was an old woman. Stuart allows that Moore was haughty and offensive in all intercourse he had with the Spaniards.)

He looks upon Cuesta as a doubtful character, full of intrigue and ambition. The quarrel between him and Valdes, (Don Antonio Valdes—1744-1816): has been productive of much mischief. He is very popular in Castile and his present appointment is owing entirely to the clamour of the people in his favour. Had the *Junta* assembled in Madrid as it was originally proposed, he has no doubt that the people would have compelled them to have named Cuesta to head the army.

The loss of Spain he ascribes to the influence of O'Farril who was so highly esteemed by all the officers in the army. To him may be imputed the hesitating, irresolute conduct of Solano, Espiletta, Amarillas, Filanghieri, and several others of that class. Besides the general estimation in which he was held in the army, he formed a great party in consequence of that opinion in his favour and attached the young officers who were best informed and most zealous in the service.

The dispassionate and benevolent character of Jovellanos, considering all he has suffered, is very remarkable; there is such a mixture of dignity and mildness that it is impossible to avoid feeling the strongest inclination towards him of love and admiration. He views the active scene into which he is thrown with philosophical calmness, and should he see the cause he has espoused succeed he will enjoy the victory without triumphant exultation; and should it fail, he is prepared to fall without despondency or sinking in abject despair. Were he some years younger, he would attempt to direct the Govt, and begin by destroying their *Junta*, which in its form is vicious; it wants the promptness of Monarchy and the energy and confidence of popular Govt.

The D. of Infantado injured himself in the public estimation by his conduct at Bayonne, where he used to *submit* to associate with Savary, and pass his mornings playing at tennis, apparently cheerful and unconcerned at the dreadful web which was weaving to entangle his country, king, and friends. It was entirely owing to his advice and to that of Escoiquiz that Ferdinand VII acted as he did, although many persons believe that he remonstrated against his entrusting himself in the hands of Napoleon before his title was acknowledged.

12th.—The French have fallen back from the Mancha upon Toledo to the amount of 17,000 or nearly 20,000. It is not known how much of this may be destined against Cuesta. That general is threatened on his flank by troops from Coria and Plasencia. Letters from Sr. Robt. Wilson. He still keeps his position at Ciudad Rodrigo. Jovellanos said a *poste* had arrived from Romana, full of the most *amarga*, (bitter), complaints against Moore, his haughtiness, insolence, ignorance, and want of skill. A copy of these complaints has been sent to the Sec. of

State for Foreign Affairs. The retreat through Galicia abounded with instances on the part of our troops of every species of outrage and violence upon the poor inhabitants. Mr. Frere received accounts from England, by Cadiz, to the 14th Jan. He says 4000 troops under Gen. Sherbrooke are coming out immediately to Cadiz.

★★★★★★

Canning in his dispatch to Frere, dated Jan. 14, states that the British Government considered that the South of Spain was now the most important place in which to assist that country. Four thousand troops had therefore been dispatched under General Sherbrooke, with orders to go on to Gibraltar if not admitted into Cadiz. They only reached the latter place, however, just as Mackenzie was leaving, and were taken by him to Lisbon.

★★★★★★

14th.—Went to the Franciscans, and by good luck got into the cloister where are the famous Murillos. The finest without all comparison is the 'Death of Santa Clara'; I scarcely think any of those in the Caridad excel it, but unfortunately the moisture of the air to which it is exposed, has considerably injured the picture. The figures of friars standing before a Pope are also an exquisite performance. The sides of the small cloister are covered by Murillo, but these are his masterpieces. A 'Concepcion' in the church; a fine altar-piece carved by Mertunes. A Walloon regt. quartered in this spacious convent.

Ld. Hd. received a note early from Jovellanos, in which he mentions the arrival of the *poste* from Cuesta during the night, containing the acct. of the enemy being in motion near the bridge of Arzobispo, but *todavia*, (nevertheless), not in great force. Cuesta had been interrogated by the *Junta* as to the meaning he affixed to the bridge of Arzobispo being *intransitable*, (impassable), he explained by saying that from the strong fortified position he has taken the French cannot penetrate by it to the southwards.

★★★★★★

Notwithstanding Cuesta's assertion Lasalle's cavalry were able to cross the bridge on Feb. 19, and force Trias' division which was opposed to them to take refuge in the mountains. The French, however, soon retreated over the river, and Cuesta again remained undisturbed for another month on the line which he had taken up south of the Tagus.

★★★★★★

Mr. Walpole from Cadiz. Sir John Moore was wounded by a cannon ball. He very gallantly, at the head of his own regt., was supporting the 50th and 42nd out of Coruña to cover the embarkation. He spoke after his wound to Col. Graham. It required such an end to redeem his reputation.

16th Feb.—Jovellanos wrote a few lines to mention, and with concern, that Infantado had not complied with the orders of the *Junta* to go to Seville. From various circumstances it appears that nothing can be more unfortunate for the duke than the *mal entourage* and his own irresolution of character.

There is much disgust expressed in this place against the Central *Junta*; it is said by its enemies that Gen. Cuesta is abandoned, and that they would rejoice at hearing news of his defeat. People also talk big that if that disaster should happen Cuesta would march against the *Junta* and dismiss them from the administration of public affairs. All make in exception in favour of Jovellanos, whom they say always proposes good measures but is overruled by Garay and others, who consequently are become obnoxious. These complaints come from the provinces also, where the *Junta* are accused of ignorance and incapacity, and blamed for the selfish objects they have in view.

It is even said that gold is amassed and not issued from the Treasury, in case on the approach of the French the *Junta* should be compelled to fly, and this hoarding would furnish them with a supply. Capmany dined with us, also Quintana, Rodenas, Mr. Luttrell, Mr. Pearce. Saragossa still held out on the 8th, though completely invested, nor were there any thoughts entertained of its surrendering. (Zaragoza had been invested for a second time since the middle of December. The actual siege was commenced on Dec. 20, and lasted until Feb. 20, on which day the remnants of the garrison marched out).

Don Francisco Ferras y Cornel, who is the nephew of the Minister for War, who is himself an Aragonese and was in Saragossa during the sixty-one days' siege, and who came from thence only lately, says there were upwards of 30,000 infantry and 800 cavalry in the city. A population of 60,000 souls, with a prodigious proportion of women. Bread in abundance, but meat and forage is scarce. An attempt was made to throw in some succours, under 5000 men, but they were baffled, and entirely cut off.

Joseph has issued orders to raise 40,000 men by conscription; this has had a good effect already, as many to escape it have fled to Romana, and 2000 already have reached Ciudad Rodrigo. Persons from Madrid attest the departure of Joseph from thence; some say he is gone to Valladolid, others to Toledo. If the former, it is to be out of the way of the population of Madrid; if the latter, it will be to take the command most likely of the force destined to act against this province. It is believed that the Galicians, especially about Orense, have risen in arms against the French.

★★★★★★

A general rising, encouraged by La Romana and fanned by the local priests, took place early in February throughout Galicia, and added seriously to the many difficulties which Soult had to face in his invasion of Portugal.

★★★★★★

Infantado still remains with the army; he does ill to contest with the Govt, he has promised to obey.

17th.—Went to see the mosaic pavement at Italica. On our return met 600 cavalry well appointed, but moderately mounted, making on towards Cuesta. Many of the trees about town are felled in order to deter the enemy from using them should they approach near enough to assault city. Works are going on; the lines are extensive, but the English engineers think them very badly constructed.

18th.—A *poste* arrived from Cuesta with the intelligence of the French having passed the bridge of Arzobispo, with what design is unknown. Genl. Trias had taken a position at Garvin. In evening found Jovellanos, and Hermida, the Minister for *Gracia y Justicia*. He had received a most desponding letter, dated 16th, from Cuesta, who laments his own situation from whom so much is expected; that his means are inconsiderable to oppose the force which is opposed to him, that he can only depend upon 12,000 men, and the enemy exceed 24,000. He concludes by advising him to recommend himself to God, who alone can work miracles.

★★★★★★

Don Benito Hermida (1736-1814) was a judge for some years, but abandoned his profession for politics, and held high office until 1803, when he was disgraced for his opposition to certain measures of Godoy. He took a leading part in the affairs of the nation after the abdication of Charles IV. He was a fine linguist and musician, and was a skilful lawyer.

★★★★★★

The account of Saragossa is alarming. Napoleon weary of the tedious manner in which Moncey was pursuing the siege, ordered Lannes to take the command, and carry the town by *vive force*. The French are in possession of the outworks, and a battery in the town which commands a Spanish fort raised in a convent. Palafox complains of having such unequal powers of artillery; the calibre of his not exceeding *pieces of 8.*

Went in the eve. to Mde. Osuna's. She had received a letter from Perico, dated 13th, Almagro, where he was with an advanced guard of 11,000 men under the D. of Albuquerque, detached from the main army of Urbina to assist Cuesta; they were to be at Ciudad Real on 14th.

★★★★★★

This statement that these troops were detached to 'assist Cuesta' is somewhat misleading. The help was only indirect, *i.e.* to keep the French busy, and prevent them from reinforcing Victor who was opposed to Cuesta. It was, according to every authority, after the affair at Mora on Feb. 18 and his subsequent retreat to Manzanares, as mentioned later, that Albuquerque was detached by order of the *Junta* with 3500 infantry and 200 cavalry to join Cuesta.

★★★★★★

Infantado has not yet given up the command; he wishes to remain with the army and act only as colonel of his regt., but this will not be permitted. I am sorry he holds out still.

Blake arrived tonight from Portugal, full of griefs against Romana probably, as he quitted him abruptly at or near Orense. A courier from Vienna, which he left on 10th, brings the account of the bakers having received orders to prepare ammunition bread, and the artillery horses to move onwards. On the 12th at Trieste the Russian ships were getting ready to move out of the harbour.

19th.—Palafox has written to Col. Doyle, who transmitted a copy of the letter to Mr. Frere. It is dated the 7th Feb. He says he foresees they must perish within the walls, which he is prepared to do, but that it is hard to fall without any attempt having been made to relieve him. Their situation he represents as deplorable, and refers him to the bearer for other particulars. The circumstance he would not write was that a contagious fever was raging amongst the inhabitants. Doyle is resolved to go with the force which is to attempt to force its way with

81

a convoy of provisions.

The division of the Central army which has advanced to assist Cuesta was at Yebenes on 15th.

Reports of the Galicians having risen in many parts against the French, and to have cut off corps convoying supplies. In Val de Orsas they have killed 84 cavalry and taken 19, with the plunder of Genl. Marchand.

★★★★★★

The approach of Marchand's division, belonging to Ney's corps, forced La Romana to evacuate Orense and move south to Chaves and Monterey; in which neighbourhood he was continually forced to change his headquarters owing to want of provisions.

★★★★★★

Romana estimates the loss of the French in their pursuit of English through Galicia at 14,000. Romana writes a private letter, date, 7th, to Jovellanos. On the 12th in his *poste* he mentions that in consequence of the favourable reports from Galicia, he had resolved upon return-ing thither, and had already reached Monterey. I feel he is sanguine, but he adds that he expected in a week to have 3 divisions of 10,000 men each.

Quintana's *manifiesto* on Europe appeared today. Jovellanos at-tempted to read it, but he was so affected that he could not pursue the lecture. It is written in a most masterly style, and in the appendix the letters from Murat to Dupont are annexed. They add, if any additional proofs were required, to the certainty of the base system of treachery and perfidy which were pursued by the French towards this country.

★★★★★★

Quintana was appointed head of the secretariat attached to the *Junta*, and was personally responsible for many of the orders and manifestos issued at the time by that body.

★★★★★★

20th Feb., Monday,—Cuesta is not so well disposed towards the English as he was previous to their retreat from Galicia. Lt. Ellis, who is returned from his headquarters, left him on acct. of the coolness of his reception and manner.

Fernan Nuñez, who is just come from his regt. at Ecija dined here, also Quintana, Paiz,—*auditor de guerra* in Romana's army in the north—and Mr. Luttrell, (a natural son of Lord Carhampton, the well-known wit and poet. He was a frequent visitor at Holland House in later days.).

Fernan Nuñez is in a bad state of health, and from his appearance and the strong symptoms he has of a pulmonary disorder, I fear he is in a declining state. He lost in hard specie in his house at Madrid, one million 8000 *reals*, money he had raised for his regt., besides all his papers, many of which were valuable as they would throw light upon many of the transactions previous to capture of Ferdinand VII.

General Blake came with Don Francisco Ferras y Cornel in eve. His manners are plain and simple, his whole appearance military and prepossessing. He expects very little from the Galician peasantry, unless they should be assisted by regular troops and commanded by some able leader. He reckoned the French force which pursued the English into Galicia at between 28 and 30,000.. Romana's loss in retreat arose more from sickness, hunger, and desertion than from the attacks of the enemy, with which it does not appear he ever was engaged. I questioned him as to the succour he expected from Santander; he said he was greatly disappointed at their not arriving, as he had been long led to expect them (another proof that the original destination of the British troops was to have been at Santander). He praised Lefebvre, (Duke of Dantzig), whom he reckoned the most enterprising general who had been opposed to him; the French operations were much brisker after Lefebvre assumed the command.

Blake evidently took the by roads through Portugal to avoid touching Cuesta's territory; he entered upon the high road at Santa Ollala. He mentioned the strange impudence and assurance with which the French assert the greatest falsehoods in their bulletins, not only in falsifying and misrepresenting accounts of battles and engagements, but really in describing actions which never took place, and boasting of victories gained and prisoners taken, where there never was even a Spanish patrol. He gave one or two instances, and named the places where such examples had occurred.

Romana in a confidential letter to Jovellanos, which he entrusted to Lord H. to read and even copy, estimates his loss in his retreat from Leon, owing to fatigue of body and mind and putrid fevers, to not less than ii colonels, one general of division, and a great number of subaltern officers of distinguished merit. He uses very strong language about General Blake and Martinengo, whom, he says, shamefully *fled*, abandoned, and seduced from him many officers, and taken the military chest. His army, he states to be at present about 8000 men, but without arms, ammunition, or generals. He has been assured the

French lost from 4,000 to 5,000 men in the action at the Puente de Burgo, (Coruña), and that had not Moore been killed, and the 2nd-in-command wounded, they would in probability have been greatly cut up, nor would the English have retreated.

21st.—Cuesta has removed Trias from his command, for not attacking French when they crossed bridge at Arzobispo. *Junta* have already sent to Cuesta 2000 muskets two days ago, and are to send him 2000 more tomorrow. Cartaojal has removed his headquarters to Valdepeñas. No certain news, but some unpleasant stories about the surrender of Saragossa.

22nd.—Jovellanos told us the contents of Cuesta's *poste.* Body of French, 4000, attacked one of Cuesta's advanced posts, consisting of 300, in which the Spanish commander was killed after having employed the enemy near 3 quarters of an hour. They were driven back to Alia. The French, Cuesta imagined, were pushing on to Guadalupe with an intention of pillaging the convent, but if that should be their object they will be foiled, as the riches of the convent and all the monks have been removed.

From Ciudad Real Perico writes to Dss. of Osuna on the 17th it was supposed in the army that an attack was to be made upon Toledo. General Blake has received orders from the *Junta* to serve in Cataluña, where, as Reding is the oldest general, he will only act as 2nd-in-command. I asked him when he first knew that he was not to be succoured from Santander, his answer:—'Only when I heard the English had landed at Coruña.' Had they even landed at Santander when they did at Coruña, he would have been saved, as the French did not begin their attack till full 10 days after the troops might have been landed, refreshed, and ready for action.

******

Reding died early in March from the wounds received at the Battle of Valla on Feb. 25. Blake on his arrival at Tarragona found himself in command, and received the post of commander-in-chief of the *Coronilla*—Aragon, Valencia, and Catalonia.

******

Dn. Francisco said they had been busily employed in going through the business of Genl. Eguia, who is now confined in the Cartuja; the accusation against him is that he did not defend Somosierra on 29th. Cuesta wishes the trial to be deferred in order that he may be sent to him; he is reckoned an able military character, and Cuesta complains of the total incapacity of most of those under him.

★★★★★★

General Eguia was head of the 'Army of Reserve' and held the command of the troops collected for the defence of Madrid against Napoleon's advance in Nov. 1808. His subordinate San Juan was in charge of the division entrusted with the defence of the Somosierra. Eguia later became second-in-command under Cuesta, and succeeded the latter when he was obliged by failing health to resign after the Battle of Talavera.

★★★★★★

23rd Feb.—Went to the cathedral with the Canonigo Cienfuegos; Jovellanos joined us during our stay in the cathedral. . . . There is a public library belonging to the cathedral, which is open at fixed hours daily for the benefit of the public. It contains some useful reading books; above the bookcases are a range of portraits since the first Archbishop of Seville down to the present. The first was the son of San Fernando, the present is the Cardinal de Bourbon, brother of the Pss. of the Peace, and son of the Infante Don Luis.

Quintana, Rodenas, Mr. B. Frere, Mr. Pearce dined. Luttrell eve. During dinner Sangro (the Galician deputy) arrived. He appeared excessively dejected; he had a bad voyage from England, and heard at sea off Coruña the deplorable retreat of the English army from Galicia. He thinks the *Junta* are not acting wisely here, and desponds of any good arising unless their discussions are public and their representation more numerous. Romana is still at Oimbra, but is very sanguine about the state of the public mind in Galicia. He has advised the Bishop of Orense to return and fulfil his duties there. His secty., Cacciaperos died at Orense of a putrid fever. He complains of Blake's flight. The French are said to have lost all their horses in Galicia, and have been compelled to mount their men on mules and asses in order to transport them back to Castile.

24th Feb.—Albuquerque with 1000 horse surprised a corps of French cavalry of 400, commanded by a Gen. Dijon or Dejean, took a hundred prisoners and the general *equipage.*

★★★★★★

This was the affair at Mora on Feb. 18: The French losses were probably not so large as here stated. The French commander was General Digeon. Jourdan in his *Memoires* remarks that Albuquerque was responsible for a false statement of facts in his

85

dispatch to the *Junta*, which caused great elation at Seville. This is evidently the version believed and quoted by Lady Holland

✶✶✶✶✶✶

The Spanish infantry ought to have come up and surrounded the town of Mora, by which the escape of the enemy would have been rendered impracticable, but the guides who conducted them mistook the way, and they went by Yebenes, which caused the delay of half a day, and the *coup manquéd*.

There was a serious disturbance at Cadiz. The pretext was that 1500 Poles, who were made prisoners in Dupont's army, should not be allowed to garrison the town, and the people rose and shut the gates against them. They also seized the person of Villel, a member of the *Junta*, and but for a Capucin who interposed for his personal safety, he would probably have been destroyed. He had offended the people by interfering with their amusements, and even dresses; they accused him of treachery and being upon the point of betraying Cadiz to the enemy. The *poste* arrived from Seville during the scuffle, and the mob insisted upon seeing the dispatches; fortunately the contents referred solely to the fortifications of the town, &c. The people entrusted him to the custody of the Capucins.

✶✶✶✶✶✶

The Marqués de Villel had been sent to Cadiz as Special Commissioner, and it was to his treatment of the people that this *émeute* was due. He appears to have considered that the reverses of the Spaniards were due to the decadence of their habits and customs, and took drastic steps to try and find a remedy. Colonel Leslie, of Balquhain, in his *Military Journal* mentions that none of the British rank and file on the transports in the harbour were allowed to land in the town, but that the officers continually came ashore and were received with enthusiasm by the inhabitants. See also Appendix C.

✶✶✶✶✶✶

They then drew up a series of their grievances; among those enumerated is that persons favoured by the P. of the Peace still retain their offices, that accused persons were not tried, and various other points. Heredia, who was placed in some office by the P. of the P. at Puerto Santa Maria, was murdered by the populace, (head of the coastguard, and unpopular for his severe measures against smugglers); and orders that Caraffa and the ex-Viceroy of Mexico and another prisoner should undergo their trial immediately. The temporary Govt, is en-

86

trusted to a *Capucin* friar and Felix Jones, the Govr., (an Irish officer in the Spanish service. He was military governor of Cadiz). Several edicts and *bandos* are issued. One is that no foreign troops whatever shall enter the town of Cadiz, but that the artillery officers of their faithful ally the English shall come into the town and examine the state of the works, there being a suspicion entertained by the people that the *Junta* have ordered the fortifications to be so constructed that the enemy may not find any impediment from them.

25th, Seville.—Albuquerque's movement meets with general disapprobation—*cosa de muchacho, (foolhardy).* There is a conjecture that an English Colonel Whittingham, who is in correspondence with Mr. Frere, has made him push on beyond the limits prescribed by the *Junta.* Cuesta *se quexa mucho,* (makes many complaints), he expected the reinforcements to join him by 22nd.

Blake is clearly of opinion that Moore might have defied the power of France if he had taken his position in the valley of Vierzo between Villafranca and Manzanal. He could only have been attacked by the enemy in front; the nature of the country prevented his being flanked. Capmany read us a proclamation he is going to publish in a few days.

Arriaza, the poet, has made his escape from Madrid; he came in the disguise of a *mayoral,* (shepherd). Also several other persons have got away both from Bayonne and Madrid.

26th, Sunday.—Sangro, Mariscal de Castilla, Mr. Pearce to dinner. Eve, Jovellanos, Conde de Campo Sagrado, Mr. B. Frere, Mr. Pearce. Blake considers Moore's first alarm of being flanked by the French by Mondoñedo through the Asturias as too ridiculous to have been a serious opinion; he allows that the enemy might have entered Galicia by the pass of Sanabria, but rejects the probability of their doing so, as artillery could only pass with difficulty, and the attempt was too hazardous for them to make. He saw Ld. Paget only once, but, from all he collected from the Spanish generals and officers, is positive that of all the English generals Ld. P. was the most averse to the retreat. It was also considered as an unpopular measure amongst the inferior officers and troops.

27th.—Rodenas, Quintana, Mr. Ellis, Pearce, dinner. After the action at Mora, Albuquerque fell back upon Consuegra, where he was briskly attacked by the French, who had received by forced marches reinforcements from Madrid, Aranjuez, and Toledo, to the amount of 12,000 infantry and 2000 cavalry. The retreat of the Spaniards was made in good order; the cavalry covered the rear, and he reached Villarta with the loss only of four or five men. He has joined Urbina's main army at Valdepeñas. The Spanish cavalry had greatly the advantage over the French. This circumstance has put them into great spirits here; besides they consider this diversion as having operated in keeping Cuesta free from an attack, which from the force collecting at Talavera would probably have taken place almost immediately.

Great complaints of Frere, whom they accuse of *mauvaise foi,* and say he has pushed the affair of landing troops at Cadiz with malignity. He wears the patience and takes up the time of the *Junta* in making long-winded speeches full of equivocal expressions in confused and unintelligible Spanish. Garay has resolved to conduct all business in future by notes. The *Junta* have peremptorily refused to allow the admission of the English troops into Cadiz. Frere assured them arms were embarked on the 18th Dec. for Spain, and their not being arrived has filled them with suspicion against Frere, whom they suspect of asserting facts without having any authority to do so from his Govt.

28th.—The English troops afloat before Cadiz are to return to Lisbon! It seems now that Mr. Frere, who said he had no authority over them, can dispose of them as he likes. Jovellanos speaks of Frere's conduct as having been intricate and violent; they all appear dissatisfied personally with him, because Apodaca's dispatches, which are subsequent to those Frere has received from his Govt., do not state the wishes of the English Ministry to be at all urgent with respect to the occupation of Cadiz by English troops.

1st March, Wednesday.—Col. Doyle's last letter to Mr. Frere was dated 22nd Feb. Saragossa had not then fallen. He mentions their being in possession of positive information of French troops having left Spain. Mr. Tupper (the partner of Price, an English merchant at Valencia) writes from Valencia that several of the Swiss Cantons are in insurrection, as they do not choose to have Berthier imposed upon them for a king. (One of Berthier's recent honours was his appointment as Sovereign Prince of Neufchâtel). The French papers breathe war in very hostile articles against Austria. They give a copy of Hope's dispatch upon the embarkation at Coruña, at which, as he terms it victory, they very fairly sneer, and hope the English may always enjoy such glories.

Some persons think that it was the D. of Infantado's intention, had he succeeded in getting to Madrid instead of being so cruelly cut up at

Ucles, to have in concert with Cuesta destroyed the Govt, of the *Junta* and restored the Council of Castile to its splendour and functions. He is the President of that Council, and Cuesta is also a member.

2nd March.—A report of Castaños having been murdered in a village by the people on his way to Algeciras.

Arriaza is a writer of considerable merit; he published some pretty verses, and had lately rendered himself conspicuous by the *Prophecy of the Pyrenees*, and a *National Hymn* in honour of the Battle of Baylen. He could not get away from Madrid when it was first occupied by the enemy, and he remained tolerably at his ease, in consequence of its being given out that all men of letters and science might remain and should be protected. He was to his dismay, however, informed that the French sought him and had resolved to shoot him. He escaped being arrested by his presence of mind, for on perceiving two suspicious men waiting for him at his house door, he passed on, took refuge with a friend, and got out of the town in the disguise of a *mayoral*. This was very difficult for him, as he is uncommonly short-sighted and wears spectacles constantly. He was suspected at Toledo, but after some risks and many alarms he arrived here about a week ago.

Napoleon was accompanied in his journey into Spain by a clever man of the name of Edouville, a French emigrant, who had been kindly received in Spain when of the age of 12 years. This man, who is a mixture of literary and military character, has given him a great insight into Spanish manners and customs. He read aloud, and translated as he read, Capmany's first *Centinela*; some passages he wished to skip, but Napoleon insisted upon the whole. Arriaza was a great friend of the O'Farril; he is, like all the others who knew O'Farril, astonished at his conduct, and convinced that he is full of remorse for the mischief he unintentionally has caused, (by taking service under the French). O'Farril, Mazarredo, Azanza, and Urquijo act together; the other part of the Ministry headed by Cabarrus, whose adherents are Arriba, Romero, &c. Arriba is a man of very extraordinary talents, who owes his situation entirely to his own assurance and enterprise: his office is Grand Judge. Romero is a very able man, draughted from the corps of *abogados*, and is placed at the head of police.

The French officers when among themselves and talking over the state of the war in Spain bore testimony universally to the military talents of Blake, whom they said after a severe day's fighting, in which he was outnumbered and obliged to retreat, never lost one piece of cannon; and when he retreated at night he disappeared, and was always found the day following in the best position. After the Battle of Zornoza, in which Blake showed great talents. Napoleon asked O'Farril, 'Who is that Blake?' '*Sire, c'est un bon militaire, et un parfait honnête homme.*'

Cuesta mentions in his *poste* that a French *parlementaire* appeared at the bridge and announced the fall of Saragossa. The report is not entirely discredited, though considered by Cuesta as an artifice of the enemy to ascertain the state of the bridge. Story of Castaños quite unfounded. He arrived at Algeciras amidst the applause of the people, who retained a grateful recollection of his good govt, when he commanded there.

3rd March.—D. of Infantado came to us; he is thin and altered.

4th March.—Cuesta relates, in his *poste* of today, a ridiculous circumstance, which if it was meant as a stratagem of the enemy to ascertain the state of the bridge, ended fatally for their *employé*. A man from the French posts appeared dressed like a priest when officiating at mass, and announced himself a messenger from the Virgin. The sentinel levelled his piece, fixed, and shot the holy ambassador dead. It was a whimsical incident and not very intelligible.

5th.—Blake set off on Friday for Tarragona, by the way of Malaga, where he intended, if a good opportunity offered, to embark. A malicious story circulated against him, which had been even laid before the *Junta, viz.* of his sketching the fortifications from the summit of the Giralda, marking certain points, and expressing concern when the paper was carried off by a gust of wind. He had made an outline of the works. He was perfectly at liberty to do so, but Don Francisco Ferras, who ascended the Giralda in his company, declares the whole story to be a fabrication. Changes meditated in the Govt.; Council of Castile likely to be revived. Talked of Infantado's views. Infantado obliged to go to Cadiz to his mother, who is unwell; has promised to return as speedily as possible.

7th March, Tuesday.—Saragossa fell on the 21st and 22nd. (20th and 21st. Oman says that about 8000 peasants and soldiers marched out of the town). Palafox had given the command to St. March, as he was attacked by the epidemic of which he was dying. Genl. O'Neille was dead, and St. March confined to his bed dying. (St. March's appointment was ill taken, and Palafox handed over the supreme command to a *Junta* of thirty-three persons—*Oman.*) The garrison from 30,000 men was reduced to 5000; the general ration had long been 4 ounces of bread and a small allowance of oil. The French army was reduced to 16,000 men. The town yielded to the mode which the French pursued of undermining and blowing up every house in succession.

Reding met with a smart check, and has been compelled to fall back upon Tarragona. He was wounded in 5 places. Col. Doyle also is ill of the contagion; it is feared that in the Army of the Centre there prevails an epidemic, and as they are ill provided with medicines and surgeons, there is great reason to fear it may occasion havoc and spread over the country. The enemy are withdrawing from the south of Madrid, and Cuesta writes that he shall construct pontoons in order to cross the Tagus, from which it should seem that both the bridges of Almaraz and Arzobispo are destroyed. The French fleet are out, (this was the Brest fleet, it was partially destroyed by Lord Cochrane in the Basque Roads during a night attack on April 11). They write from Cadiz that an English fleet under Duckworth is in pursuit of it. Arriaza came in eve., and was very pleasant.

8th.—A mysterious letter from Gen. M. who had informed me a few days ago that his destination was to the eastward, but that within 2 hours of giving me this notice he had received intelligence that the enemy were in a quarter where he did not know they were, and that he was going to meet them. (General Mackenzie, the commander of the British force lying off Cadiz, which was now ordered to return to Lisbon, and join Wellesley's army).

A deputy arrived from the Asturias, which he left a fortnight ago. He represents the force there at about 30,000 men, armed and disciplined, and ready to repulse the enemy at every point. (Mr. Oman mentions a dispatch—Frere to Lord Castlereagh—of March 34, in which it is stated that the Asturian *Junta* reported that they had over 20,000 men under arms).

Cuesta is jealous of Romana having dignities which he claims as having been conferred upon him by Fernando VII, the Captain-General of Castile, &c., &c. Lobo came this eve. He left London on 22nd Feb.

★★★★★★

Don Rafael Lobo y Campo, Spanish sailor. He was sent to London in 1808 as secretary to the Mission from Seville, and remained as secretary at the Embassy. He put himself in communication with La Romana, in Denmark, and assisted in person in the escape of the Spanish troops. He died in 1816.

★★★★★★

Jacome, (a member of the *Junta* of Seville, and one of the deputies sent to England in 1808 to seek assistance against the French), and his nephew are also arrived. The arms and saddles will soon come. The day he left London it was generally believed that Lord Castlereagh was out, and Ld. Wellesley was to come in, (as Secretary for Foreign Affairs in place of Canning).

Thursday, 9th March.—Dn. Francisco Ferras, Capmany, Rodenas, and Don José Manescan.

Manescan, (one of the judges of the Supreme Court), is a friend of Rodenas's. He is an *oidor* of Valencia, and distinguished himself considerably during the disturbances in that city, especially in his decision of character and readiness to punish offenders. He sentenced to death 38 offenders in one morning. They amply deserved punishment, as they were of those who had burst open the prison doors and butchered 300 defenceless French prisoners, and were also instrumental in the murder of poor Saavedra. He is reckoned very clever, and full of fire and enthusiasm. He joined loudly in disapproving the mode of administering justice here, where a French spy detected and convicted is to be secretly strangled tonight in his prison, and his body to be exhibited tomorrow in the *Plaza*, with a label affixed to describe his quality, country, and offences.

Cuesta is impatient for the arrival of the pontoons, which are prepared at Badajoz. He intends to pass the Tagus and give battle to the enemy. The Govt, have it in contemplation to decree a national mourning for the loss of Saragossa of 9 days, public funeral orations, and extensive privileges to the town for its glorious and never-to-be-forgotten resistance. Quintana is busily employed in composing this solemn and affecting appeal to the feelings of the public. The French have not ventured to enter the town yet, partly from fear of the epidemic, and perhaps some apprehension of the expiring hand of an unsubdued patriot.

Jovellanos brought the Asturian deputy. The state of that principality is very promising. Ballesteros commands a division of 10,000 men; he is greatly beloved of the soldiers, who chose him by acclamation, and whenever he exposes his person they entreat him to be more cautious for their sakes, as without him they could do nothing.

★★★★★★

Ballesteros' division was that part of the Asturian force which had not followed Blake to Leon after the Battle of Espinosa, but had retired to their own mountains and remained quietly there. The *Junta* had been recruiting largely in the province and had nearly 20,000 men in April, but had done little or nothing towards the common cause. This force was told off to watch Bonnet's division near Santander.

★★★★★★

Matarosa, (the Conde de Toreno), &c., are at Gijon, and very active in these disturbances. Went to Mde. Osuna's; Ld. Hd. and Ld. John to La Villa Manriques' *tertulia*. No particular news.

Friday, 10th March.—Sr. Robt. Wilson still continues collecting men at Ciudad Rodrigo. By offers of reward he gets Polish and German deserters, and if they bring arms he adds considerably to the recompense. Genl. Sherbrooke and his troops are off Cadiz.

Jovellanos has been occupied in preparing materials for the re-establishment of the Council of Castile, a revival which the *Junta* have in view. He told me that it was an error to suppose that Council had any pernicious tendency against civil liberty: that previous to the formation of the Central *Junta* it had usurped powers it did not possess legally, but that the Cortes had always been a favourite object in it: that it was indispensable to have a tribunal of *dernier report*, and useful for the internal administration of affairs to have a supreme authority to superintend its political economy.

★★★★★★

The effete Council of Castile had seriously discredited its importance by the ignominious and unhesitating surrender to Napoleon's wishes in the matter of Joseph's appointment as King. It was superseded by the Central *Junta* in Oct 1808, after a long wrangle as to the legality of the powers of the newly elected body.

★★★★★★

Wednesday, 15th March, Seville.—Received a letter from Capt. Parker in which he informs me of his being in the Tagus, having brought out General Beresford to Lisbon for the purpose of disciplining the Portuguese levies.

Perez de Castro is gone to succeed Tenorio as *chargé d'affaires* from the *Junta* at Lisbon. He is a very clever man; the first declaration of war from Aranjuez was written by him, and the whole of that celebrated work to which Cevallos has affixed his name is also his composition. (Lady Holland evidently refers to Cevallos' pamphlet on the affairs of Spain and the events of Bayonne, which he published in London in 1808). He also went in disguise to Bayonne and obtained an interview with Fernando VII, and facilitated the escape of some of his companions in the *segretoria de estado*, (State prison).

★★★★★★

William Carr Beresford (1768-1854), raised to the peerage in 1814 as Lord Beresford. He took part in Sir John Moore's retreat, and having then returned to England with his troops, he was sent out to Portugal to reorganise the military forces of that country.

Arteche speaks of Don Evaristo Perez de Castro as Spanish representative in Portugal.

★★★★★★

The pontoons which are gone from Badajoz to Cuesta are magnificent of their kind; they cost 14,000,000 *reals*. Upon the River Tietar there has been a little affair which terminated to the advantage of the Spaniards, who made several prisoners. Cuesta has now 22,000 men, well equipped and disciplined; upwards of 2000 cavalry in excellent condition. His headquarters are at Deleitosa to be nearer the enemy, who seem to be making some demonstrations towards the bridge of Almaraz.

From the intercepted letters it appears that the French in Salamanca are ignorant of Soult's position in Galicia, from whence it is inferred that the *Gallegos* have cut off all communication between that army and the French corps which are dispersed about Castile. The *Lively* frigate went into Vigo, and cut out some English small craft which had been captured by the French, The country from thence to Santiago is in insurrection, and if the people had more arms and ammunition, they might make an effectual resistance to the French. The French attempted to cross the Mino on boats; the Portuguese allowed them to advance, and then opened a brisk fire from some masked batteries which they had erected. (This was on Feb. 26 at Campo Saucos, about two miles from the mouth of the river. The French failed ignominiously to effect a landing on the other bank).

Romana is still in the neighbourhood of Oimbra; the accusations against him are numerous, the accusers respectable, and the points plausible. He learnt at Sorèze too much of the French *légèreté*, and I

94

greatly fear his statements partake more of that quality than is befitting they should upon such important matters.

17th March, Friday.—Lord Carlos Doyle, for so he styles or allows himself to be styled, writes from Tortosa that the French have behaved with the greatest inhumanity to their prisoners at Saragossa, stripped them literally naked, having robbed them of everything. Palafox is alive, and when able to be moved is to be conducted to Bayonne; he was delirious when the French officer came to his bedside, and was ignorant of the surrender of the city. (The French officer tried to insist on his signing orders for the surrender of two other towns, and when he refused threatened to have him shot. He was taken to France and confined in close captivity at Vincennes until the end of 1813).

Reding is at present at Tarragona with 8000 men; Lazan at Tortosa; the French at Fraga. The French have fallen back in La Mancha to the neighbourhood of Yepes, Dos Barrios, and other villages, which they occupied before the affair at Mora. At Valencia there are 14,000 men embodied, but only 4,000 musquets to arm them with. The French fleet are in Basque roads, closely blockaded by Ld. Gambier. General Sherbrooke is arrived at Lisbon with the troops originally destined for Cadiz. The convoy with provisions and clothing for the Spanish Army is arrived at Cadiz; the arms unfortunately are not on board any of these vessels, though mentioned as belonging to that convoy.

Hermida told Ld. Hd. that he had been making great exertions in the section of Grace and Justice to procure some modification, if not abrogation, of the decree against the Liberty of the Press; but that notwithstanding all his efforts, he had hitherto been unsuccessful. His chief ally in the section is Jovellanos; the principal opponents are Riquelme, (one of the members from Aragon to the Central *Junta*), and the Archbishop of Laodicea, (one of the members for Seville, and Bishop Coadjutor of that town). The latter is a narrow-minded, timid, feeble man, but being the only archbishop in the *Junta* he is a sort of head of the clergy, and being also a member of the provincial *Junta* of Seville, he acts in the doubly capacity and has greater influence.

Quintana represents Garay as being totally under the control of Jovellanos (but this I doubt). Calvo is one of the most able and eloquent men they have. (Don Lorenzo Calvo de Rozas, an intimate friend of Palafox, and his representative on the Council at Madrid in September). He was originally a small merchant in Madrid; he failed in his business. He placed himself by the side of Palafox in Saragossa, brought into the town amidst the balls of the enemy a timely supply of provisions. He wrote that famous proclamation signed by Palafox, in which he makes Napoleon responsible for the safety of Ferdinand and throws out a hint of favour of some Austrian Prince. (This proclamation was issued at the time of the first rising in Zaragoza, and was dated May 31, 1808). Upon his first admission to the *Junta*, it was expected that he would take the lead, but he lost himself entirely by making a proposition on behalf of Palafox, whom he proposed should be Regent.

18th March, Saturday.—The Council of Castile has been re-instated by a decree of the *Junta*, but the members who are to compose it have not been summoned, nor have the powers been defined. Infantado, who is the President, considers himself as slighted, whereas the re-establishment of it was, I believe, chiefly done with a view to please him and make him a station worthy of his consequence, and as a compensation for the loss of the command of the army.

Dn. Francisco Saavedra is the *Ministro de la Hacienda*, (Chancellor of the Exchequer). He is a stout man, apparently about fifty-two or three, but he is in reality a year older than Jovellanos. The upper part of his face, his brow, is very fine and has the same commanding and animated character as that of the late Ld. Lansdown; the lower features have a more set appearance, indicating a sort of suffering. This they have acquired since the severe illness he had, which the vulgar ascribed to poison administered by the queen during his ministry. The place he now holds is excessively laborious, and he quite sinks under the fatigue. It must be very ill organised, because he told us that full two hours every day, from 5 till 7, he employed solely in signing his name.

When the queen broke the administration up, Jovellanos was sent into the Asturias and Saavedra exiled to Puerto Santa Maria. The intrigue which occasioned their downfall is not exactly known; some ascribe their failure to Saavedra, who advised a line of conduct about the P. of the P., without activity and energy to enforce it. He recommended in order to get him out of the way, that he should be sent to travel with an honourable commission to all the Courts in Europe. The queen, who though displeased, angry, and jealous, and wished him to be mortified, could not bear his absence, and to avoid parting sacrificed those very persons she had been exciting to act against Godoy. Jovellanos praises the integrity and candour of Saavedra, whom he seems to admire and love very affectionately.

19th March, Sunday.—An extraordinary messenger arrived this morn. early from Cuesta with the alarming account that 12,000 Frenchmen had crossed the bridge of Arzobispo. The Spaniards behaved perfectly well; they defended the River Ibor, and with great order and bravery retired to Campillo.

★★★★★★

The French advance must have come somewhat as an unpleasant surprise to Cuesta, who had been himself gaily talking of advancing across the river. Victor crossed the Tagus on March 16 with Ruffin's and Villatte's divisions at Arzobispo, while Leval's Germans crossed at Talavera. The Spaniards under the Duque del Parque made a long and determined resistance against this combined force, but fled in confusion when the enemy came to close quarters.

★★★★★★

Cuesta is satisfied with the conduct of his troops. The French are without artillery, it being impossible to convey any across that bridge. Previous to dispatching the news hither, Cuesta had sent to apprise Albuquerque, who is at Ciudad Real, of the necessity of his supporting his right, which they hope A. will feel and advance without orders from Cartaojal's headquarters. Cuesta has 4000 cavalry. The opinion and belief in the Govt. is that the French force on the line of the Tagus is not above 28 to 32,000 men, and not above 4000 cavalry. Urbina, some say, already has 6000 cavalry. Cuesta, they say, writes in spirits; he is at the Puerto de Mirabete.

An officer who has made his escape from Saragossa, gives a melancholy acct. of the condition of the inhabitants and the state of the city. The latter is chiefly a heap of ruins, and the inhabitants are dying as rapidly as they did in Andalusia of the yellow fever. Lannes has placed guards in the churches in order to protect the plate, that no one may share the plunder with him.

20th March, Monday.—M., Mde. Ariza dinner. Great anxiety prevailed for the arrival of intelligence from Cuesta, which was not of a nature to dispel alarm. The French have crossed at Almaraz, and their force altogether consists of 27.000 men, a force superior to Cuesta's. The bridge of Almaraz was yielded scandalously by Henestrosa, either from cowardice or treachery, but the other points were bravely fought.

★★★★★★

Henestrosa's position opposite Almaraz had become impossible owing to Victor's success at Meza de Ibor, and Oman states that Cuesta sent orders to his lieutenant to abandon the position. Cuesta's force retreated without danger to Truxillo, but Henestrosa only got away with difficulty, yet managed to inflict two decided checks on the enemy during his retreat.

★★★★★★

Cuesta is afraid the enemy may attempt to push on and intercept him from Truxillo, where his magazines, &c., are. His plan was to abandon Mirabete and reach Truxillo last night, but there was a bare possibility of the enemy getting there before him. His intention is to fight his way through and reach the passes of the Sierra Morena, so as to cover Andalusia. The moment is critical: one false movement in tactics and the whole cause is lost.

At length the arms are arrived at Cadiz, 30,000 musquets, &c., &c.

Jalon, an officer sent from Valencia, gives a good report of the state of the public mind there. They have 4000 men armed with *bad* muskets, and 12,000 clothed, trained, and embodied who have none, and as many more enlisted who have no clothing and are not drilled.

There is a foolish, prating Baron Crossard from the Austrians; he has no mission, but is allowed to come in order to see the armies. According to the private letters and public papers, the English public are only occupied with the disgraceful business of the D. of York, (the scandal about Mrs. Clarke), against whom some women of no character and some men of bad character have brought forth very severe charges of corruption if they should be substantiated. Spain, the reverses of the English Army, and the failure of the measures of ministers, seem all forgotten in the superior interest of examining women of the town at the Bar of the H. of Commons.

21st March.—The news from Cuesta has revived the drooping and almost expiring hopes of the Spaniards. Cuesta began his retreat at ½ past ten on the night of the 18th from Mirabete; he effected it in excellent order to Truxillo, without sustaining the loss of a single piece of cannon or any of his baggage or ammunition. His headquarters were at Santa Cruz de la Sierra, and his *avant* guard at Truxillo; the enemy had an advanced post at Torrecillas. His intention was to maintain himself at Sta. Cruz until he knew what were the movements of the army of Albuquerque in his favour. The opinion now is that the enemy are not in great force, that they hardly equal, and certainly do not exceed that of Cuesta. From great despondence, the spirits of the people are rising almost too much.

Great complaints of the English military adventurers who go to the Spanish armies and interfere and meddle. Infantado sent away one when he discovered that he was not employed by the English Govt.—a Col. Whittingham. The consequence has been that he has traduced and injured the Duke in every possible manner.

23rd March.—Cuesta, conscious how exposed his situation was if the French should advance and get on his rear, resolved to fall back and avoid active operations, in order that the Army of the Centre might have full opportunity to pursue its operations. He found considerable difficulty in repressing the ardour of his troops, who are very desirous of advancing in this affair as well as in that of Consuegra, (Cuesta was awaiting two valuable reinforcements, hence his unusual show of caution). It is evident that the Spanish cavalry is far superior to that of the French.

Albuquerque left Ciudad Real at ½ past four in morning on the 19th, with the intention of proceeding to Guadalupe to support Cuesta. Urbina was to follow up this movement, and to attack the French at Toledo, where they are said to be 700 *weak*; but I much fear the Spaniards are sanguine and credulous about the forces of their enemies. Ld. Hd. has had a letter from Romana. He was attacked at Chaves by a considerable force, and at the close of the affair they came to the bayonet; he has fallen back. Ciudad Rodrigo is terrified, and an attack is hourly expected.

Cuesta continues retreating, he has fallen back upon Medellin, where he intends to maintain himself to give scope to the movements of the Central Army. The Spanish cavalry has again had a brilliant pursuit and victory over the enemy at Miajadas; the regts. Infante and Almanza are named for their bravery. (This was the second of two successful skirmishes with the enemy, which were planned by Henestrosa during his retreat. The French lost over 150 men killed and wounded. The first took place on the 20th at Berrocal).

Cuesta adds that but for the appearance of a column of infantry, the enemy would have lost every horseman. These regts. are part of Romana's dismounted cavalry who were in Germany, and left this place about a fortnight ago equipped and tolerably mounted. This skirmish happened on 21st.

The 40th regt., (the British regiment which had been sent from Elvas to Seville in February), have orders to march to Elvas next Monday. Gen. Sherbrooke has about 4000 men freshly arrived at Lisbon. Cornel, the Minister of War, applied to the English Minister, Frere, to allow the 40th to take the post of Sta. Ollala; I know not what has been the answer. Great succours in clothing, &c., are arrived at Lisbon from England; the people are quite enraptured.

Blake is to be appointed Capt.-Genl. of Aragon and Valencia, and to have one half of Lazan's army put under his command, and to collect near Teruel. Very pleasing accounts of the successes of the *somatenes* and *miqueletes* in Catalonia. Two thousand men have advanced from Sta. Ollala to join Cuesta, (three regiments from Badajoz under the Marqués de Portago), and the same number of raw troops have gone from hence to supply their place at Sta. Ollala. They write from Gibraltar and Cadiz that in an English frigate which passed the straits an Austrian and Russian courier were on board. Good news if true: great rumours of Austrian war.

24th March.—Duque del Infantado, Chev. Ardelberg, Arriaza, Dn. Francisco Ferras y Cornel. Cuesta's *poste* of today is still dated from Medellin, but it is supposed that he intends to fall back upon Campanario, in order to secure his junction with the Duke of Albuquerque, who on the 16th left Ciudad Real and joined Gen. Echavarria at Almodovar del Campo. Their corps united consisted of 8000 infantry and 500 cavalry, and it is reported, for it is not authentic, that his advanced guard was in Guadalupe on the 21st.

★★★★★★

Albuquerque does not seem to have picked up any of Echavarria's force, and joined Cuesta with the seven regiments of infantry and one of cavalry from Cartaojal's force—a little over 4000 men in all. Arteche says that Cuesta expected a reinforcement of at least 10,000 men.

★★★★★★

Urbina has marched towards Aranjuez with 4,000 or 5,000 cavalry and flying artillery. The infantry and remainder of his army will follow; they were in Valdepeñas and Manzanares. The French south of Madrid are said to be considerably weakened and disheartened.

Freire, the Galician, called with Sangro this eve. He reports unfavourably of Romana's conduct and of the state of his army.

It is not accurately known how many French have crossed the Tagus; Cuesta at a rough guess estimates them at 26,000. Those who know Cuesta are very much pleased at a little trait of liveliness, a disposition very foreign to his nature in general; for when he dispatched the courier who arrived today, he gave him himself the dispatches and gravely asked what he thought of his army, adding '*Diga á Sevilla que no tengan cuidado*,' ('Tell Seville not to be afraid'). The *Junta* are perfectly aware that the first fruits of a victory will be their complete annihilation. Cuesta will fall unmercifully upon them and assume the Govt, himself. Already some of his officers write loudly in his praise, and of the necessity of constituting him *generalisimo*.

25th March.—My birthday. Cuesta dates from Campanario on the 23rd. His nephew had come from the advanced guard of Albuquerque, which was within 4 leagues of him. Cuesta intended to go on to Higuera to meet Albuquerque who was at El Valle. That district is remarkably fruitful and abundant, and will furnish *viveres*, (provisions), and straw, especially for the cavalry, and it is chiefly on that acct., to replenish his supplies, that he goes thither.

Various rumours about Romana and his army; some say he is already at Astorga on his way to the Asturias. At Chaves there is reason to fear he conducted himself very ill *sans coup ferir*. He as usual has quarrelled with those he acted with, and Silveira the Portuguese general and he mutually accuse each other of great errors.

★★★★★★

La Romana's refusal to leave Spain and enter Portugal to assist Silveira, the Portuguese general, certainly had the appearance of cowardice and treachery, especially as neither they nor their men were on good terms. But in reality it was the wisest line La Romana could have taken. He was thus enabled to draw off his force, which was hardly fit to take the open field, practically unharmed, and could place himself on Soult's flank and rear—the very position from which the latter had wished to dislodge him. His skeleton rear-guard, it is true, was intercepted and dismembered by Franceschi, but his main force was safe, and keeping within the Spanish boundaries he moved by easy stages into Galicia.

★★★★★★

Went in the evening to the Condesa de Condamina's, Jovellanos, Freres, and D. of Osuna. Jovellanos has been confined to his house nearly a week with a painful complaint, a *divieso* or boil, in his thigh. I had refrained from calling out of discretion, but I longed so much once more to enjoy the charms of his conversation, that I went. He is cheerful, and was very pleasant. Hermida's daughter is just arrived from the neighbourhood of Saragossa. Had the besieged possessed a greater stock of gunpowder, they might have destroyed the French who had lodged themselves in the convent of St. Augustin by undermining them, but their quantity was very small, and all they used was manufactured in the town.

The epidemic raged universally. Ten canons of the cathedral died, and when this was alleged as a reason for capitulating, Palafox still protested in favour of death to infamy. The French in order to conciliate the Aragonese have declared that Saragossa shall be exempted for 6 years from all contributions whatever, that all the monasteries shall be abolished and the edifices demolished, so that the materials may be used by the inhabitants to repair and rebuild their houses destroyed by the siege. Palafox, they say, in the infirm state of health in which he is, was compelled to go to his balcony and view the execution of his friend and preceptor, Dn. Ignacio de Asso. They required the Auxiliary Bishop to preach a sermon of thanksgiving for the conquest in the church of Our Lady *del Pilar*. He is a clever man, and will either not comply or do it in a tone that will not please.

26th March.—Cuesta's *poste* of the 24th is from La Serena, and the junction with Albuquerque is considered as effected. The distance between them is only 4 leagues, and the officers ride over from headquarters. The enemy seem to have remained without any change of position at Miajadas. Cuesta has received intelligence of the enemy having sent out of Madrid on the 14th 12 pieces of heavy cannon for battering walls. This ordnance is coming down to the army of Estremadura, and Cuesta is convinced that they intend to besiege Badajoz; he rejoices at this probability, as he is confident that he shall be able to cut off their retreat and seize their magazines. Ferras is all eagerness that Cuesta should attack without delay, as the Spaniards do not fight so well when they wait to be attacked. He reckons the force of that army now with Albuquerque, the supplies from Badajoz, St. Ollala, and this place, 33,000 effective men.

Very contradictory rumours about Romana; some say he is recalled and coming here, others that he is at Astorga, and some say at Lugo. He has quarrelled with the Portuguese, and the whole of his conduct betrays a degree of flightiness that has hurt him in the opinion of those most disposed in his favour. His *intendente*, Heras, is the man who in fact does all.

27th March.—The French have not advanced beyond Miajadas, but from some observations of the spies they were preparing to go on to Merida. The French have evacuated Reus in Cataluña, and a few of their regts. have returned to France; this gives great strength to the report of an Austrian war.

Quintana gave a curious acct. of the fears of the Govt, in case Cuesta should gain an important victory; indeed so fully are they aware of their own weakness and unpopularity that to avoid Cuesta's seizing upon the Govt., they would at the time of announcing publicly his successes issue an edict for assembling the Cortes. This Garay told him yesterday was resolved upon.

By a letter from Valdepeñas, it appears that Cartaojal has surprised and routed a Polish regt. of cavalry at Yebenes. (This was the most northerly point reach by Cartaojal in his foolhardy dash on Toledo. It is true he routed this Polish outpost and killed or took 100 men, but he was forced to retreat to Ciudad Real on Sebastiani's approach. The latter then most unexpectedly pressed forward towards that town, and in the rout which ensued the Spanish troops were very severely handled before they could reach the shelter of the mountains).

28th.—We dined with Jovellanos, who is still confined to his house. Our party consisted of Garay, Campo Sagrado, Hermida, and the two nephews of Jovellanos. Cartaojal has found, as I always dreaded, the enemy much stronger in the Mancha, and accordingly the scheme of reaching Toledo is renounced. The enemy are in great numbers at and about Consuegra. Garay had received accounts from Portugal that about 17,000 French had penetrated to Braga and were advancing upon Oporto. The populace at Oporto had risen in a most disorderly manner, broke open the house of Bernardino Freire, and murdered him and his *aide-de-camp*. Poor man! they accused him of being a traitor, the common cry when the armies fly, as those of the Portuguese do generally.

★★★★★★

Bernardino Freire was murdered by the populace at Braga, not at Oporto. He was dragged to his death from the gaol, where his second-in-command, Baron Eben, chosen by the troops as his successor, had placed him in the hope of saving his life. He had certainly shown little courage or foresight in his efforts to oppose the advance of the enemy.

★★★★★★

The runaways said nothing but the want of powder prevented them from gaining a complete victory over the French.

29th.—Cuesta in his paste of the 27th complains of the small numbers furnished by the Andalusian armies; the force brought by Albuquerque not exceeding 3500 infantry and 300 cavalry, in lieu of 8,000 or 9,000 men promised to him. The advanced guards have been engaged with the French near Medellin, and it is said that a column of the enemy has been detached towards Merida. Garay told us that Cuesta was very much discontented at the smallness of the succours, and wrote excessively out of humour.

Cartaojal is much censured by the *Junta* for advancing without his infantry, having left it at Valdepeñas without instructions how it was to march. Garay spoke warmly against him and said it should be a severe *carga*, (reprimand).

30th March.—Cartaojal writes a confused and unintelligible letter from the Venta de Carolina. A division of his army under Moreno, has been attacked and defeated! In consequence of which he made the whole army retreat to Viso and Sta. Cruz. Thus this army, which was to seize Toledo and conquer Madrid, has fallen back upon the Sierra Morena. The cavalry he entrusted to the most inefficient general, Perellos, but omits mentioning where they were. The *Junta* of armament has removed back to Carolina.

The *poste* of Cuesta did not come in at the usual hour.

31st.—The accounts arrived very late from Cuesta last night, bringing the acct. of a most disastrous result from a successful and brilliant commencement. On the 28th, between Don Benito and Medellin, he attacked the enemy, and had at first greatly the advantage; his infantry and artillery drove the French in every direction, but a regt. of cavalry called by that inauspicious name for Spain, Maria Luisa, yielded to a charge of the French cavalry, and nothing but confusion and disorder ensued.

★★★★★★

Victor drew up his army in front of the town of Medellin, and Cuesta placing all his troops in the front line, which allowed only four men deep, advanced without any reserve, with the intention of enveloping the French by their longer front. At first the Spanish tactics were successful and the French were forced back, but as soon as their advance was checked the thin Spanish line wavered and fell into confusion. After this the end soon came, and though the Spanish cavalry to a large extent escaped owing to their cowardly behaviour, the infantry were decimated by the French cavalry. The Spanish losses were probably about 8000 men.

Mr. Oman states that it was the 3 regiments on the left flank which behaved so badly and threw their comrades into disorder. These were the 2 regiments from La Romana's army, and a Toledo regiment which rode over Cuesta. He also mentions that the Maria Luisa regiment was in the centre of the line, and behaved well in preserving some of the right wing from the French.

★★★★★★

Cuesta was thrown from his horse and bruised, but did not sustain any material injury. He writes that had he died he should have at last had the satisfaction of seeing the French turn their backs. He was nearly taken, and to avoid it threw off his general's uniform and put on the coat of a private soldier.

An officer from Cartaojal's army says his loss did not exceed 800 men, (Arteche computes the casualties in this action at 2000, besides the same number of prisoners). Those prisoners taken at Yebenes are brought away, but it was from all accts. a disgraceful retreat, and shows a complete want of all military knowledge and common presence of mind on the part of Cartaojal.

April 1st, Seville.—We were to have set off today, but the violence of the rain, thunderstorms, &c., prevented us. Cuesta writes from Campillo on the 30th. He was too sanguine as to collecting his *dispersos*. The cavalry were ordered to Llerena, he was to put his *cartel-general* in Berlanga, and he intended to form a semi-circle in order to collect the fugitives. Jovellanos has recommended some salutary and judicious measures to the *Junta*; his moderation and firmness at this juncture is very striking, and he may easily derive a greater degree of influence from it over his terrified colleagues than he acquired in their days of prosperity. He has advised great publicity towards the people, and publication of all the pastes as they arrive.

Garay read a letter from Lisbon in which he is informed of the retaking of Chaves by the Portuguese general Silveira, who surprised a corps of French who had been left at Chaves; they have killed 200 of them, and driven the rest into a castle where they cannot maintain themselves above three days.

★★★★★★

Chaves had been taken by Soult early in May, after La Romana had moved away and left Silveira to his fate. The latter had collected the remnants of his army in the mountains, when the French advanced on Oporto, and on the very day that Soult defeated Eben at Braga Silveira reappeared at Chaves with 6000 men. Only one company of able-bodied Frenchmen had been left there, the remainder being either sick or unreliable legionaries. The commandant retired into the citadel, but surrendered after 5 days, when 1200 men fell into the hands of the Portuguese.

See Appendix B.

★★★★★★

2nd April.—Just as we were going to set off, I was taken ill rather in an alarming manner and obliged to go to bed.

Cuesta's last *poste* is written in a very desponding state. He is at Berlanga and means to proceed to Llerena, but is not sanguine at all as to the probability of collecting together as numerous a force as he had expected. The French entered Merida on 30th and remained there on the 31st. He still believes their object is Badajoz. All the assistance which can be given is sent from hence already.

Albuquerque arrived this evening from Cuesta's army. Mr. Jackson brought us an account from Alicant written by the Austrian Consul that Ld. Collingwood had issued orders that Russian vessels were not to be detained. Russian vessels in the Tagus preparing for sea.

3rd.—Cuesta's cavalry are almost all assembled at Llerena, but unfortunately his infantry come slowly. He is to retreat towards St. Ollala. The French advanced parties for foraging have been as far as Almendralejo. He still believes the French intend to attack Badajoz.

The accounts of Cartaojal's army are as bad as possible. He made a scandalous retreat before an inferior force. The *Junta* are so much displeased at this conduct that he is to be recalled immediately, and Cuesta is appointed Commander-in-Chief, with Albuquerque *ad interim* 2nd-in-command, until Venegas can be found, who has been confined by illness at Valencia.

★★★★★★

General Francisco Venegas, who as Infantado's second-in-command was actually in charge of the force defeated at Ucles. He may not have been entirely to blame in this action, as his commander left him unsupported in the face of a vastly superior force of the enemy. All authorities, however, agree in belittling his military skill, and in all probability the 'Army of the Centre' was exchanging a better commander for a worse. Colonel Whittingham writes from Aldea del Rio on April 9: 'General Venegas has taken command of the army of Sierra Morena, and the Count of Orgaz that of the division on their march to join General Cuesta and which will pass through Seville. The D. of Albuquerque having no longer any command will return in a few days to Seville.' (*Holland House MSS.*)

★★★★★★

The *Junta* have appointed the Archbishop of Mexico to be Viceroy of that country; Cisneros, who is already there, to be the Viceroy of Buenos Ayres, and another marine officer who has conducted himself well, to Caraccas. They had, at the formation of their *Junta*, desired the American provinces to elect deputies to represent them in the *Junta*.

4th April.—Cuesta still at Llerena with a very small number of infantry. He ascribes their dilatoriness to the swelling of the torrents, which must have prevented their joining. The enemy remain at Merida.

Cartaojal's magazines have fallen into the hands of the enemy, and the want of forage has compelled him to place his cavalry at Ubeda.

5th April.—Cuesta has placed his headquarters at Monasterio, and placed advanced guards at Fuente de Cantos and Santos. The French have been at Zafra. The French have evacuated Viso and Visillo in La Mancha. Vives writes that he keeps the French *escarmentado*, (beaten troops), about Ciudad Rodrigo, that Romana is at Ponferrada, and Brigadier Wilson at Alcantara. Romana Ferras calls the *duende*, (Will-o'-the-wisp); he is here, there, and everywhere. The Portuguese have taken the castle in which the French had shut themselves up after the affair of Chaves. The Gallegos have summoned Vigo, and only given the French 24 hours to consider, which they must from the smallness of their numbers comply with.

★★★★★★

Vigo was blockaded by the Galicians soon after Soult's advance into Portugal. They were assisted by two English frigates, which arrived on March 23. Five days later the French surrendered, stipulating only that they should remain prisoners in British hands.

★★★★★★

A party of 400 cavalry have summoned Badajoz; the governor made a spirited and vaunting reply.

6th April.—Cuesta mentions that the enemy has retreated from Almendralejo and gone in the direction of Lobon and Talavera. Cornel, the Minister of War, thinks the Governor of Badajoz is a man of firmness but totally without talents. From a note which Campo Sagrado wrote to me this eve., it appears that the official return of the state of Cuesta's army is as follows: 2971 cavalry, 6702 infty., besides 200 cavalry soldiers without horses. (These figures tally closely with those in a letter from D'Urban to Cradock, quoted by Mr. Oman, of date April 8). He has also from 3,000 to 4,000 recruits, and at St. Ollala there are more. His disperses are assembling, and many have reached Cordoba already.

7th April.—Before I set off, I went to take leave of Jovellanos, who is still confined by his boil. He seemed very much concerned at our going. Nothing had arrived from the armies; however he promised to let us hear regularly the bulletins from thence. We quitted Seville at 2 o'clock; I never felt more regret at leaving a place, the loss of society, and interesting information. It reminded me of the going out of the late Ministry, as to me the chief pleasure of their being in office was that I knew sooner and better what was going on.

11th April.—Entered Cadiz at ½ past four. Duff and Lobo called. Went to the play. Dss. of Hijar and Feman Nuñez came to see me in my box.

13th April, Cadiz.—This place so insufferable that as we cannot go by Gibraltar, we have wisely determined upon returning to Seville for 10 days. Admiral Purvis called; very obliging, and promised assistance about frigates, &c. We *cannot* embark till after 7th May. Dined at the Dss. of Infantado's.

15th April.—Set off with great satisfaction from Cadiz. Slept at Pta. Santa Maria.

16th, Pta. Santa Maria.—Set off at 12, the weather not too hot, and going in a northerly direction made it very pleasant, as the sun was not so powerfully upon my head. News from armies continues good, as far as great force being collecting. Cuesta, with the army of the Carolina which is now passing through Seville, will have 26,000 infantry, and 6000 cavalry. (These figures nearly tally with Napier's account. Mr. Oman gives 20,000 infantry and 3000 cavalry as the correct estimate). Victor is entrenching himself at Medellin. After dinner called upon Mrs. Gordon; her daughter Mrs. Dos very pleasing. Complaints against Frere universal; Spaniards full as much as English. They want an ambassador and a man of consideration and rank. Mr. Cranstoun said the complaints were so strong that application had already been made for his recall.

17th April, 1809, Xeres.—Set off from thence at ¼ before 11; met Mr. Gordon equipped in the *Andaluz* peasant dress, well-mounted, waiting to show his farm, which lies partly by the roadside, and is very extensive; he manages it under the direction of a Scotch bailiff. The weather was very cold. Spoke, at the Venta del Cuervo, to Major Evatt on his return from Seville to Gibraltar. The only news from Seville is that Urbina cannot be found; some think he has absconded to the enemy, others that the Govt, wish him to escape punishment, and have connived at his concealing himself in some convent. The popular feeling is very strong against him.

19th April, Seville.—Jovellanos and Ferras to dinner. Eve., Quintana, Capmany, Perico came; Wiseman, Col. Whittingham. The latter accompanies the D. of Albuquerque, who is now here but on his way to join Cuesta with a reinforcement of 7000 infantry and near 3000 cavalry. Venegas has still from 15 to 16,000 effective infantry and 1500 cavalry. The French are entrenching themselves at Merida; they have been reinforced by 6000 men from Salamanca, who on their way took possession of the bridge of Alcantara, in consequence of the *Junta* of Badajoz having withdrawn, when their town was threatened with a siege, their forces from thence. (This was Lapisse's division, which had been kept inactive near Salamanca by Wilson's small force for two months. They reached Merida on April 19. Alcantara was sacked and the inhabitants treated with the utmost cruelty).

Pedro Giron very much improved; manly, military appearance, greatly esteemed in the army, and beloved by his officers and soldiers. The opinion of the best informed military men is against the translation of the war from La Mancha to Estremadura; in the latter the cavalry cannot be subsisted so well, and the present positions are

109

unfavourable to their operations. Wiseman criticised Cuesta's mode of attack, the disposing the army in a long line without a corps of reserve, and his cavalry, with the exception only of 200, all on one wing. This was the case at Medellin and will ever be his tactics, as he is obstinate and determined upon persevering in his own plan. The steadiness of the infantry was astonishing, and even with the hottest fire playing upon them they continued advancing with greatest firmness and regularity. The loss of the Spaniards is estimated at 5000, that of the French at 3000. (Mr. Oman computes the Spanish losses to have been at the lowest 7500. There is great uncertainty about those of the French. Sémélé and Jourdan put them at 300, others at 4000 and 2000).

All concur in believing that the result of a pitched battle will always be fatal to the Spaniards from the superior discipline and manoeuvres of French, but that in skirmishes and guerrillas they will always succeed, both in infantry and cavalry. W. speaks handsomely of Venegas, though all Albuquerque's partisans are discontented at present with him. He throws the whole blame of the affair of Ucles on the D. of Infantado; that action was the most fatal to the Spaniards. They lost 9000 of their best infantry, including the greater part of veteran regts., which were surrounded and entirely cut off. Venegas had frequently apprised Infantado of his danger and that he should inevitably be surrounded; he even sent an *aide-de-camp* to headquarters at Cuenca to expose his situation, but he neither received assistance nor a reply to his application. The enemy were three times his number when they attacked him.

All parties agree that nothing could be more scandalous than the flight of Cartaojal, who fled from an enemy but one-third equal to himself. All the letters from Cataluña and Aragon state the retreat of the French. Blake in his letter to Ferras corroborates this report, and adds that many corps of their army have passed through Irun, (the result of the Austrian war). Jaca, in Aragon, was sold to them by the treachery of the commanding officer.

20th April, Seville,—Intercepted correspondence has been brought in; the letters of most interest are from King Joseph and Jourdan to the French commanders, especially to Sebastiani. Joseph declares it is not his intention that any operation against Seville should take place until Victor has communicated with Soult, and then the attack is to be a combined one from Estremadura and La Mancha. (This was Napoleon's own plan of campaign. Soult was to capture Oporto, communicate with Victor when nearing Lisbon, join with him in Estremadura after capturing the Portuguese capital, and advance in combination against Seville)

A Visconde de Quintanilla, (deputy for Leon, his information as to the numbers of the British was quite correct), who is just come from Lisbon, declares that the English army amounts to 25,000, a fact much to be doubted. Frere has an official account of 14,000 men, but no more.

An officer who had escaped from Aragon gave many instances of the cruelty of the French towards their prisoners. The garrison of Saragossa was marched to Bayonne with a French column, the prisoners who halted and could not keep pace with them were shot; he saw 140 lying dead on the road. This fact corroborated by Whittingham and Don Francisco.

It is in agitation amongst the members of the *Junta* to take some steps towards convoking the Cortes. A decree or manifesto sketched by Garay is to be drawn up by Quintana, and to be published immediately. This excellent measure is owing to our venerable friend Jovellanos, who has never ceased urging the necessity of the proceeding. However the period of the assembling of the Cortes will be remote, one year at least.

21st April.—Perico brought the D. of Albuquerque, whom I was glad to see. He is low in stature, his head is full one-fifth of his height, his long face does not afford a very intelligent countenance; his eyes are remarkably small but rather lively, fair light hair. His manner denoted neither the silliness of character imputed to him by many, nor the great superiority of talent ascribed to him by others. He complained of Cartaojal not having given him the detachment he was ordered to supply, which if he had obtained, the battle of Medellin would have been a second Baylen.

The French have abandoned the bridge of Alcantara, and the Spaniards, Portuguese, and a few English under Sr. Robt. Wilson have taken possession of it. The Conde de Montijo, who was arrested at Granada for an absurd tumult excited by himself to invest him with the authority of Capt.-General, is arrived here; the whole affair was so foolish that it will not lead to any consequences.

★★★★★★

D. Engenio Eulalio Portocarrero y Palafox, VII Conde de Mon-

111

tijo, son of Don Felipe Antonio Palafox and Da. Maria Francis-
ca de Sales Portocarrero y Zuniga, Condesa de Montijo in her
own right. A turbulent, discontented reactionary, he was always
at the head of any movement directed against the more sober
members of the *Junta*. In this case, he was banished for the time
being, first to Badajoz (not San Lucar, as is stated by Arteche).

★★★★★★

22nd April.—The guerrillas of Cuesta have made a handsome
prize, 14,000 merinos belonging to the Conde del Campo de Alonge,
which were going with French passports to the north of Spain, also a
number of brood mares.

23rd.—Dined at Jovellanos'. Party consisted of Garay, Campo
Sagrado, Jovellanos' nephews. Garay very much delighted at the approbation bestowed upon him for the share, and it seems to have
been a powerful one, in bringing about the measure in favour of the
Cortes, his mind being well imbued with Jovellanos' opinions upon
that subject. For Jovellanos, besides his declaration at Aranjuez, had
very recently during his late illness delivered in again in writing his
opinion. He had proposed a few nights ago without any previous
concert in the *Junta* the convoking the Cortes. Campo Sagrado told
me that he occupied himself with observing the effect produced upon
the countenances of many present who had, under the influence of
Florida Blanca, rejected the proposition for assembling Cortes when
proposed at Aranjuez by Jovellanos, (during the early sessions of the
Supreme *Junta*), and he observed great surprise, but no very decided
opposition.

Calvo who had rejected the scheme at Aranjuez, upon finding it
likely to be carried, adopted the plan with eagerness and made a flam-
ing speech, declaring that unless the measure was adopted by the *Junta*
he would take minutes of the proceedings and lay before the public
the salutary scheme which had been rejected by them. The most hostile to the project are Valdes, the archbishop, and Riquelme, whom
Jovellanos calls an *athlète* against it; there are also several others. Campo
Sagrado described the meeting at Aranjuez upon the subject to have
been very animated; a dispute arose between Jovellanos and Florida
Blanca, in which the former was about resigning, and would have
done so but for the disasters of the campaign.

Calvo is a suspected character, always ready to fall into the current
and with sufficient dexterity to see in time which way it is likely to

flow.

Jaca, in Aragon, which had been sold to the enemy by the treachery of its governor, has been retaken by the inhabitants headed by the apothecary of the town. Fresh reports of the French withdrawing from Spain.

Sebastiani has written to Jovellanos and Saavedra with offers of accommodation, telling them the cause of the insurgents is lost, &c. I have copies of the letters.

25th.—Jovellanos, Garay, Quintana, Rodenas dined. Ferras, eve. Garay very lively and amusing; a quick, open, frank, clever man.

Reding so ill of the epidemical disease which rages in his army that his life is despaired of, and the command of the army is assumed by Coupigny. The manifesto and decree which is drawn up by Quintana is at present undergoing the considerations of the section of the *Junta*. It is reckoned too long and rather full of poetry. Some ascribe the acquiescence on the part of the *Junta* to the fear of Cuesta.

26th.—Nothing fresh from either of the armies. French couriers are daily intercepted, and the valise containing the letters is brought here; 100 *doblones* is the reward. The armed peasantry contrive to kill even the hussars who escort them. Victor has received reinforcements from La Mancha. The French are said to have collected a force of 18,000 men at Saragossa.

27th.—Ld. Hd. and Ld. John dined at the regimental mess of the 40th regt. Ferras and Perico eve. Ferras gave a statement of the force at the armies. The French have evacuated Barcelona, taking with them all their plunder and prisoners, leaving only a small garrison in the *Ciudadela*. It is said they have shaped their course towards France by the way of Vich. Coupigny has detached a corps under Wimpfen to annoy them on their march, and the *somatenes* are very active. (St. Cyr moved out to Vich on April 18, to save his store of provisions in Barcelona, and at the same time to cover the preparations which were going forward for the siege of Gerona).

28th.—Six valises have been brought to Govt, within 4 days. In Estremadura the peasantry are formed into regular bodies who harass the enemy and cut off their communications in every direction and intercept their correspondence. These lost letters are of use to Cuesta, by giving the military details of the positions of the force of artillery, &c., and their intended movements. A corps of 1400 men has been sent from Victor's army towards Caceres, and another detachment is gone to Madrid.

29th.—Jovellanos gave us the news of the arrival of Sr. Arthur Wellesley at Lisbon.(He arrived there on April 22, and a week later moved out and commenced his advance to meet Soult, who was then in the neighbourhood of Oporto). General Doyle who, *par parenthèse*, was never within hearing of a musket being fired off, gave some acct. of Saragossa. The *artillera*, the heroine whom Mr. Vaughan mentioned with so much praise, was killed in the 2nd siege by a cannon ball, as were 3 other women who had been inspired by her courage and followed her example. Palafox was insulted by the French and cruelly treated; they removed the surgeon who attended him, and placed a Frenchman in his place. In his room there were several drawings done by the celebrated Goya, who had gone from Madrid on purpose to see the ruins of Saragossa; these drawings and one of the famous heroine above mentioned, also by Goya, the French officers cut and destroyed with their sabres, at the moment too when Palafox was dying in his bed.

30th April.—News came today of the death of Reding at Tarragona, and also that Coupigny had been ill of the same contagious fever for 3 days. Also that General Vives has died at Ciudad Rodrigo of a pleurisy; only five days' illness. Considerable solicitude as to the nomination of a President; the election is to take place tomorrow. Jovellanos excluded himself in the paper upon the Cortes which he wrote at Aranjuez; he wishes to name a President out of their body, and would choose Saavedra. There is an apprehension that Valdes may be chosen, and he is reckoned to be the worst that could be named. Altamira is objected to from his excessive nullity.

1st May.—Altamira (Marquis de Astorga), has been chosen for the Presidency, and perhaps it was the most judicious choice, as they could not have Jovellanos, and by not choosing one out of their body neither could they have had Saavedra.

2nd May, Seville.—Cuesta mentions the arrival of wagons with 70 wounded at Victor's headquarters, but has no guess from whence they came, unless they are the victims of the holy crusade, or that there has been an affair with Brigadier Wilson. It is said, but not from authority, that the bridge of Alcantara has again been evacuated. The Govt, are somewhat displeased and a little disconcerted at Frere's behaviour in urging fresh plans of military operations, considering that Miguel Alava has only just been dispatched with full instructions from hence and from Cuesta to Lisbon, to concert with Genl. Wellesley for a combined plan of campaign. This conduct of his, and some expressions which he dropped inadvertently, give reason to apprehend that Wellesley's orders from home are to consider the defence of Lisbon as the chief object of his expedition. Frere, without waiting to hear the result of Alava's communication with Wellesley, is pressing a project in which the D. of Albuquerque shall have an independent command in the Mancha, but the *Junta* very judiciously reject all such plans until they hear what are to be the movements of the English Army. The *Junta* have complimented Cuesta with the nomination of a successor to General Vives, and it is supposed the Duque del Parque will obtain the appointment.

★★★★★★

Duque del Parque-Castrillo (1755-1832). He served Joseph for a short time, but soon took service with his compatriots. He was in command of a division at Meza de Ibor and Medellin.

★★★★★★

The spirit of the Aragonese remains undaunted still. At Molina de Aragon after repulsing the French in several successive attacks, when they found an irresistible force coming against them, they resolved to abandon the town and withdrew with their families and portable effects into the mountains, and continued there until the French chose to evacuate the place.

At the Castillo de Albuquerque near Caceres, in Estremadura, the inhabitants upon being demanded to furnish rations for 2000 men, said they had no answer to make to such requisitions but from the mouths of their cannon.

The priests headed by a bishop and several dignitaries of the Church have established a sort of crusade in Estremadura against the French. The initiated wear a cross upon their breasts, like those worn in the Holy Wars against the *infidels*, and the pious crusader is consecrated for engaging in such a sacred cause, and Heaven is promised and certain reward if he falls in the contest. It is wonderful the havoc these enthusiasts make amongst the enemy, and Victor has complained to Cuesta of this cruel and irregular mode of warfare. It well becomes a Frenchman to complain after what they have inflicted and are inflicting upon the poor priests, and indeed upon every class and denomination of the community in Spain.

Col. Whittingham confirms the report of the excellent state of Cuesta's army, and the exactness of Ferras' numbers—25,000 infantry, 3000 cavalry beyond Monasterio, and 3500 on this side under the command of Albuquerque. Provisions are abundant and there is no sickness, but the cavalry want forage.

3rd May.—No further decision was made in the *Junta* last night than to defer the discussion upon the subject of the Cortes to the 14th of this month, and then every *vocal,* (voter), the *Junta* is to deliver in his opinion and vote in *writing* on the subject.

General Wellesley is marching on towards Oporto, and carries every soldier, Portuguese and English, he can gather. Alava writes in praise of his activity and frankness, but seems disappointed that no positive promise of assistance is made to support Cuesta.

Antillon is a geographer, and has just published a statistical survey and description of Spain; he is clever and well-informed, it is said, upon *la physique.* He is an Aragonese, and was in Saragossa during the first siege, and near it latterly. He confirms the stories of the cruelties and murders committed by the French in violation of the terms of capitulation. He is remarkably unpleasant in his manners, and has filthy tricks which might prove he was akin to Belsham.

★★★★★★

Don Isidoro Antillon (1777-1820), professor of history and geography at the Colegio de Nobles, and the author of various works on geography, astronomy, and history.

★★★★★★

The *Semanario politico* (*sic*) is going to be revived, and he in conjunction with Blanco are to be the writers.

★★★★★★

Don José Maria Blanco y Crespo, more commonly known as Joseph Blanco White (1775-1841), son of Don Guillermo White, an Irishman by birth and British Vice-Consul at Seville. Quintana had established the *Semanario patriotico* in Madrid in 1808, and when it was removed to Seville the editorship was offered to White and Antillon. Their free style of writing, however, frightened the *Junta*, who put a stop to the publication of the journal. White soon after (1810) went to England, where he took up his abode, and later became editor of the *Español*, a periodical which lasted for four years, being published in England and circulated in Spain.

Quintana told me that it was suspected that Frere was averse to the convoking of the Cortes, and that Garay this morning had been betrayed into some degree of warmth and refused him the paper which had been submitted to the sections, upon the pretext that it was not yet an official piece, not having been decreed by the *Junta*.

4th May.—Ferras told me that 14,000 French from Saragossa under Marshal Mortier were proceeding by the way of Burgos to Galicia to assist Ney and Soult. He also told us that the French had contrived to get into Barcelona a convoy of 30 transports, escorted by 5 sail of the line; the latter, owing to the shallowness of the water in the harbour, did not attempt to enter. (These ships came from Toulon, under convoy of Admiral Cosmao). These vessels have probably brought stores and supplies for the garrison, and perhaps a few troops.

I told Frere that he was accused of being unfriendly to the Cortes; he admitted that he objected to their mode of proceeding, and certain it is this clamour for reform in England has revived all his old anti-Jacobin terrors.

5th May.—Cuesta in his *poste* of today expresses great ill-humour against the English, whose armies, he says, are never exposed. This opinion is given in consequence of the letter he received from Gen. Wellesley, who does not seem to fulfil all the flattering expectations which had been raised by Don Miguel Alava's *first* report.

6th May.—The Queen of Sicily has returned to the Spaniards all the jewels which the Pss. of Asturias had given back to her family, and also 5000 muskets, 3000 of which are arrived already at Alicante.

7th May.—The Madrid *Gazette* at length announces the commencement of hostilities between Austria and France.

8th May.—The corps which was under Vives in the province of Salamanca has met with some successes. They have taken possession of Ledesma, and pushed on their forces into Avila. Coupigny sends two *postes* in which he mentions that the French were attacked near Vich and lost 1400 men, and that the garrison of Barcelona had made a sortie but had been repelled with some loss. (No movement of any importance can be traced about this time, but the French were continually being harassed by the bands of *somatenes* and *miqueletes* which took such a prominent part in the warfare of this north-east corner of Spain). He also mentions Lord Collingwood having divided his fleet into two squadrons, one directed towards Toulon, and the other towards Gibraltar to watch the Straits.

Sr. Arthur Wellesley was at Coimbra on the 2nd, and expected to be joined by his whole force on 4th. Silveira has maintained himself at the *Puente* against a corps of Soult's army and effected a junction with 4000 of Beresford's army.

★★★★★★

Silveira had gallantly kept 9000 French under Loison in check at the bridge of Amarante for a whole fortnight, but was driven back on May 3 and his force dispersed. He took refuge at Lamego, and was not joined by Beresford's flanking column until May 10 (*Oman.*)

★★★★★★

A strange story of an intercepted letter of Victor's to Frere. Jovellanos has received a long letter from Blake in which he states all the difficulties of his situation, and gives a plan of campaign which he thinks more advisable than that proposed by Reding, but which is incompatible with the orders he received from the *Junta* of clearing Cataluña; he presses the necessity of making the seat of war in Aragon. The *Junta* have sent him a *carte blanche*, and he is Captain-General of Aragon and Commander-in-Chief of the 3 armies.

10th May, Seville.—Ld. Hd. received a letter from Adl. Purvis, apprising us of the arrival of the *Ocean* off Cadiz harbour, adding that he advised us to lose no time, as she was to proceed to England with dispatches. Accordingly we determined upon setting off tomorrow.

Ld. Hd. had a long letter from Sr. Robt. Wilson, (see Appendix B). Lapisse's division got from Salamanca to Alcantara in consequence of the cowardice of the Portuguese, who fled when they were ordered to advance. The peasants defended the bridge of Alcantara five hours. He mentioned that from an intercepted letter of Kellermann's it appeared that Ney and Soult had quarrelled in consequence of the expedition of the latter to Oporto, which had been undertaken without the approbation of Ney, whose plan was first to subdue all Galicia. (Relations became very strained between Ney and Soult over this point, but the latter had Napoleon's instructions to push south, and he could but obey).

Kellermann was stationed at Valladolid with cavalry to watch Romana and the Asturias, and keep down the spirit of the people at Leon who were ready to rise. We dined with Jovellanos, his nephews, Monasterio, Mde. Santa Colomba, Hermida's daughter, and her husband. Eve., Capmany, Quintana, Rodenas, Paiz, Ferras, Arriaza, Gallegos, Malo, &c., &c., and Frere to supper.

11th May.—Quitted Seville with extreme regret quarter before 11. A short time after reaching Utrera a most melancholy accident occurred; Joaquin, our coachman, whom we took at Coruña, was stabbed by one of our own *carreteros*, of the name of Martin, who drove our own cart and Portuguese *machos*, (mules). The blow was aimed at the heart, but fortunately only pierced the lungs; for near half an hour Mr. A. was very doubtful whether the blow was mortal or not. The poor fellow instantly demanded a confessor and the sacraments. After being administered his agitation of mind subsided greatly. The assassin was thrown into prison and the *Justicia*, personified in the *carregidar* and *escribano*, (notary), took the depositions of the wounded man and the witnesses; they stripped the assassin of all his property and secured his effects, which were carefully registered by the *escribano*. What his future lot may be is uncertain, owing to the extreme tardiness of the Spanish law proceedings.

12th May.—Set off at 4. Reached the Venta de San Antonio about the *oracion*, near eight. The people of the *venta* were under some alarm in consequence of a troop of horsemen who had been committing great depredations on the high road in the morning; the robbers were supposed to be lurking in a house under the ruins of an old tower about ½ a league off. As the *banditti* in Andalusia often force the solitary *ventas* to admit them, our soldiers immediately secured the only two gates of entrance, and it was determined that we should remain the whole night in order not to encounter the danger of being attacked. I went to bed, and our party supped at a table just at the foot of my bed and opposite to a small grated window (without glass) which opened to the country. At about 10 o'clock, just as supper was coming in, I heard the sound of a horse, followed immediately by another. Jokingly I said to Charles, 'Hullo! here are the robbers!'

Ld. Hd. jumped up immediately and ran to the window asking, 'Who goes there?' The answer was not calculated to set us at rest, '*Caballeros, no tengan cuidado, Senor,*' ('Gentlemen. Don't be afraid. Sir,'). In an instant the soldiers and servants and muleteers put themselves into a posture of defence, for 6 or 7 horsemen had arrived at the front gate, and were clamorous for admittance; fortunately no shots were fired, and when a parley was obtained it seemed that this was a party of

13 from Espera in search of the robbers, who had plundered a house there and committed various excesses. We were not without apprehension, even after they were admitted, that we had let in the rogues. However they proved to be what they really pretended. The alarm was very great and justifiable; every face was blanched from fear. The reason for their surrounding the *venta*, and posting themselves at the gates was from a supposition that the robbers might have quartered themselves there for the night, and unless so circumvented might effect their escape.

13th.—On our road we met a person belonging to the house of Gordon, who told us that a convoy of 70 vessels were come from Malta, and put under the *Ocean*, which was not to sail for some days. In eve. the *nuncio* and two other persons called upon us.

14th May, Pta. Sta. Maria.—I was resolved not to return to the villainous *fonda*, and with some difficulty we got by favour into a private house belonging to Mr. Vaughan (who is at Gibraltar) upon the Alameda, and was, I think, formerly occupied by Ly. Westmorland. The Sheridans and Mr. Campbell called.

★★★★★★

Tom Sheridan, R. B. Sheridan's only son (1775-1817), who died at the Cape of Good Hope while acting as Colonial Treasurer. He married, in 1805, Caroline Henrietta Callander, the novelist, and by her was father of the three noted beauties, Mrs. Norton, Lady Dufferin, and the Duchess of Somerset. He had been ill for some time, and was travelling abroad for his health.

★★★★★★

The *Ocean* is very much out of repair, and though safe, would yet from its rolling and being so strained terrify me excessively, besides the passage would from the convoy be at least 6 weeks. Frere is recalled, and Lord Wellesley is named to succeed him. Ld. Grey made a severe attack upon Frere for his letters to Moore. Ministers hardly made any defence for him.

15th May.—Dined alone. Mr. Campbell very obligingly has offered us his house, which is larger and cooler. We moved in the eve. Duff who had been over to the *posta* with Sir John Cradock (who is gone to Seville) brought us letters from Jovellanos and Ferras. (Cradock was offered the appointment of Governor of Gibraltar when superseded in Portugal by Wellesley).

There have been several skirmishes in the Mancha, all in favour of the Spaniards. In Estremadura the French are retiring towards Truxillo, and Cuesta's advanced guard is in Santos.

★★★★★★

Owing to a rumour that the head of a Portuguese column had reoccupied Alcantara, Victor moved against that place with Lapisse's division, and had little difficulty in reoccupying it, as the force was in reality a small one of 2000 men—part of the Lusitanian Legion, under Colonel Mayne. (*The Loyal Lusitanian Legion During the Peninsular War* by John Scott Lillie and William Mayne is also published by Leonaur). Victor did not remain, but withdrawing the main body of his troops to the neighbourhood of Caceres he rejoined them there.

★★★★★★

Venegas' have reached Infantes. Blake in a *posta muy reservada* tells the *Junta* that he has had an offer of being put into possession of one of the gates of Montjuich *moyennant* 10 millions of *reals* and a secure refuge in Spain. He has acceded to the proposal, and it is approved, as the advantage is well worth the money.

★★★★★★

Blake had personally little or nothing to do with the conspiracy which was hatching in Barcelona for the purpose of ejecting the French. He was far away, engaged in the campaign which resulted so unsuccessfully for him in the Battle of Alcañiz and Belchite. Doubtless, however, the reports of his lieutenant, Coupigny, would be forwarded by him to the *Junta*. The plot was frustrated by two Italian officers who were approached and feigned willingness to help, but who told all to Duhesme, the governor. The ringleaders were arrested before the appointed time, and the whole scheme miscarried.

★★★★★★

Jovellanos says the opinions delivered on the Cortes on the 14th were so long that the time was consumed in hearing them read.

Romana has dismissed the Provisional *Junta* of Oviedo by military force; he ordered grenadiers to lock the doors of the room in which they usually assembled, and prevent their meeting. (The *Junta* of Oviedo had refused to furnish the necessary supplies for La Romana's army; hence his arbitrary action. From the report of an eyewitness, he marched 50 men into the Council Chamber and ordered them to clear the room).

The precedent might prove fatal to the Central *Junta* itself, especially if Cuesta were younger.

18th May, Cadiz.—Ld, Hd. and John dined on board the *Atlas* with Adl. Purvis. Victor is retreating towards Alcantara, either with an intention of making an effort to assist Soult, or to meet with Mortis, whose division left Saragossa supposed with the project of getting into Castile. Cuesta is pursuing, but slowly, as he is afraid this movement of Victor's may be a stratagem to draw him into the plains; accordingly he keeps towards Badajoz, (see Appendix E).

The majority of the *Junta* are for calling the Cortes, and declaring to the public their intention.

19th May.—Conde de Fernan Nuñez dined. Jovellanos sends a bulletin daily of all events. He laments as a lover of the fine arts the loss of that magnificent work, a specimen of the taste of the age of Trajan, the bridge of Alcantara, which was destroyed by the Portuguese and English on the approach of Victor's army. As a military operation it was judicious, but one of the finest works of antiquity b thus demolished, and owes its destruction to those modern Vandals, the French.

★★★★★★

The bridge was not demolished when Victor attacked Mayne on May 14, as the mine was not completely successful. The French were able to cross in sufficient numbers to drive back the defenders, and it was not until June 10 that Mayne, having reoccupied the position, finally destroyed the arches.

★★★★★★

When the French found the bridge blown up, they fell back, and are on their march to cross the Tagus higher up. Cuesta pursues slowly. Albuquerque was ordered forward with his cavalry, and doubtless will harass the enemy greatly on their march.

Ballesteros made 700 French prisoners at San Vicente de la Barquera, and killed many in the action; they also were drowned in making their escape over the river.

★★★★★★

No mention is made by any authority of an action about this date. In fact Oman states that Ballesteros only left his lair in the mountains at Covadonga on May 24 in order to annoy Bonnet by his raid on Santander. This was entirely successful, and the numbers of French losses correspond closely with the fight above mentioned. The date given by the Spanish historians of the capture of Santander, however, is June 10. Ballesteros unfortunately for himself lingered in the town, was caught there two days later by Bonnet, and his army cut up and dispersed with a loss of 3000 prisoners. Can it be that rumour had forestalled the event by a whole month? There is an authentic parallel in the case of the Battle of Bailen. It was reported in Galicia on June 24, and Wellesley touching at Coruña on *July 20 en route* for Portugal heard of the battle in Andalusia on the very day on which it took place.

★★★★★★

For want of boats he could not follow them, otherwise he would immediately have got to Santander where the French have only 4500 men. It is supposed that he must be in possession of it by this time.

Romana was on the 9th at Oviedo. Jovellanos does not disapprove of his proceedings against that *Junta*, where I believe he acted in the capacity of delegate from the Supreme *Junta*. The *Junta* was thwarting Romana in all his regulations about the army, which by robbery and secret intrigue they would soon have destroyed. A report here that Blake is coming upon Cuenca to threaten Madrid. Also a story of Josef's having withdrawn to San Ildefonso.

20th.—By a letter from Mr. Hoppner at Seville to Mr. Campbell, it appears that the French column 10,000 strong, who were marching upon Alcantara, fell back upon the news of the destruction of the bridge, and are now at Arroyo del Puerco. (Probably Lascelles Hoppner, younger son of the painter, who was sent to Seville with dispatches and remained some time studying the pictures of Murillo. He was shortly after shut up in a lunatic asylum—*Autobiography of Blanco White.*)

Another division is gone directly from Merida to Almaraz. Cuesta's headquarters are at Fuente Maestre, nor does it appear that any part of his army has crossed the Guadiana.

Quintana writes, not in great spirits, that the Cortes will meet in the course of next year, and sooner if circumstances permit. The analysis of the opinions delivered on 14th are not yet made out. Plans of reform and internal govert. are in the meantime to be prepared for the Cortes when they meet.

21st May.—Great rejoicing at Seville in consequence of the news from Portugal. (Wellesley's successes at Oporto, and Beresford's at Amarante, see Appendix D).

There was a great function at the theatre, a salvo from Purvis's ship, and patriotic songs. An official announcement of the taking of Santander, which Jovellanos is afraid is premature.

French to the number of 400 or 500 are shut up and fortified in a convent at Merida, and they are in momentary expectation at Seville of hearing of their surrender, as Zayas has already summoned them. (The French—two battalions of Germans, had no difficulty in holding their own, and the Spaniards speedily retreated upon an alarm being raised of superior forces moving against them).

Cabezas, the deputy from Asturias, who was recommended to Ld. Hd. by Jovellanos, gives a sad acct. of Romana's qualities as a general, though praises his gallantry as a soldier. It is to be regretted that the Central *Junta* have not recalled him, as he does infinite mischief, having contrived to disorganise the army, disperse and reduce it to a small force, nor allowed them whilst he was with it to fire off a musket; he is so disliked in Galicia that he probably will never venture himself there. His army is at Lugo under a good officer of the name of Mendizabal. (This paragraph is incorrect in most of its particulars, but has been retained in the text as an example of the jealousies of the time and the false statements which are apt to obscure the truth).

22nd May, Cadiz.—Lobo, who was so greatly dissatisfied with the *Junta*, is now quite won over by his being named to the command of a frigate and sent in it on a mission to Constantinople; his violent patriotism has subsided, and instead of finding him quite furious at the delays about the Cortes, he soberly observes that too much time and reflection cannot precede such an important measure as the convoking them.

23rd May.—The accounts from Seville do not fulfil all we had expected. Zayas, instead of seizing the French whom he had summoned in Merida, is at Lobon, where he intends to pass the river with his cavalry; he can retreat upon Badajoz if the enemy should attack him with superior forces. Jovellanos says, '*Lo que nos, da alguno cuidado es la division de Bassecourt, cuya direccion era a Truxillo, y desde este se ignora. Pero Cuesta no teme.*' ('That the division of Bassecourt gave us some alarm; it had gone in the direction of Trujillo, and its whereabouts afterwards was unknown. But Cuesta was not afraid.')

Alava is returned from Portugal; he praises both Cuesta and the English Army, especially the cavalry of the latter. A *contrabandisia*, (smuggler), and his gang have taken the French general Lasalle and a Col. Artan, killed all their escort, and stripped and robbed them entirely. (This story must be a Spanish fabrication. General Lasalle was present at Medellin on March 28, and was recalled a few days later to take charge of a division in Germany. De Cléry in his *Memoirs* mentions that Roederer met him at Burgos on April 28, and from a dispatch it appears that he was at Ebersdorf on May 19).

Sir John Cradock, Ld. Ebrington, and Col. Reynell called; he is just returned from Seville whither he made an excursion. He was not pleased with Frere, who was as usual negligent, did not present him to the *Junta*, and with difficulty to the President. He has all the appearance of a broken-hearted, wounded man; I admire his not being able to dissemble his feelings.

He said he had resigned the appointment given to him of Governor of Gibraltar. He confirmed the account of the discontent and insubordination which is said to exist in the army of Soult. The English forces he rates much lower than we had hoped, in all only 20,000, cavalry included. General Mackenzie is with a force at Abrantes, and some troops are left in Lisbon; then St. Arthur Wellesley has not above 16,000 or 17,000 men with him. Beresford and Silveira between 7,000 and 8,000. The quarrel between Ney and Soult has been most destructive to the operations and the French arms in that quarter.

Ld. Hd. received his letters from Seville. In the eve., Jovellanos. Ferras, and Capmany. *The French have returned to Merida.* The *poste* from Cuesta had not arrived. Venegas is still at Sta. Elena, and the enemy in their former positions. No *poste* from Blake, from whence they infer that he is in motion. It is at length finally settled that the Cortes are to meet in the course of next year and sooner even, if circumstances shall admit, and this is to be announced immediately to the country by a short and simple decree. Admiral Berkeley has sent gun-boats to Abrantes.

24th May.—Sr. John Cradock sent to Ld. Hd. Ld. Castlereagh's dispatch and private letter, and his answer relating to his removal from Portugal and appointment to Gibraltar.

★★★★★★

May 24, 1809. Allow me to ask your perusal of the enclosed as the question may arise why I am sent to Gibraltar, leaving the army I lately commanded in Portugal before the enemy. I cannot blame ministers for any act that either give the appearance or reality of more success, but perhaps it was not fair to me for five months to leave us to our fate in Portugal with no other instruction than "to maintain our situation until compelled to evacuate." While distress, danger, and disgrace were our lot the command was consigned to me; when all is changed it was given to another. Lord Castlereagh's letter to me is a private one.—Sir J. Cradock to Lord Holland.

★★★★★★

Ld. Castlereagh's letter is written in a most disgusting manner, full of the jargon of the H. of Commons, and he labours throughout to give a very false impression. By way of consoling Cradock he tells him that the eyes of Europe will be diverted towards Gibraltar, as the struggle will be there and he may acquire as much of glory as the commander did in 1782 and more than at the head of an army. A thorough false, tricking letter. Cradock with feeling and spirit declines the inactive station of Gibraltar. It was a cruel mortification that he should be withdrawn at the very moment he was, for he had commenced active operations and was actually on his march towards Soult. He told Ld. Hd. very confidentially that on the 22nd April a colonel in the French service passed from the French quarters at Aveiro to Col. Trant and applied to him for a passport to return to France.

★★★★★★

The officer was Captain Argenton, adjutant of a Dragoon regiment. He was conducted to Lisbon by Major Douglas, an English officer in the Portuguese service, and Beresford, and had an interview with Wellesley who had just arrived. He was sent back to Oporto, but saw Wellesley again near Coimbra on May 6. He was betrayed to Soult, however, on his second return to the French camp, and was thrown into prison. The plot therefore entirely miscarried, as Soult acting on his information, arrested the ringleaders. Argenton in his examination mentioned Wellesley's presence and the movements of the British force, and thus ruined Wellesley's hopes of surprising the French. Nothing was done to the conspirators, and Argenton himself escaped to England.

★★★★★★

Upon being questioned whether he was a deserter, he replied that he could hardly be called one, as he withdrew with the knowledge of almost all his brother officers; for, with the exception of Soult himself and three other officers, all were heartily tired of the war and ready to embark in any measures for the restoration of peace upon the Continent, and were even inclined to compel Napoleon to comply with this measure. He added that this feeling was pretty general in the army, but the Imperial Guards alone were so firmly attached to Napoleon, that no assistance was to be expected from them. This col. advised C. to collect every soldier in the country and press forward upon Soult, whom if they could surround and offer a capitulation of a safe retreat into France for his army, he was certain the offer would be accepted, and the troops once returned to France would there manifest the disposition he knew they had to act against Napoleon. C. sent this off to ministers, and when Sir A. Wellesley arrived he communicated this information, upon which, however, he did not implicitly rely. Wellesley naturally enough felt averse to any sound that resembled that of Convention, and judged it best to compel Soult to see England than to permit him to return to France. Upwards of one half of Soult's army is composed of foreigners; Ld. Hd. suspected that the name of this colonel was Melzi.

Jovellanos writes from the *Junta*, where Campo Sagrado was reading Cuesta's *poste*. Zayas was opposite to Merida, preparing to ford the river, and recommence his attack upon the old convent. Henestrosa is at Almendralejo and Torremegia with the cavalry. Bassecourt is at Campanario and Medellin. The French are at Truxillo, Alcuescar, Merida, Arroyo del Puerco, and Brozas. General Mackenzie with 16,000 men and cavalry. (General Mackenzie was detached by Wellesley with about 12,000 men to hold Abrantes, and resist any advance of Victor's troops in the direction of Lisbon). Sr. John C. says he may have 10,000, and that he has two regts. of English cavalry.

Soult is hemmed in by Wellesley; his army can only escape by dispersion. Sickness both in Soult and Victor's army to a very great extent.

25th May.—A messenger who left Madrid on the 10th May told Fernan Nuñez that he had witnessed an *alboroto*, (disturbance), on the 6th, in consequence of the condemnation of four criminals, who were to be executed in the Plaza de la Cebada. A pardon was granted at the foot of the gallows to one, because he was a Corsican and countryman of Josef's; the others were Spaniards. The people were incensed at the distinction and were riotous. No blood was spilt.

Nothing fresh from Cuesta; he assured Alava that he should keep his word to Wellesley, that he would not engage with Victor until the destruction of Soult's army was completed. Zayas had fallen back on the approach of a superior force. Vessel arrived from Lisbon, which it had left on 21st; no accts. of fresh successes. Mr. Jackson writes to me from Seville, that Soult had retired towards the Mino, and that Wellesley was in full pursuit of him.

Napoleon released the Prince of Castelfranco, (D. Pablo Sangro y de Merode, 1740-1815, Spanish general, and Ambassador in Vienna until 1808. His wife was Dowager-Duchess of Berwick), from his prison and allowed him to choose his retreat. He selected Vienna, and sent to Madrid for his wife to join and accompany him thither; however upon the news of the Austrian war, Castelfranco was thrown again into prison, and the princess arrested at Bordeaux.

26th May.—The Madrid *Gazette* of the 6th claims a victory over the Austrians between Landshut and Ratisbon on 21st *ulto.* (the Battle of Echmuhl, on April 22). . . This account is most likely to be a good deal exaggerated, yet the rejoicings at Boulogne and elsewhere confirm the report of a victory.

Cuesta and Victor continue nearly in the same positions. The French have not re-entered Merida. Zayas is preparing to ford the river to renew his attack on the old convent. Albuquerque is at Zafra. The French have placed 1000 horse at Miajadas to keep their communications from being cut off with Truxillo. Campo Sagrado in his bulletin mentions an intercepted letter from Victor to Soult, which states that on 29th April (day letter was written) his infantry consisted of 20,741, cavalry 4762, besides artillery. He apprised him of his plan, which was to penetrate by Almaden del Azogue. In consequence of this intention Bassecourt with the 5th division has been ordered from Campanario to Monterubbio. Victor's plan most probably was to make a junction with Sebastiani. It is said that Joseph has quitted Madrid and joined the army in the Mancha.

Perez de Castro sent off an extraordinary to Seville from Lisbon, giving an account of the surrender of Soult and his army. (This was of course incorrect. Soult was able after many hardships to draw off the remains of his army into Galicia). There is no official account from Oporto, but the details in the private letters are so circumstantial and bear such marks of truth, that Castro is satisfied with the fact. A small *bark* came in today from the Bayona Islands. An English frigate told her on the 18th that Soult and his army had reached Barcellos, and that Sr. A. Wellesley was following closely. A vessel from Malta brings an acct. of a splendid victory fought near Venice between the

Austrians and French, in which the former were successful. The news came from Trieste on 20th. The story is too dramatic. The catastrophe is brought about by the Archduke John, who wounds the Vice-King Eugenio, and then after three days hard fighting and reverses the Austrians are finally victorious. This news is published in an extraordinary *Gazette* at Gibraltar, but it seems to want confirmation.

★★★★★★

The Archduke John inflicted a signal defeat on Eugène Beauharnais on April 16 at Sacile, near Pordenone. The French commander, however, does not appear to have received any wound. The successes in Italy were more than counterbalanced by Napoleon's rapid advance to Vienna.

★★★★★★

29th.—Alas! all the glorious news which had been so positively asserted for some days was quite overthrown by the accounts from Seville. Jovellanos says the news from Portugal is not so successful in the result as they had been taught to expect. Soult with ¾ of his army has escaped into the mts. of Orense; he sacrificed the remainder of his army, his baggage, artillery, &c. Wellesley was going to fulfil his promise to Cuesta, (to move his troops to assist him, as soon as Soult had been dealt with), and was to cross the Mondego on the 25th or 26th. Mortier appeared at Salamanca and threatened Ledesma; he has fallen back no one knows whither, but it is conjectured that he will attempt to form a junction either with Victor or Sebastiani. Cuesta has applied for Mackenzie with his corps to come from Alcantara to prevent Victor's *salida*, (sally), into Castile. Sr. John Cradock says this request will not be complied with, as the English Army has positive instructions not to operate in detached corps. Victor was making some movements towards Almaraz.

Romana, foolish fellow, instead of collecting and reinforcing his army with the troops he might draw from the Asturias, was on the 12th of this month at Oviedo, squabbling and disputing with the Civil Governt. In La Sierra Morena there has been an action *muy bonito* with the guerrillas. Blake has taken Alcañiz, and the whole plan and conduct of affairs was judicious and brilliant.

★★★★★★

In Aragon, owing to successes achieved by the Spanish irregulars at Monzon and Pomar, affairs began to look well for the Spaniards. One of Grandjean's brigades under Laval was forced by Blake to evacuate Alcañiz on May 18. His army at that time amounted to about 10,000 men. Suchet at this juncture took up the command of the French troops in Aragon, and at once marched with 8000 men to attack Blake. The battle took place near Alcañiz on May 23, and resulted in a defeat of the French, who lost at least 700 men and retreated in complete disorder.

★★★★★★

There is to be an extraordinary *Gazette* upon this success. Mr. Jackson sent me an abstract of Sr. A. Wellesley's letter to Frere, dated Oporto, 22nd. He followed Soult beyond Braga to Salamonde. He came up with their rearguard and took 600 prisoners under the command of Loison. On the 27th he and his army were to be at Coimbra. He refers Frere to Mr. Villiers's letters for details, but these letters have not yet arrived. About ¾ of the French Army has escaped, without cannon, ammunition, or baggage.

No news in the Seville letters from the armies. Jovellanos begins to be afraid that Cuesta, who has rigorously kept his word not to attack whilst Wellesley was goings on to Oporto, will consider his promise as sufficiently fulfilled and begin attacking immediately. The day of San Fernando probably will excite him to some attempt of the sort.

30th May, the day of San Fernando.—Intelligence from Blake, the defeat of a body of French who had marched from Barbastro to punish Monzon, followed by the evacuation of Barbastro. This last was sent to me by Don Francisco, and is contained in a letter from his uncle, dated Lerida, 22nd. It seems that 1300 French had crossed the Cinca in order to punish Monzon, were not only foiled in that object, but prevented from returning by the swelling of the river, in consequence of which 600 of them were made prisoners, and the rest including the commander, a Great-Cross of the Legion of Honour, killed or drowned. (Habert was the French general in command. He seems to have been one of the few who escaped capture. His attempt to recapture Monzon from the insurgents, who had driven out the French, took place on May 16).

In consequence of these disasters, those who remained at Barbastro evacuated that city on the night of the 29th. In several towns of Aragon the French have had public rejoicings for the taking of Seville. They are said to have abandoned their intention of besieging Gerona.

Jovellanos is discontented at the choice of the commissioners for the Cortes; the five are Jovellanos, Caro. Castanedo, the Archbishop of Laodicea, and Riquelme.

★★★★★★

By a proclamation issued by the Central *Junta* on May 22, the Cortes was to be called together ' early the following year or earlier if circumstances permit.' The method of procedure was to be left to five members. Arteche places a different construction on the respective attitudes of the commissioners from that stated by Lady Holland. He remarks that Riquelme and Caro were opposed in their views to the other three members).

★★★★★★

31st May.—Jovellanos writes shortly, as he had spent the whole of the San Fernando in ceremony though the day was melancholy, for certainly without having any great love for Ferdinand there is something very dismal in passing a day in his honour in festivity, whilst he, poor fellow, is cut off from all intercourse with his countrymen and confined in a foreign country. I do not believe, however, that these were Jovellanos's feelings when he said the day was not *de alegria*, (festive); he was probably more annoyed at the election of the Commission of five. He says Cuesta writes that he has *certain* intelligence that Mortier is returning into France with his division; in his army nothing new has occurred, nor in that of the Sierra Morena. Ld. Hd. has a letter from Quintana and Blanco very full of complaints and dissatisfaction at the decree for the convocation of the Cortes, which they call barren, cold, and formal. They are even unreasonable in grumbling at Jovellanos, to whom they ascribe very much of this delay, but in which they accuse him *à tort*. Sr. John Cradock, &c., sailed in the *Surveillante* for Gibraltar. Ld. Ebrington and T. Sheridan rode over to Gibraltar, leaving his good little wife. My rheumatism very troublesome.

2nd June.—Letters from Jovellanos, Ferras, and Quintana, containing an acct. of a very brilliant affair of Blake's with the French near Alcañiz on the 23rd May. Ferras enclosed Maldonado's relation of the battle, which as he was present, is interesting. The French, commanded by Suchet, who had succeeded Junot, attacked him four times and were vigorously repulsed. At one moment, owing to the great superiority of the French in cavalry, the Spanish line was thrown into so much disorder that Maldonado and Burriel seeing the danger to which the general was exposed, advised him to save himself '*que no habia remedio, aun hay remedio dixo*'; and with a company of infantry only he encouraged and sustained the artillery, and the rest followed his example and saved the day. The French lost one piece of cannon,

131

500 killed, 100 prisoners; they abandoned their positions and retired towards Saragossa.

The siege of Gerona is begun, but the garrison are full of spirits and confident of success, and have made several successful sallies. (The siege of Gerona in Catalonia was actually commenced on May 24 by Verdier. The place, which was commanded by Alvarez de Castro, held out till Dec, 10). A slight advantage under Grimarest in the Sierra Morena. When Cuesta's *poste* came away, Zayas and Bassecourt were engaged with the enemy. Cuesta believed that the French were preparing to cross the Tagus at Almaraz. Romana was in the Asturias on the 15th with 7000 troops, ill equipped and provided. He has 6000 men in Vigo, and the remainder of his army near Lugo. He has written to Wellesley that if he destroys Soult, he will demolish Ney, but if they form a junction Galicia and the Asturias will be lost.

Most melancholy details in the Madrid Gazettes; the bulletins of the French Army in Bavaria from the 24th to 27th April. On 19th and 23rd actions between French and Austrians which finally terminated in the total expulsion of the latter from Bavaria, with loss of 30,000 prisoners, 100 cannon, baggages, ammunition, &c. The Archduke Charles had fallen back to Bohemia, the French had passed the Irun, and Napoleon promised his army to be in Vienna in a month. (The campaign of Abensberg, Echmuhl, and Ratisbon. Napoleon had only left Fans twelve days before the Austrians were driven from Bavaria).

3rd June.—The French from their movements appear disposed to retreat upon Almaraz. They have already abandoned Miajadas. Jovellanos says the Commission of five was chosen by secret votes. His was the first name that came out. He admits that Riquelme and the archbishop were chosen by the enemies of the Cortes, but he is satisfied that he can defeat their intentions by devoting himself entirely to the trust committed to him, and supported as the cause of liberty is by the public opinion, he feels confident of triumphing over any opposition that may be made to him by others of the Commission. King Joseph has been at Toledo, where he did not meet with a single *viva* from the people; he returned to Aranjuez.

4th June. —A vessel from Gijon in five days brings the bad news of the French having penetrated into the Asturias, and reached the neighbourhood of Gijon on the 19th, which place was preparing to defend itself; many women and children and old persons had escaped on board some English transports and other vessels on the coast, and that Romana had embarked his army in order to convey it to Ribadeo in Galicia, so as to get into the rear of the French. This vessel says that the French Army is Ney's, who has evacuated Ferrol and took the Asturias in his way to France for the sake of plunder, but this is mere report.

★★★★★★

This was one section of the concentric advance planned by the French, in order to envelope and destroy the scattered Spanish forces in Galicia and the Asturias, by the simultaneous advance of three columns moving from different bases. The attack on Oviedo and Gijon, undertaken by Ney, was completely successful. La Romana was taken by surprise, retreated hurriedly to the coast, and embarked without his troops. Oviedo was occupied by the French on May 19, and Gijon on May 20.

★★★★★★

A splendid illumination at the theatre in honour of George III, and a representation of the escape of Romana and his army from the Isle of Fünen. A dull performance.

5th June, Cadiz.—Ferras says the *encomienda*, a military *comandancia* at Peso Real in Valencia, which the *Junta* have given to Blake, is worth 60,000 *reals*. He complains of Caro at Valencia, who does not support Blake with supplies and cavalry, and adds that the family will ruin Spain, for Romana has fled from the enemy in the plains. Jovellanos knew of the French having possession of the principal *Juntas* in the Asturias; he laments over Gijon, and adds that their former *Junta* would not have abandoned them as Romana has done!

★★★★★★

Oman (vol. ii. 414) combats a somewhat similar suggestion made by Napier. The reinforcements supplied from Valencia seem adequate, and compare favourably with those sent by other provinces.

★★★★★★

There are official accounts of the French having been driven from Santiago on the 23rd by Don Martin de la Carrera after a severe defeat, and of a battle near Lugo on the 19th, in which they were defeated with great loss by Don Nicolas Mahy, and compelled to shut themselves up in that town.

★★★★★★

General Mahy had escaped westward from the advance of Ney's

133

column, and being unpursued set himself to attack the isolated French garrisons left in Galicia. He attacked General Fournier at Lugo with 6000 men, drove him into the town, which he was about to attempt to assault when Soult's unexpected arrival from Orense with the discomfited remains of his Portuguese army drove him to take refuge in the mountains. At the same time Martin la Carrera with a small body of regulars from Puebla de Sanabria joined the insurgents who had attacked Tuy and Vigo, and advanced against Santiago. The French commander Mancune met them outside the town, but was defeated with the loss of 600 men, and driven to Coruña, where he was joined in all haste by Ney and his victorious force from Oviedo.

★★★★★★

There are official communications from the respective generals and conveyed by English cruisers to Lisbon to Perez de Castro, who forwards them to the *Junta*. There is a subsequent acct. of the surrender of Lugo on the 24th, but it rests entirely on the testimony of a Portuguese officer, who added that Mazarredo was in Lugo. Mahy's letter of the 20th mentions the departure of Ney with all his scattered parties from Old Castile towards the Asturias, which he meant to plunder on his way to France, whither he was going, and that he had already reached Cangas de Tineo. He adds that he could not besiege Lugo for want of battering cannon, and meant to take a position near Mondoñedo to watch the motions of Marshal Ney.

A letter from Zafra of 31st from Col. Whittingham, which mentioned that Victor was concentrating his forces at Torremocha.

Jovellanos enclosed a bulletin from Campo Sagrado. Cuesta has a *terciano*, (tercian fever), which is not yet become malignant: O'Donoju, (Cuesta's chief of the staff), writes for him. Two English colonels from Wellesley's army had reached his headquarters in order to concert a plan of operations. The English Army was to leave Coimbra on 1st June, but from the badness of the roads and the want of shoes it would not arrive till the 15th or 16th. The amount will then be 20,000 infantry, 4000 cavalry, 6 brigades of artillery. (The whole total of English troops which entered Spain was about 22,000—*Oman*. The leading brigades did not enter Spain till July 3).

June 7, Chiclana.—Jovellanos sends an extract from the *Moniteur*, 11th May, which announces the appointment of Ld. Holland to the embassy of Vienna; it adds that his *Seigneurie* must lose no time in getting there, as he may find another sovereign than the one he is sent to. Jovellanos is annoyed at the delay of Wellesley, and is full of suspicion and discontent, and complains that he has exacted a promise of forbearance from Cuesta. Ferras says there are no further details from Blake, about whom he feels the greatest anxiety; he probably bas advanced to Caspe. Reinforcements of cavalry and infantry are sent off already from Valencia. Nothing from Cuesta.

8th.—Hot day. Arriaza, Iglesias, Caceres, and Dan, Arturo Gordon called Monday. Eat an early dinner, and went in eve. to Cadiz. Crossed the bark which is very ill contrived. The toll of the bark is due to the Duke, and but for Solano, who sacrificed the convenience of the public to favour Medina Sidonia's interests, who as *Señor* of Chiclana has the profits of the ferry, the public might have had an excellent stone bridge; the whole scheme was propounded, but for the above reason was dropped. Duff told us that the profits to Villafranca upon the tunny fishery at Conil last year were 90,000 *duros*, but as the market was over-stocked they do not mean to get as many fish this year. In Catalonia the tunny fish had a great consumption, but that market at present is closed to them. Cuesta continued so ill that he had not been able to see the English colonels sent by Gen. Wellesley. Eguia has the supreme command at present. The French are concentrating at Merida. Some say they are waiting for pontoons from Madrid to cross the Tagus.

9th.—By Jackson's expression of they say that Wellesley is to be at Badajoz, it seems as if he doubted the truth of the report. Cuesta is impatient to advance. The Lisbon *Gazette* reports that Soult's army was pursued to Allariz near Orense. By a letter from the Duque del Parque of 30th, Ciudad Rodrigo, it seems that the French are in force at Salamanca, Avila, Valladolid, having abandoned Ledesma from the increased force of the Spaniards in that quarter.

Madame de Hijar has just heard that Napoleon, who had given permission to Castelfranco to choose any place for his residence out of Spain, has again ordered him to be arrested, and he is to be confined as a prisoner at Gaeta because he had chosen Vienna for his retreat. His wife, the Dow. Dss. of Berwick, who had obtained permission to join him, is detained at Bordeaux *gardée à vue.* The Marquis of Santa Cruz is already in his prison at Finistral in Piémont. The French entered Vienna on 12th May.

10th.—Infantado called; he wants to speak with Ld. Hd. confiden-

135

tially. Ld. Wellesley is to come out in the *Donegal*, (he arrived off Cadiz on July 31), and brings Cevallos. (Cevallos had been sent to England by the *Junta* as their agent).

12th June.—*Poste* of last night this morning. No news from armies. The official returns, Mr. Jackson writes to me, were from Cuesta as follows: 28,000 infantry, 7000 cavalry well mounted, besides artillery and unequipped troops. Venegas has 19,000 foot and cavalry altogether. The English cols, who are with Cuesta are Bourke and Cadogan. (Richard Bourke (1777-1853), assistant quartermaster-general to the British Army in Portugal, and afterwards Governor of New South Wales. He was made K.C.B. in 1835. Henry Cadogan (1780-1813), *aide-de-camp* to Sir Arthur Wellesley, He was killed at Vitoria.)

Albuquerque left Zafra on the 9th to proceed to Villanueva de la Serena and Don Benito, in order to reinforce Bassecourt, who was at Medellin threatened with an attack from Miajadas. Zayas was preparing to renew his attack on that eternal convent in Merida. Bassecourt advanced first; had a skirmish with the French on the 8th half a league beyond Medellin.

★★★★★★

Mr. Jackson to Lord Holland: 'June 12, Seville. On the 8th the 2nd regiment of Hussars of Estremadura (*alias* of Maria Luisa) belonging to Bassecourt's division and advanced half a league beyond Medellin, was vigorously attacked by 80 horse, who came within musket's shot supported by a body of 400. Their Colonel Ribas attacked the first who offered themselves with the greatest intrepidity, and Bassecourt says he saw them entirely turned, so that no one would have escaped, had not the principal body charged ours and obliged Ribas to retire, which he did in such order that they dared not venture to pursue him. We lost only 3 killed and one wounded; the enemy 40 of the first and 70 of the latter.' Albuquerque had 1400 men with him.

★★★★★★

Very severe *solano* or *levante* wind which affects everybody; I have suffered greatly from a fluxion in my head and cheek. Mr. North, Ld. Lewisham, Mr. Fazakerley dined; I was too ill from pain and went to bed.

14th.—No company on acct. of my illness. Cuesta writes that the enemy were preparing to come upon Merida or Medellin, which compelled him to divide his forces between these two points. (The news of Soult's retreat had just reached the French, and the retirement behind the Tagus was only commenced on this date, June 14. It was more due, however, to the lack of provisions south of that river than to any fear of the British advance). He has made the first division march to support Bassecourt at Villanueva de la Serena, and has given the command to Eguia, remaining himself with the rest near Merida. On the 11th he had a letter from Sir A. Wellesley apprising him of a French division having returned upon Alcantara, where the Portuguese commander had *cortado el puente*. The French had got a letter of Cuesta's to an officer at Alcantara, which fortunately contained nothing but instructions not to destroy the bridge until the last extremity. Some English have reached Portalegre. Wellesley has assured Cuesta that he will co-operate with him, and march if expedient north *los Pirineos*. Romana was at Orense on the 4th between the Mino and the Sil acting on the defensive, whilst Soult had reached Lugo in the most deplorable condition with his army. Ney had returned from the Asturias. Mortier had dispatched 6000 men to Leon, (to join Kellermann. He was not long allowed the use of them for Mortier sent for the division back in a hurry to assist in repelling the expected advance of Wellesley towards Salamanca).

★★★★★★

After his escape by sea from Oviedo, La Romana landed at Ribadeo and joined Mahy. Seeing, however, that the Spanish troops were thus confined in a corner, he decided to move to Orense, and slipped past Soult, who had plenty to do at Lugo with reorganising his battered force and quarrelling about future movements with Ney.

★★★★★★

16th.—Arriaza at dinner. Col. Doyle gave us an acct. of Ward, whom he had left at Gibraltar more out of humour and discontented than ever. He has made an enemy and furnished matter for a joke wherever he has been. Doyle has received an exact acct. of the Valencia forces which left Valencia to join Blake on the 2nd June—7000 infantry and 800 cavalry; of the latter he says there is one regt. equal in excellence to any in the Spanish service. Also an admirable officer whom Blake is determined, whenever an opportunity may offer, of raising to the rank of *Mariscal-de-Campo*: Valcarcel is his name. The letter from Jovellanos which ought to have arrived last night came this morning. He is not ill. It gives an acct. of the evacuation of Merida by the French; the 300 in the convent were escorted out under the cover of 2000 cavalry, and have withdrawn to Alcuescar. Zayas occupies Merida, and Henestrosa has orders to advance with his infantry to Almendralejo, and his cavalry to Calamonte.

Romana writes his disgusting proceedings from Orense, where he is on the defensive with 9633 men. Soult has formed his junction with Ney, who has evacuated the Asturias.

★★★★★★

La Romana had taken the sensible resolve never to engage the enemy in force if he could avoid it. How much better would it have been had other Spanish generals done likewise I From a letter, however, in the Record Office (June 9), quoted by Mr. Oman, he appears in this case to have intended to fall on Key's flank, but was deterred from doing so by the presence of Soult at Monforte.

Soult and Ney had decided, after much squabbling at Lugo, to undertake the reduction of Galicia, and arranged a plan of campaign accordingly, which the former appears to have had no intention of carrying out. He in fact took the first opportunity of marching away to Leon, leaving Ney to undertake a task which was quite beyond his power with the force at his command.

These movements of the French refer to the earlier sweeping movements mentioned earlier.

★★★★★★

Campo Sagrado, in his bulletin, mentions that the French had entered that principality in two corps, one under Kellermann by Paxares, the other 6000 under Ney by Ibias. A curate! acted as guide to the latter corps, which proceeded so secretly and rapidly that it had reached Salas and Cornellana before its entrance into the Asturias was known at Gijon. Campo Sagrado is highly incensed against Romana, whom he thinks highly deserving of punishment, and wishes much to have it inflicted; for according to his own statements there were 6000 good troops under Ballesteros and 5000 under Worster, but he gives no explanation or justification of his conduct in first suppressing the *Junta*, and then in neglecting and abandoning the defence of the province.

17th.—A packet from England came this morning with papers and letters to the 6th June. Very dismal accts. from Austria which have depressed us all, as when that country is subdued Spain must be overrun by legions of fresh invaders flushed with victory and conquest, and what can she do against such physical superiority?

G. Lamb is married to Caroline St. Jules. D. of D. behaves very kindly. They are to live in a house of their own, as he wisely intends to pursue his profession. (Honble. George Lamb (1764-1834), fourth son of Peniston, first Viscount Melbourne. He was a lawyer, but employed his time more in literature and politics than in his own profession).

Ly. Isabella Fitzgerald, is married to Chabot, the son of Jarnac, a bad marriage, which Ly. L. Conolly with her usual good-nature is endeavouring to reconcile the family to. (Lady Isabella Charlotte Fitzgerald, fourth daughter of William Robert, second Duke of Leinster. She married Major-General Louis Guillaume de Rohan Chabot, Viscomte de Chabot, and died in 1868).

Tierney and Sr. Francis Burdett had some sharp words together in the H. of Commons, (on Curwen's Reform Bill, May 26), but the latter made a submission, else Tierney's towering passion would have ended in a duel between them.

General Wellesley writes on 13th of June from Abrantes and promises a junction in a few days with Cuesta; and entreats in the meantime that no action may be hazarded. There are symptoms of retreat in Victor's army, and some of his troops have passed the Tagus. The English still want shoes. Jovellanos has very kindly released Capmany from the drudgery of the *Gazette*, and employed him in enquiries and researches about the Cortes.

18th June, Cadiz.—Went off early in day to Pto. Sta. Maria, partly with the intention of changing the air, and partly with a view perhaps of proceeding again to Lisbon by the way of Seville, for there is no chance of sailing from Cadiz. Admirals Purvis and Berkeley have quarrelled, and ships do not go from their respective stations; and Ld. Wellesley's arrival grows doubtful and even his returned ships may not take us or may not go back to England.

19th, Puerto Santa Maria.—I had letters from Rodenas and Ferras, Ld. Hd. one from Jovellanos. The army of La Carolina is resuming its old positions. Victor returning across the Tagus, and Cuesta in pursuit of his rearguard. The Conde de Noroña had an action with the French at Puente de Sampayo immediately on his arrival in Galicia, in which he repulsed them four times and finally gained the victory.

★★★★★★

It was the reduction of this force of insurgents and regulars in the south of Galicia which was occupying Ney when he heard of Soult's departure from the provinces. Alone he was unable to make any impression on these Spaniards safely ensconced behind the Oitaben, and he finally retired to Lugo. The Conde de Noroña had been given command of the force which had done so well at Vigo and Santiago; 2500 men only were regular troops.

★★★★★★

The Spaniards at Seville are very much dissatisfied with Sir A. Wellesley, whom they accuse of not advancing and of not allowing Cuesta to advance. He first complained of want of shoes, and now he grounds his delay upon want of money. He was still at Abrantes. Sebastiani has moved to Consuegra.

Ferras accounts for the smallness of Blake's army at Alcañiz because he had left a strong garrison at Tortosa; he thought by this time his numbers would be doubled. On the 7th his headquarters were still at Samper. Strange to say the English king has refused to accept of the 4000 merinos, which at Frere's instigation the *Junta* had offered him. Poor creatures, they have already sailed. B. Frere is to remain as secty. to the embassy with Lord Wellesley. Ly. Wellesley does not for the moment come out.

20th.—The accounts from Jovellanos and Jackson from Seville are too excellent almost to admit of belief; if true in the smallest degree, Spain may yet be saved. An *extraordinary Gazette* from Tarragona has arrived giving a minute and circumstantial account of a great *defeat* sustained by the French commanded by *Napoleon!* in person on the Danube on the 22nd and 23rd of May. (The Battle of Aspern, where Napoleon was repulsed and driven back to the island of Lobau). It is said that this is corroborated by private letters from Paris, and by a bulletin in which they admit their loss to amount to 3000 men.

Victor is *bona-fide* retreating, and Cuesta is in full pursuit; the last accounts from Cuesta were dated Miajadas; Eguia at Sta. Cruz de la Sierra, and actions had taken place between the S. light troops and 5000 French stationed at Ruena and La Coimbre (?). Some random accts. of the English army. Venegas has advanced to Manzanares, and recovered the positions so scandalously abandoned by Urbina. The road being *libre* from Seville to Badajoz, we have resolved not to loiter on this coast, but to proceed to Lisbon and there get a passage home.

23rd June, Xeres.—Letters from Jovellanos and Ferras, by which it appears that the French have abandoned Truxillo, leaving magazines of com and flour behind them. Cuesta is at that city, his advanced

140

guard at Jaraicejo. There have been skirmishes with the French rear-guard, but of no importance. Nothing of the English. Blake still at Belchite on the 12th. Headquarters of Venegas at Valdepeñas. Jovellanos is alarmed at the probable junction of Victor and Sebastiani. 12th bulletin of French Army acknowledges losses, but no very accurate official particulars have yet been received.

Mr. Gordon is very well pleased with the advantages which the *Junta* have accorded to Xeres, *viz.* the establishment of an *aduana*, (custom house), which shall render them independent of Cadiz; of the trade direct with America; and permission to make a canal from Guadalquiver through its territory to the Bay of Cadiz, which when completed will enable them to have a dock above Puerto Real to ship their goods without being exposed to delay from the bar of Sta. Maria, which is oftentimes impassable for several days together. Cadiz will suffer if the scheme is ever realised.

24th June.—At Seville we found the city gates blocked up by batteries, and great precautions of course were necessary to wind our way through the embrasures, &c. Took up our abode in the Dueñas, (the Marquesa de Ariza's house), our rooms are insufferably hot, the house is filled, Mde. Castelflorido, her husband, and the Marqués Ariza. Jovellanos, Ferras, &c., in eve.

25th June, Seville.—Jovellanos, Ferras. Sad news of Blake's defeat on 18th at Belchite after repulse from Saragossa.

★★★★★★

Blake after collecting his reinforcements advanced from Alcañiz on Zaragoza, but was attacked at Maria by Suchet, who profited by the faulty dispositions of the Spanish commander, and drove him from the field. Blake retreated in good order to Belchite, where he again drew up his forces to oppose the enemy on the following day. As far as can be ascertained an accidental explosion of Spanish powder-wagons was the primary cause of the disgraceful *sauve qui peut* which followed. The Spanish Army, already shaken by the events of the previous day, thought they had been treacherously attacked in the rear and fled in the utmost confusion. Their actual loss was not great, but the army simply scattered all over the country, and it was months before it was reformed.

★★★★★★

27th.—Blake's *poste* very affecting; seems to have been cruelly betrayed and abandoned by the Valencians. An intrigue of the *grandees* suspected.

On the 26th there was a very interesting discussion in the *Junta* upon the business of the Cortes, whether the representation should be of the whole nation, or from the three classes the *bravo militar, clerigo, pueblo*; the leaning was in favour of the latter. Several members entered with their vote a protest of reservation, to object in case they thought the proportion of deputies from those classes too great.

Poor Blake has written a touching letter to the *Junta*, which I have not yet prevailed upon myself to read, for the calamity has truly affected me. He gives no details. The Section of War took the deposition of the courier, who declares that the action only lasted one hour, beginning at 6 and ending at 7; that the dispersion was complete, and that the general and his staff were left *entirely* alone. The Valencian reinforcements had reached him in part, for O'Donoju, the col. of the regt. of Olivenza was killed. (Arteche quoting Toreno says that Colonel Juan O'Donojú was taken prisoner).

From various circumstances it seems evident that he was sacrificed and betrayed scandalously by a party of officers in his own army. Caro, the brother of Romana, who is the popular head of the rabble of Valencia, excited underhand a tumult in the city to prevent his going with the succour ordered for Blake.

★★★★★★

General José Caro, La Romana's youngest brother, Governor of Valencia. He had in the province and with the local *Junta* immense influence, which was always employed to oppose the authority of the Central *Junta* at Seville and to thwart their actions.

★★★★★★

Lazan is suspected of conniving at the treachery, and to be one of the intriguing *grandees* who intend to endeavour to overturn the Govt. He has evaded the orders of the *Junta* who recalled him lately. The plot is deep, if the conjectures are well founded. Lazan wanted the Capt.-Generalship of Aragon; Caro has long been trying to be confirmed as such in Valencia; Villafranca by intrigue obtained that of Murcia; and Montijo has struggled for that of Granada, which, however, in the attempt to gain, he has entirely lost, and got himself arrested and confined to Badajoz.

Bauza with great dexterity has contrived to make his escape from Madrid with his family and all his most valuable papers, and to conceal the rest so that the French can have no access to them—his materials for a map of the province of Spain bordering on the Pyrenees, Malespina's voyage, the drawings and various materials for S. America, &c. Laborde, who had been employed upon the *Voyage Pittoresque d'Espagne*, persecuted him. (Alexandre Louis Joseph, Comte de Laborde (1773-1842), who accompanied Lucien Bonaparte on his mission to Spain as *aide-de-camp*, and remained there to obtain materials for his work, which was published in 1808).

The French officers are very corrupt and money will procure any testimony. For five guineas he got a certificate from a *mulatto* colonel to declare he was 60 years of age. He describes the people of Madrid and of every place which he passed through as equally hostile to the French as this. He says, what they all do, that the French have no power over any part of Spain but just where their armies are in possession.

Cuesta has received his famous pontoons from Badajoz; but they have sent him only 18 boats, whereas 22 is the complement, consequently he undergoes great difficulty and delay in passing his troops.

★★★★★★

Cuesta had advanced to Almaraz, when Victor withdrew his troops north of the Tagus to Talavera. He repaired the pontoon bridge there, which had been destroyed by the French. Victor had intended to hold the line of the Tagus, but sheer want of provisions drove him to retire behind the Alberche.

★★★★★★

The enemy seem to have evacuated their positions on the opposite shore of the river, so he has no obstacle to encounter in crossing the river but the embarrassments which arise from want of boats. From a letter just received by Quintana from Venegas' army it seems that Sebastiani has been greatly reinforced; if from Victor's army the news is good, but if from Aragon or elsewhere it is alarming.

★★★★★★

The reinforcements did consist of troops lent by Sebastiani to Victor, and of part of Joseph's own force at Madrid. Venegas had to beat a hurried retreat, and was not caught, though his rash advance merited such a fate. Joseph pursued him as far south as El Moral.

★★★★★★

King Pepe has taken the command; probably he did not like to trust himself in Madrid, stripped of troops, alone amongst his faithful vassals. Venegas, in consequence of this information is falling back upon Despeña Perros.

I spoke to Campo Sagrado upon this sad disaster which has befallen Blake, adding how much it was to be wished that he might receive every consolation which could be afforded him from the Govt. He spoke with the utmost feeling, and said the charge of writing had been entrusted to him by the *Junta*, and that his friends might be satisfied that everything should be done to mitigate his anguish of mind and prove that he still retained their confidence. I hinted that in order to acquit him to the public, the blame ought to be thrown where it was deserved, for to conceal the treachery of those who had betrayed him was in fact sharing it in part.

Veri, (Don Tomas de Veri, member of the Central *Junta* for the Balearic Isles), who was by, joined most heartily in this; Campo Sagrado acquiesced equally warmly, but it was evident that he was not allowed to act upon that subject as he wished. Veri gave me a copy of poor Blake's *poste*; it is very affecting, and evidently written under a feeling of the utmost despondency. He declined all future command even if the *Junta* would entrust any to a man of such a *mala estrella*; he will serve his country as a mere soldier, declines the *encomienda*, and only requests a moderate pension for his family merely for their maintenance. He gives no details of the action, but from the ambiguity of some of the expressions he glances at treachery in those about him.

The D. of Infantado has determined upon publishing an account of his whole conduct. His opinion against the abdication of Ferdinand is very strong, and would have cleared him from many aspersions had he been judicious enough to have made it public at the time, instead of entrusting it to Cevallos, who to make his own case more *saliente*, (remarkable), concealed Infantado's. The D. of Albuquerque in a pet has thrown up his command, which, considering that he is in face of the enemy, is scandalous. He is discontented with Cuesta, and angry with the *Junta* for not giving him a separate supreme command. Jovellanos is displeased with Frere, who never ceases to urge the *Junta* to make him C.-in-Chief. This is a part of the grand plot of the *grandees*. Ld. Hd. dined with Infantado. Before we set off Jovellanos and Infantado were with us.

30th June, Fuente de Cantos.—We are lodged here in the house of the Conde de Casa Chaves, a member of the *Junta* of Badajoz. The females of this family, as did the others of the town, fled into the *Sierra*

144

whilst the French were in the neighbourhood. It does not appear that any French reached this place. A small party went to Zafra, but on finding the inhabitants were disposed to make resistance, they withdrew. The *Condesa* of this house is a relation of Venegas; she seems a mild, well-behaved person. Her husband is very unpleasant, and treats her with the utmost harshness; she submits to the lowest household drudgery whilst he takes his *siesta* and with his Order at his button struts like a person of importance.

1st July.—Our host and many persons of substance are proprietors of the *merinos*. The Marquis of Enseñares from Zafra came over in consequence of hearing that we were likely to go there; by some strange jumble they conceived Ld. Hd. was a great purchaser of wool, and they set off their stock of that commodity for the best advantage. 1500 French came to this place (Los Santos). They only remained two hours in consequence of the approach of Echevarria's advanced guards. They committed great ravages at Almendralejo. At Merida they have sacked the town, only one house is untouched; they pretend to say they only destroy where the proprietors fly, and that at Caceres where the inhabitants remained they left everything uninjured.

2nd July.—Left Los Santos at 3 o'clock. Saw on left the town and old tower and walls of Feria; very picturesquely situated. A party of French went up to the town and demanded rations, but the people retired to the old tower and worked an old cannon, which played so briskly that they forced them to retire. Reached Sta. Marta about 7 o'clock. The French to the number of 500 were quartered here for 22 days, beginning from 21st April. The women and young men fled, and many houses were quite deserted. The French cut down the olives for their encampment, and took off the doors and windows from the houses for their tents, which when they withdrew they burnt.

The young men who left the village joined with other peasants, and kept up a constant skirmishing with the advanced posts of the French. Our curate's house was not destroyed, his mother and another woman remained; she lodged two colonels, one who said he was a near relation of Napoleon's. One of them on going away expressed his satisfaction at the reception he had met with and the uniform attention he had received ; and to prove his gratitude he begged to leave a certificate of approbation, desiring it might be shown to any friend who might afterwards come to her house. The poor woman readily accepted of his offer, and accordingly received from him the following

145

certificate, which is literally copied in orthography, &c.:—

Malheureux Espagnols, votre ignorance et votre fanatisme font tout votre malheur. Si vous éties plus alacres vous series peutêtre plus justes, moin ferosse plus sivilisées, et par consequent plus heiareux et plus estimables.

Till Mr. Allen translated the meaning of the words, the people were fully persuaded they possessed a high compliment in their favour.

3rd July, Sta, Marta.—We only lay down for a few hours and proceeded on our journey early. The *alcalde* told us that in consequence of the great alarm and fright produced by the arrival of the French at Sta. Marta, much sickness had ensued, haemorrhages, and the death of most of the young sucking children whose mothers had fled in great trepidation on foot amongst the mountains. At Los Santos Ld. Hd. received a letter from the person who is to lodge us at Badajoz, to know exactly at what hour we should arrive, in order to receive him in a manner suitable to his rank. This is terribly disagreeable, and entails great *ennui* for me. At Sta. Marta the *Junta* of Badajoz sent us out a guard of honour on horseback to escort us. Saw to the left Nogales, where a body of peasantry amounting to 5,000 or 6,000 repulsed the French who went to demand rations. Upon the road before Albuera we met Proudman, the messenger, who was on his way from Sr. A. Wellesley to Seville with dispatches.

Wellesley left Abrantes on 26th, and was to leave Castello Branco yesterday, 2nd July, and according to his report was to march 10 days onwards. About a league from Badajoz, two members deputed from the *Junta* came in a coach and six, escorted by a troop of Dragoons, to meet Ld. Hd. They got out in the middle of the high road, and made him a set speech, which when concluded they invited us to go into the coach, an honour I of course declined, but Ld. Hd. was resigned to his fate and went with them. A vast crowd was assembled in and about the town to greet our arrival, and we got out of the carriage amidst innumerable *vivas* at the house of the late Conde de Torre Fresno, which had been prepared for our reception. In the eve. we had a *refresco*, and all classes and descriptions of persons came: the Capt.-General d'Arcé, the *Inquisidor* Riesgo, whom we knew at Valladolid and who is the president of this *Junta*. Fireworks and music on a stage erected opposite to our windows, on which the portrait of Ferdinand VII was exhibited occasionally amidst the applauses.

4th July, Badajoz.—I had a severe cold which served as a pretext to keep me away from the clamorous festivities which Ld. Hd. was compelled to undergo; there was a dinner consisting of 30 persons, and noisy toasts full of patriotism and compliments. John was better, and we dined in my room together. Late in eve. I went in the saloon, and was pestered with civilities, fireworks, drums, &c. All these honours were owing to our friend Garay, who, from a mistaken notion of doing what was civil, overpowered us by all these troublesome attentions.

I hear that the *Junta* of Badajoz are dissatisfied with the Central *Junta*, and in order to see their downfall are very eager for the Cortes. Ld. Hd. obtained promises to see the Conde de Montijo, who is strictly confined under a strong guard on acct. of the accusations against him by the *Junta* of Granada for having excited a tumult in that town. He is a clever man, quick, eloquent, and designing, and has got himself many partisans even at Badajoz for he represents himself as an object of persecution, and indeed the *Junta* have been inconsiderate in sending him to the centre of his own country to a hostile *Junta*.

The Capt.-General, d'Arcé, told me of some atrocities of the French; one committed most cruelly *par gaieté de coeur*. At Brozas they dressed an old man of seventy in women's clothes, and compelled him to dance till he dropped; then stabbed him with their bayonets, and afterwards burned his body. This *Junta* intends to make a collection of all such horrors which can be authenticated, and publish them. They have also established a Commission to look into the abuses committed during the residence of the French in the towns which they have now abandoned, for it seems that many worthless inhabitants purchased the goods and valuable effects of his more unfortunate neighbour.

5th July.—We left Badajoz at ¼ before 6. I was terrified at one of the honours destined for us, a *salve* from the balconies (?); accordingly I set off at full gallop. Ld. Hd. was obliged to the last to hear their civilities, and came in the carriage with the two deputies who were appointed to receive Ld. Hd. as far as the River Cayo, the limit of the kingdom. We got to Elvas at 8, and lodged in the house of Mr. Fletcher.

6th July, Elvas.—Left Elvas at 6. . . . The Governor of Badajoz forwarded by a postillion a letter from Don Francisco, who mentions having heard from Blake and Maldonado. The discomfiture of the former seems to be still a mystery. In the former actions his troops

147

appeared full of confidence and enthusiasm, and the enemy expected to make their way out of Aragon, when in an instant, without even discharging their pieces and only two rounds from the enemy, Blake was deserted by his whole army, and whether this desertion was owing to treachery or to panic is still unknown. He is gone to Tarragona with Maldonado, and has left Lazan at Tortosa, and Roca at Morella to collect the fugitives. Cuesta's advanced posts had reached within a league of Talavera, but on finding the enemy in force, and understanding that King Joseph was advancing from La Mancha to Toledo at the head of a considerable reinforcement, he meant to send back the main body of his army to recross the Tagus on the 29th, securing the bridges, and leaving his advanced guard on the other side of the river, and there to wait for the arrival of the English.

8th July, Evora.—We were most kindly received and lodged by the archbishop in his palace, which is very large, and contains some handsome, lofty, well-furnished rooms. The archbishop, (D. Fray Manuel de Cenáculo Villas Boas), is a very remarkable man for his learning and piety. He is 86 years of age; he was originally a Franciscan friar, but from his great learning and excellent qualities was selected by Pombal as the fittest person to be the preceptor of the elder brother of the P. Regent, a young man about whom the greatest hopes were entertained, but who unfortunately (it is said) for the glory and welfare of Portugal, was cut off in his prime at 25.

★★★★★★

Dom José, eldest son of Queen Maria I. He married his aunt Da. Maria Benedictina, and died in 1786. His next brother, Dom João, was appointed Regent after his mother had finally lost her senses

★★★★★★

He is a venerable figure, but so old, that he reminded me of the body of John II which is preserved in the coffin at Batalha.

Evora was one of the towns which in consequence of the resistance made in Spain against the French, followed that example, and in July 1808 rose and formed a sort of *Junta.* Junot, in order to intimidate and prevent the spirit of resistance from spreading, detached Gen. Loison with a strong force of 10,000 troops upon the pretext of marching to relieve Dupont in Andalusia from Lisbon, but in fact to chastise and suppress these provincial Govts. Loison was lodged in this palace, and on first seeing the archbishop he spoke very roughly, and told him three times over that his life was forfeited for having issued a decree against. the D. of Abrantes (Junot); however he became calmer, and gave his word of honour to the archbishop that his palace should be respected and nothing plundered in the general sack which was to be made of the town.

However, notwithstanding this sacred promise, he himself accompanied by some officers and soldiers forced open a private door, and broke into a cabinet of medals and antiquities, &c., and plundered the collection of all the gold and silver medals, of which he had a very valuable series, leaving the copper and bronze untouched. Not satisfied with this, he rifled the drawers and coffers in which were deposited some trinkets and golden crucifixes, &c. These of course were taken, but the wood-work torn and cast away; heaps of MSS. were destroyed, and the shreds and remains are now left in a heap as a curious vestige of the rage and mischief of the French. A priest, the *grand vicaire*, assured Ld. Hd. that Loison *himself* stole from a table whilst the Archbishop was sleeping his Episcopal ring, and saw him (Loison) put it into his pocket. There was regular battle between the Portuguese and some Spaniards who had come to their assistance and the French without the walls of the town, and Loison then gave it up to massacre and pillage. 800 of the inhabitants were killed, 57 secular priests, and 10 monks.

After dinner we went to the library, which is built by the archbishop, and the collection, which is valuable and extensive, is made entirely by him; he probably designs to annex it as a bequest to the archbishopric. Beside the collection of medals and coins of which the French plundered him, and of rare manuscripts which they destroyed, he has some very pretty fragments of ancient statues, which were found in digging both here and at Beja (he was formerly Bishop of Beja), also some curious inscriptions, &c.

9th July.—We dined at an early hour with the archbishop; he had appeared much affected at the sight of the portrait of his pupil, and I was anxious, without absolutely asking, to know some particulars respecting the character and death of that prince. Accordingly we found him very willing to dwell upon the subject, and also about the character of Pombal. To that minister he owed his appoint, of preceptor to the young prince, and his see of Beja. He spoke highly of his talents as a statesman, and of the charms of his conversation as a gentleman or man of the world. On the accession of the present queen, the

149

archbishop was dismissed from his employment about the prince, and Pombal was disgraced, but the prince continued to correspond regularly with him.

★★★★★★

Maria I and her husband Pedro III were entirely governed by her mother Da. Marianna Vittoria, widow of King José, who hated the Minister Pombal, and obtained his dismissal from office.

★★★★★★

He praises highly his talents, disposition, and acquirements; is satisfied that had he lived this country would have been in a very different situation. He was married to his aunt, a person of very extraordinary abilities; she is now living and has accompanied the Royal family to the *Brésils*. The archbishop represents the present Princess of *Brésil*, (Da. Carlotta Joaquina, eldest daughter of Charles IV of Spain and Queen Maria Luisa. She was born in 1775), as a woman of very wonderful knowledge and learning.

In one of the saloons of the palace there are some curious old pictures representing the birth and life of Christ; they are the works of a Greek painter, who is said to have been brought into Portugal by Isabella, an Aragonese Princess, when she came to marry King Diniz nearly 600 years ago. The drawing and composition is very good; the present archbishop has had them cleaned and refreshed, but great care was taken not to destroy the original design in any way. (Several pictures are said to be by Gran Vasco. They were preserved from destruction by the archbishop).

Setubal, 12th July.—Capt. Smith gave us some disgusting instances of the bad govert. of the Regency, who disgrace themselves by as much bribery and connivance at peculation as any of the old Governts. He also told us that the cause of Gen. Wellesley's delay was his suspicion of the Portuguese Govt., and that he did not like to advance leaving them behind him without an English force at Lisbon; accordingly a camp to a considerable amount is now collected in that city.

13th July.—Reached Belem, where we found Mr. Villiers' carriage waiting, and from thence we went to his house and dined with Ld. John Fitzroy.

From Jovellanos, 8th July. Romana is recalled, but has permission to name his successor!

★★★★★★

La Romana was recalled from Galicia by the *Junta* under the pretext of his appointment to a vacant deputyship from Valencia. He was succeeded by the Duque del Parque.

Captain Parker to Lord Holland: 'Ferrol, Aug. 18, 1809. We had the Marquis of Romana nearly a month at Coruña and found him remarkably pleasant. I have enclosed the drawing of a monument which he has in the handsomest manner caused to be erected over the remains of Sir John Moore, which had been removed to a more appropriate place of interment, and deposited with military honours. The *marquis* marched about a fortnight ago towards Villa Franca, where he will, I believe, leave the army and proceed to Seville, having I understand, been recalled by the Central *Junta*, as he meditated an attack on St. Andero with a division of the army.'

★★★★★★

What feebleness in the Govt! Jovellanos and —— very much discontented with their colleagues in regard to the Asturias, and other things. Jovellanos thinks for the sake of *decoro* and his own feelings he shall ask leave to go to the baths. No progress about the affair of the Cortes. Great efforts are making to collect an army for Blake. An army of rescue is forming between Xenil and Guadalquiver, and that in consequence of the number of public papers, addresses, etc., the *Gazette* is in future to be published twice a week. Wellesley and Beresford have quarrelled about the patronage of the Portuguese Army. Major Berkeley writes to his father, the admiral, that the difference is very striking in their comforts since they have entered Spain, better than when they were supplied by their own commissariat in Portugal; they have wine and excellent bread and all supplies in abundance, and yet they are marching through the *worst* part of the worst and most uncultivated province of Spain.

17th.—We are to sail in the *Lively*, commanded by Capt. McKinley.

19th.—Our accommodation was excellent, and what was equally important, Capt. McKinley was one of the most obliging and kindhearted men I ever met with.

On the 10th of August got into St. Helens and landed in a most boisterous gale and high sea at Portsmouth. Remained the whole day, set off the following, and slept at ——, and on 12th reached Holland House.

151

Appendices

Appendix A
Lord Paget to Lord Holland
No. 1

Private

Astorga, Nov. 24th, 1808.

My dear Lord,—I am very sorry to be obliged to assure you that I think there is no chance whatever of your being enabled to remain in Spain. It is but too true that Blake's army has been beaten and totally dispersed. He is said to be at Leon without troops, where Romana also was yesterday. Letters have been written by their desire to Sr. D. Baird to state the fact pretty much as it is, and to engage him to provide for his own safety. The French have had their cavalry dancing all over the country. They have been at Valladolid with 1200 of them and two pieces of artillery, and are said to have had the same number at Mayorga. They have withdrawn them from the latter place and had, on the 22nd, concentrated 14,000 men at Rio Seco. Sr. J. M. is no doubt by this time on his march to Ciudad Rodrigo, as in his last letter written, I think, on the 21st, he states his intention of retiring from Salamanca the moment that the French move from Valladolid, and that they have already done this, I have no doubt. He considered then all hope of junction as nearly at an end, and directed Sir D. B. to retire for embarkation.

In consequence the army has begun its retreat to the position of Villafranca. The Light Brigade of Infantry stay here as a rearguard, and I also shall remain. The cavalry will continue to move forwards.

We are, alas! in the most critical and the most melancholy of all situations. I do not mean in respect to the danger in the act of retreating. I have no apprehension on that head. But it is most melancholy to be sent to assist in the defence of a country, and to be obliged to abandon it without the power of making an effort, and this is really the case. The following is the state of the Spanish armies. Blake's is totally vanished. The Estremadurians were beat at Burgos and dispersed. In a letter from Graham, which I have read, who was with Castaños's army, he says that it does not amount to more than 20,000 men, and that that of Palafox's is about 10,000; that both are ill-equipped, half-naked, and not in a state to keep the field, and I am sorry to say that I hear of no reserves, no enthusiasm in the people. In fact there positively does not exist any Spanish corps with which any part of the British Army can form a junction.

Sr. J. M. will retreat upon Lisbon, as will, no doubt, Hope if he can; but as he cannot yet have joined Moore, having made a very circuitous march by Madrid, I should not be at all surprised if he were to be put in the situation of being obliged to retire upon Gibraltar. We shall fall back upon Vigo, as the only chance of saving the horses, by waiting in Bayona or even transporting them to the islands until transports arrive for them; but always, however, liable to be over-pressed and to be obliged to destroy them and to save the men. You will remember what I stated as likely to happen; I am not therefore surprised, but sadly grieved. All I can now hope for, is that the infantry may be enabled to remain a sufficient time at Villafranca to allow the cavalry to come up, that we may then have our opportunity (and that we may not fail in it) of showing ourselves. I am aware that this can do no good to the general cause, but I am, I own, childish enough to feel ashamed of going off quietly. The British Army has been put into the most cruel situation. Ministers must have been totally deceived with respect to the situation of this country, the state of its army, and the disposition of the people. I am aware that I am writing to a Spaniard, but I really think that he will not now have much to say for his *protégés*.

What I have said respecting our retreat to Vigo is in the *strictest confidence*, because it is of much importance that the enemy should not be aware of it, as he has a shorter road to it than we can go on acct. of stores and all the various *impedimenta* of an army. This is a secret, however, which like most others will no doubt soon be generally known.

I have not been enabled to obtain any information respecting Sir G. Webster, or Lauderdale's son.

The following is my *speculation*. I am not in possession of many *facts*. The French are over-running the Asturias *tout à leur aise*, and may very possibly try to push a light corps along the sea coast. They will leave a sufficient force to keep in check but not to beat Castaños and Palafox, whilst they are pushing forwards a strong corps to prevent our junction, which having effected, it will separate and follow each of us, but particularly Moore. Madrid will soon be in their hands; there is nothing whatever to stop them. They may possibly push a corps by Monforte and Orense to try to keep us out of Vigo if apprised of our intentions, and our situation is such that we cannot march straight to our point of embarkation from the difficulty of moving the artillery, the stores, and ammunition by the short route. I think that any four of the lines of this letter read to Mr. Ward will send him off by the 1st packet, and I hope that the whole will engage you and Lady Holland (to whom I beg my best compliments) to repair forthwith to Holland House and there wait until the patriotic Spaniards are *en masse* for the expulsion of Joseph and his suite.

   Ever, my dear Lord,
    Very faithfully yours,

                Paget.

P.S.—No letters for you or Mr. Allen.

Patroles has been within 14 leagues of Madrid. Not yet at Benavente. Let them stop only one week and we will join Moore, give them a good licking. *We* will catch *Joseph*, and then retire into Andalusia and wait for a little more *Spanish* patriotism.

No. 2

                Astorga, Nov. 28th.

My dear Lord,—I wrote a short note to you this morn. by the messenger sent by Sir J. Moore, since which I have been favoured by your kind letter and Ly. H.'s kind note of the 25th. I am much in hopes that the *little panic* which was felt here is subsiding, and that things may still be done as they ought to be, for I confess to you that I have been most wretched at what was likely to be decided upon.

I do not quite agree with you in your reasoning respecting the improbability of the enemy trying to penetrate thro' the Asturias. He may do so. There is not a respectable corps to stop him, and I do not believe that La Romana is inclined to detach anything from Leon to look behind him. I now feel confident that we shall at all events attempt a junction with Moore, nor have I the least doubt of succeeding in it. This will at once cover your movement by Vigo and Tuy into Portugal, but it will not tend to lessen the probability of a corps pushing on to Ferrol, &c., through the Asturias, particularly if Romana makes the movement of which he talks, namely that of following our corps towards Salamanca. I own I would rather wish him to get into the rear of that corps which is getting towards Oviedo, and then if your Galicians would make a movement on his front, the Marquis might make a *joli coup*.

Many thanks for your letter of intelligence; some of it was new to me. Such, for instance, as the arrival of Bonaparte at Vitoria. It confirms me in the idea that he is pouring a very large force upon Castaños. I wish that army may be able to stand the shock. I own I doubt it. I know not what may be the spirit of the people to the southward, but believe me, there is very little enthusiasm this way, and I confess to you that I have but a poor opinion of the Spanish *quartier-général*. With respect to the British Army, I suspect that the orders given have been so extremely cautious, or rather that our ministers have recommended such extreme caution, that we shall only engage seriously when we cannot help it, but then I do really believe we shall perform wonders. The cavalry is suffering a good deal upon the march, not in condition, but in the feet and legs of the horses. My regiment has been sadly harassed, and owing to the stupidity, or something worse, of some of the gentlemen who were sent back to stop the advance of baggage and stores, even laid hands upon the cavalry which has been twice stopped and even sent back, and twice obliged to make forced marches to recover lost ground.

If anything particular should occur I will send a line to you to Vigo as well as to Coruña. With best compts. to Ly. H. and party.

> Believe me,
> > My dear Lord,
> > > Very faithfully yours,
> > > > Paget.

P.S.—Most happy am I to tell you that our advance is decided upon. And I am now as anxious to conceal this intention as I was the former less satisfactory one, for if we are quiet, I am not without hopes of making some little *coup* upon the march. I shall probably move on the 3rd; the *gros* corps on the 4th or 5th.

No. 3

Sahagun, Dec. 23rd, 1808

My dear Lord, I am in a violent rage with you. You are the most prejudiced man alive. You talk to a parcel of people snug upon the sea coast and who, knowing your enthusiasm for the Spanish cause, flatter *your misconceptions* of the state of this country, and from the language of such people you form your judgment of the dispositions of the Spanish nation. *'Tis one not worth saving.* Such ignorance, such deceit, such apathy, such pusillanimity, such cruelty, was never both united. There is not one army that has fought at all. There is not one general who has exerted himself, there is not one province that has made any sacrifice whatever. There is but one town in all Spain that has shown an atom of energy. We are treated like enemies.

The houses are shut against us. The resources of the country are withheld from us; we are roving about the country in search of Quixotic adventures to save our own honour, whilst there is not a Spaniard who does not skulk and shrink within himself at the very name of Frenchman. I am with an army the finest in the world for its numbers, enthusiastic, equal to every exertion, burning to engage. I have been one of the most strenuous advisers to advance and to take our chance. But why have I done so? For my own sake, for that of my comrades in arms, for the honour of the British Army, not, believe me, not in the smallest degree for the Spaniards. I have been an enthusiast for their cause; but I, as well as all the world, at least the English world, have been grossly deceived. All I have to say upon that subject is much too long for a letter, but when we meet, I will *convince* you that you too have been deceived.

Let me turn to a subject on which I can write with more pleasure and consequently in better humour.

The British cavalry has been several times partially engaged and has each time acquitted itself with the greatest honour. The 18th have made three little *coups*, in one of which Charles Stewart was engaged and did famously. In the latter (it is with the intensest satisfaction I relate it to you for Lady Holland's information) Captain Jones and Sir Godfrey Webster at the head of 30 men attacked 100 of the enemy, killed 20 and took 5 prisoners. 'Twas a most gallant affair.

I must now (as you are a great soldier) detail to you a *coup* which fell to my share. Being 4 leagues from hence with the 10th and 15th Hussars and some artillery, I learnt that General-of-Brigade the Marquis de Debelle with 700 or 800 cavalry was in this town. I ordered the 10th with the guns to march on one side of the river and to make every demonstration to engage them to quit the town; and I marched at 1 a.m. with about 400 of the 15th, picking up a Capt. and 12 of the 7th in my way, in order to get round the town by day-break. At half past 4 my advanced guard fell in with a *patrole* of the enemy, charged it and made 5 prisoners, but the rest escaping, and fearing they might be in time to prevent my plan I was obliged to push on.

I arrived exactly in time. They had formed without the town, and upon perceiving us made off. I had a great deal of manoeuvring to come up with and cut them off from their point of retreat. At length having accomplished my object, I formed and immediately attacked. They fired their pistols and received us firmly. We broke through them and the result was 2 lt.-cols., 1 capt., 10 lieuts., 170 men, 125 horses, some mules and baggage taken. Several killed, 19 wounded. I had two officers and 22 men wounded. Had I not in consequence of the *patrole* been obliged to hasten my march, by which I was forced to attack before the arrival of the 10th, I think I should have had most of them. By every testimony of prisoners they were 750. I cannot speak too highly in praise of those engaged. The attack was most regular and beautiful. The pursuit very wild. I scolded them well for it, and they answered by 3 cheers and begging I would accept from them the two finest horses taken. This is of course for your private ear. But of what avail are such things, if those for whom we came to fight will not fight for themselves. But I stop myself and having begun my letter in anger I will close in good humour, sincerely congratulating Lady Holland upon the gallantry of her son.

> Open your eyes, my dear Lord,
> > And believe me,
> > > Very faithfully yours,

> > > > Paget.

We march tonight to attack Soult and shall beat him.
We are all delighted.
Sincerely so.
Mais à quoi bon?

Appendix B

Sir Robert Wilson to Lord Holland

No. 1

> Villa da Cerves, April 6, 1809.

My Lord,—I have to lament that your Lordship's only reached me this day, as I may have appeared negligent of a correspondence which I would cultivate as a great honour and the source of much gratification. I wish it had been in my power to render your journey less inconvenient, and I shall ever regret that circumstances prevented me from receiving your Lordship at Oporto. I am afraid to indulge my feelings at the commendation of your Lordship for the resolution I embraced to continue in Spain at a moment of despondency, for I must not suffer myself to estimate the service beyond its value.

I would have been a more useful friend to the great cause, which exacts as a duty and stimulates to ambition every personal sacrifice, but my means would have been inadequate to my desires. Whilst I, however, bear any part of this contest, you may be assured of hearing whatever may be worthy of your notice as matter of fact whether propitious or adverse.

Notwithstanding the appearance of an immediate junction Soult persevered in his order to attack Portugal, relying on the intention of the English to embark from Lisbon whenever a French force appeared in the country, as his intercepted dispatch acquainted us. He left in Galicia another corps of the army, but the Imperial Guards and all the light cavalry of the army returned to France from their cantonments in Valladolid, Astorga, &c., and the last column was met at Burgos on the 12th of March. Genl. Lapisse collected on the Tonnes about 8000 men to cover Segovia and Leon, and combine with Soult whenever communication was practicable. After several enterprises to pass the Minho, Soult was defeated in that plan, and was finally compelled to make a movement against Chaves, into which place a col. of militia with 1200 troops and near 3000 troops threw themselves contrary to Genl. Silveira's order, and surrendered by capitulation the next day.

The Marquis of Romana, finding the route along the frontier of Galicia open, took advantage of this moment to break from a connection which had been imperiously forced on him and which from the disposition of the Portuguese became every day more painful and menacing. He moved forward, left a post at Puebla de Sanabria, and on the 13th of March was at Ponferrada marching without interruption towards the Asturias, where a considerable force would submit to his orders. The *marquis's* own force did not exceed 9000 armed and 7000 unarmed men. Soult pressed on from Chaves on the 14th of March, the day after its surrender, and advanced against Braga, where the people put Genl. Bernardino Freire and his two *aides-de-camp* to death on the suspicion of treason and, I fear, on the assurance of imbecility both as to capacity and personal fortitude.

The French pressed on. The troops without a leader fled, and the people, bold only in crime, emigrated en masse from this city. Gen. Silveira at the head of a vast number of militia, populace, and about 3000 regulars, taking advantage of a feeble garrison, invested Chaves and possessed himself of the place with about 1000 persons, of which probably there were 500 soldiers. The rest infirm, and followers of the army. Soult arrived before Porto on the 25th. The populace, previously alarmed, had proceeded to wreak their vengeance on about 20 persons confined in the prisons and some others, who puerile malice and no public offences doomed. On the 27th the city was summoned and the summons rejected. The bishop had left the town the day before. On the 29th, the French columns advanced, forced the batteries which had wasted their ammunition in idle cannonades that gave the enemy confidence, and occupied the city with very little loss to themselves, but much to the Portuguese, who crowded the bridge and were forced over into the river. The French hearing that the Bishop had not long departed from the Villa Nova with the public treasure, pursued, but could not overtake him.

Such is the report of the capture of this city that I have been able to collect from persons worthy of credit, but you must imagine the extent of the catastrophe by remembering the character of the city and keeping in mind that until the moment of danger there was the most insolent confidence and lawless restraint on all persons and property. Its pains and its penalties are rather indeed now a subject for satisfaction than pity, since a French taskmaster alone could *dominer* to subdue a spirit of turbulence and cruelty which prevailed without the trace of one noble sentiment or a public or private virtue.

That Soult can continue at Oporto appears impossible. He has not above 12,000. Silveira at the head of an immense multitude environs his posts, and with the multitude within the city will oblige a severity of duty that would not be long supported, whilst the British troops and the Portuguese advance from Lisbon and alarm him more seriously. The division in Galicia can scarcely aid him without abandoning the sea ports and yielding Galicia to Romana. The division from Salamanca has advanced, probably with that intention, but after a parade before Ciudad Rodrigo where my arty. killed him several men, from thence its general bore on St. Felices.

On my return from Coria, where I had gone to take the command of 2500 Portuguese and as many Spaniards, but which Cuesta's retreat prevented from assembling, I found the Agueda swollen by the rains, and therefore I resolved to take the very passage the enemy had over it. On the 1st I attacked him, carried the village, and in a sharp action of several hours killed and wounded him above 100 men, without any loss to mention on our side. I do not therefore think that he will endeavour to force his way when he finds that every step is disputed, where the country everywhere becomes more unfavourable for his progress, and where above 8000 troops *could* and, I hope, *would* oppose him, for there can be no further pretext for inaction in the Portuguese Army.

Considering, therefore, all these circumstances, and that the Austrian war is in full activity, I must hope, nay believe, that Soult has no alternative but capitulation or a very difficult retreat, probably to Zamora. Of this I am *assured* that in Portugal there are the means to annihilate the projects, if not the corps, of Soult, and of pressing the Salamanca division back on Valladolid. But not to abuse power we must use time, and if this principle be adopted your Lordship may yet visit Madrid this summer.

British interests deserved our efforts, but those who have had opportunity to know the Spaniards and investigate their worth, must feel a more generous concern in their welfare.

I have existed but by their fidelity now for three months, and I have not found one instance to justify suspicion of their disloyalty to my service, but on the contrary a thousand for admiration of their patriotism, spirit of independence, zeal, and natural courage.

I am now waiting for some instructions from Lisbon and I should suppose greater force to command than 600 men, but I must not depreciate my 600, for their conduct has been exemplary in the field, to my astonishment. I am loath to leave Spain even for a moment, and very very reluctant to cross the Duero from private considerations, but I shall not hesitate to pass there if my presence can be more useful than in this qr. We all have much to do, and, I hope, shall do it cheerily and merrily to the joy of old England.

I beg my best respects to Lady Holland and I remain
    Your Lordship's
        Most obedt. servt.,

                         Robt. Wilson.

No. 2

                         Thomar, April 20, 1809.
My Lord,—The French column which so suddenly moved from the province of Salamanca by most rapid marches advanced on Alcantara, which city defended by 2000 peasants offered for five hours some resistance. Unfortunately I could not overtake the enemy with my inf., or, weak and unsupported as I was, we should have shattered

him considerably. With the cavalry I made prisoners, but no serious impression.

I had flattered myself that a corps of 2500 men, which I had entreated might be moved forward from Salude Nova, would have checked the enemy until I could get up, and by a mutual attack he must have perished, for he was in the *cul de sac*, encumbered with a large convoy of ammunition, and conscious of his perilous situation very much alarmed. But instead of hearing that the troops advanced from Salude Nova I found that as the enemy appeared the commander had hoisted the white flag, retired to Abrantes, whilst men, women, and children left desolate every hamlet, village, and intervening town on the east of the Zezere.

Fortune and cowardice thus relieved the enemy, but the hazards to which he exposed himself by passing along the frontier of a kingdom and thro' a country that his rage for enormities scared to desperate hostility, abandoning a point where he neared Portugal and Soult in his forlorn situation, proved the urgency to Victor of his succour, and a letter from General Kellermann to Soult confirms that the orders for Lapisse's division to march to Estremadura were given in consequence of the Battle of Medellin.

I was ordered by Marshal Beresford to repair instantly to him, and so soon as I had seen the enemy pass Alcantara, and I had placed a garrison there, I repaired here, where I find General Beresford employed in an Herculean labour, but he will partially succeed. Altogether, he cannot to any solid degree, unless there is a general reform in the state, and even then much time is required for the extinction of old habits and the exercise of a new education. It is, however, always well to begin, and I hope success will crown the effort, for Portugal has certainly great military resources applicable to the interests of England.

Soult has now remained undisturbed at Oporto since his capture, rioting in spoil, but I believe daily becoming more uneasy as to his situation.

He has been obliged to extend his forces—5000 men preserve Tuy, Orense, and Braga, as many are on this side of the Duero, and the same force between Penafiel and Oporto, in which city he leaves but a very feeble garrison by day and scarcely any at night. At Zamora, Kellermann writes that there are 1500 inf. and 400 horse belonging to his corps, but Silveira with 8000 troops will actively, I hope, keep that succour in check, and indeed the peasantry of the Tras os Montes are more than equal to that service.

Ney has quarrelled with Soult, because Soult would not postpone his march into Portugal until Galicia was restored to order, and the capture of Vigo, with the general insurrection in Galicia and Romana's security whilst he intercepts all communication, as verified by Gen. Kellermann from Valladolid, proves the insufficiency of the enemy's forces in that qr. to achieve their enterprises or maintain themselves.

Genl. Kellermann in his letter to Soult moreover says that he watches at Valladolid with a considerable cavalry the Asturians and Romana and the people of Leon, who would have the inclination to rise if they dared, but that the Austrian war has recalled all the household troops of every description to France and that he is silent as to any force destined to replace them.

At Salamanca there is scarcely 500 men capable to bear arms, and I feel that fortune has been rather unkind in withdrawing me at a moment that I could have achieved what I had so long proposed, but I hope we shall be vigorous in our operations against Soult and then march into Spain; for the march alone would assure safety to the Peninsula and especially if we move boldly up the Tagus. But I am somewhat disposed to believe that there is no very great cordiality of operation in the two staffs at this moment.

Sir A. Wellesley is momentarily expected out with an army, and I should suppose orders from home would even stimulate his zeal and ambition, for if we do our duty, victory is certain and immediate, in which case I hope to see your Lordship still at Madrid. With great esteem and respect,

I remain,

Your Lordship's

Most obedt. Servt.,

Robt. Wilson.

No. 3

Zarza Major, June 20, 1809.

My Lord,—It is very long since I had the opportunity to write, and indeed I did expect to leave the Peninsula, as I was for a time removed from the Legion and the chance of serving in Spain, but a more agreeable arrangement having finally been made, I now find myself here with my Legion and attached exclusively to the British Army.

Marshal Beresford and the Portuguese troops are ordered to the north of Portugal and are to keep in check Soult and Ney, who made a movement that indicated an approach to the Tras os Montes whilst some other corps menaced Bragança, but in fact with the intention solely of diverting our operations from Victor.

The delay of the British Army, is now, I believe, terminated, and the 1st division will reach this place on the 2nd, with the intention of moving on Plasencia and Madrid if the enemy check between Talavera de Reyna and the capital. But it is supposed that Victor will leave Madrid on his left, and in all cases I expect a stem chase. It is however a most serious object to prevent the enemy from collecting his forces installed on the Ebro, and I sincerely lament our return to the Tagus for the recommencement of our operations.

Sir A. Wellesley has certainly been most eager to advance, but I have heard that he only received his orders very lately, for the Govt, was afraid of a new adventure. The Galician retreat has had many a mischievous effect. It has calumniated a gallant, generous, and friendly nation; it has erected imaginary impediments to success; it has seriously discouraged the British Army, and founded a spirit of licentiousness and rapine that excites the most painful slur and which will require the energy of Sir A. Wellesley to repress.

The Austrian successes have excited, however, great enthusiasm, and I hope that our march will be one continued and unchequered series of triumph, to console for so many years of disaster. The victory of Essling must have a propitious effect on the French army, because the foreigners composing it will now find that there is another power in Europe anxious to secure and capable to protect them, and the local effect must be great. Assuredly the evacuation of the Tyrol and the retrograde movement of Bonaparte and the Vice-King of Italy whilst revolt engages the chiefs of the Confederation and Holland, now would be a glorious moment to raise the true banner of public liberty and by the sacrifice of Galicia restore the monarchy of Poland. It would be a blow that condemned Russia to precarious European existence and consolidated the Austrian preponderance. I am however diverting into political speculations that your Lordship does not require from me, and therefore, with the promise of continuing to communicate whatever may be really interesting with regard to our movements north of the Tagus,

I remain with great sincerity and truth,

Your obedt. and humble servt.,

Robt. Wilson.

I suppose that the British Army will be 28,000 effective infy. with arty., exclusive of cavalry, on the *onset*, but the average for the campaign, not reckoning accidents in the field, 26,000 altogether. Portugal may send beyond the northern frontier about 8000 men, but with great ill will on the part of officers and the nation at large, but not of the *soldiers*.

Henry Luttrell to Lady Holland

Cadiz, March 1, 1809.

Dear Lady Holland,—It was my intention to have written to you yesterday but I arrived here with so violent a cold, thanks to the Levant wind which has affected most people here in the same manner, as totally to disqualify me both for occupation and amusement. Though not much better this morning, I write at all hazards, lest you should suppose me unmindful of my promise. The insurrection here wore, at one time, a most serious aspect. A mob very soon, if not controlled, changes its object. Disappointed in executing their vengeance on Villel, the insurgents turned their fury against the wretched man whom they murdered from personal, not political, hatred. Their next motion was to let loose the contents of the gaols, and to plunder the houses of the rich merchants. The first of these exploits they had very nearly effected, and if, in this critical juncture, the volunteers and the priests had not united in bodily and ghostly energies against them, a scene extremely like what was acted in London in 1780 would inevitably have followed.

Major Doyle, whose curiosity led him to mix with all the insurgents, tells me that they were to the last degree ferocious, and bent upon blood. The men were sharpening their knives upon the stones, and a number of women of the lower classes adding all they could by outcries and gestures to the spirit of mischief and murder among the men. Villel bad a most narrow escape. Doyle, who witnessed what passed in front of his house, gave up his life for lost. The man, he says, behaved with a great deal of firmness, and protested most strongly against the disclosure of his official dispatches. He seems to be very unpopular here. No puritan magistrate in the days of Cromwell ever made a more rigid and vexatious inquisition into the irregularities, and even the harmless recreations, of private life than he seems to have done, laying to the account of the dress and dancing and intrigue of Cadiz all that has happened unfavourable to the Spanish cause.

It is strange how extremes meet. That a zealous Catholic should think and act so like a zealous Presbyterian is amusing enough. But it will not do. Spain requires, at this crisis of her fate, men, not monks. Something no doubt has been achieved, and much, I know, is expected from the strong spirit of superstition, or religion if you will, in this country, but I believe it will wholly fail, when most relied upon. At no time do I feel stronger apprehensions for the final issue of the momentous contest now pending, than when I reflect how mainly the hopes of Spain repose on this insecure and treacherous foundation. Should you have at any time ten minutes leisure, it would be charitable to employ them in giving me some account of what is passing in Seville, a place which I shall remember with pleasure chiefly on account of your and Lord Holland's kind attentions. Pray convey to him my best regards, and believe me, dear Lady Holland,

Your obliged and faithful humble servant,

Henry Luttrell.

APPENDIX D

Account by Captain Burgh of the pursuit of Soult,
Forwarded to Lord Holland by Colonel Reynell

Convento de Tujo, 20 miles N. of Oporto,
21st May, 1809.

Our Campaign in the N. of Portugal terminated on the 18th, when we fairly saw the enemy out of the country; since that day the troops have been drawing towards Victor, who, we understand is approaching Lisbon.

The enemy retreated all night after the battle of the 12th on the road to Amarante, and the German Legion pursued them the next morning. The remainder of the army unfortunately halted that day. When the French got as far as Penafiel they heard of Marshal Beresford's approach to Amarante, and after spiking all their Cannon and blowing up the tumbrils they retreated by Guimaraens and Braga.

On the 15th our army was at Braga; the enemy left it only the day before. On the 16th we got up with their rear guard consisting of about 3000 men who were strongly posted on a hill in front of the village of Salamonde; the guards were in advance and were ordered forward to the attack supported by artillery, cavalry, and the German Legion. Sir Arthur had previously sent two comps. over the hills to turn the enemy's left; these companies lost their way, and two others were sent which occasioned some delay, and it was past 6 o'clock before the attack commenced. The guards advanced in sections along the road in face of the enemy's position.

This manoeuvre astonished them, and after receiving the first discharge of musquetry they ran down the ravines in the greatest disorder. The darkness favoured their escape; if we had had half an hour more daylight not a man could have got off, as the Portuguese had broken down the bridge in their rear. Numbers were killed by the peasantry and drowned in attempting to cross the river, 400 horses and droves of their bullocks were taken, and the only piece of cannon they had left. They have not now any wheeled carriage. A great deal of plunder had been taken by our lt. infantry and dragoons. On the morning of the 16th, 20 drags, took 50 French prisoners at Agreja Nova, and found on them a quantity of coin.

Considering the long march of near 30 miles from Braga through very heavy rain (which has continued without cessation since the 13th) upon the worst possible roads, the advance of the army only marched one league on the 17th, to Receines. No artillery could come up that day, as it was first necessary to repair the bridge.

Next day we had a most unpleasant march to Montalegre, the road was full of dead bodies of the French murdered by the peasants; their army is most sickly and consequently many stragglers who seldom escape the rage of the peasantry. We passed also about 100 horses and mules that were hamstrung by the enemy. This act of cruelty cannot be easily accounted for.

Arriving at Montalegre we found that the enemy had just left a village a few miles which was then in flames; all the towns the French passed through after they left Braga were destroyed by them, and nothing now remaining except the bare walls. The inhabitants all fled to the Mountains on their approach.

The Portuguese genl. Silveira, with between 3,000 and 4,000, had been in that neighbourhood for some days without offering any resistance. On our arrival at Montalegre after hard pressing to put his army in motion after the enemy, he wished to have some of our dragoons, but Sir Arthur positively refused, having predetermined not to pursue the enemy through the mountains of Galicia, as they were disencumbered of all kind of baggage to impede their flight.

Beresford has marched from Chaves to Monterey, and with Silveira will hang on the enemy's flank and rear. They have already lost one fourth of their army with all their artillery, &c., with the loss on our side of about 200.

You are nearer the scene of Victor's manoeuvres and better acquainted with them than we are. The army is in motion (Tilson's force is already arrived at Oporto) and there will be a grand *assemblement* at Coimbra in 5 or 6 days I believe a rapid movement will be made to crush Victor.

Lord MacDuff to Lord Holland

No. 1

Monasterio; Sunday, 24th May, 1809.

My Dear Lord,—Some time since, having mentioned my determination of visiting the armies, you expressed a wish of hearing from me. I have been here since Tuesday last, and have been employed in witnessing the discipline of the several corps along the road and around this place. The whole division in this neighbourhood were taken out by the genl. yesterday and today to manoeuvre, and formed into attacking and attacked parties. The genl. took great pains in explaining, and they seemed, on the whole, to conduct themselves like soldiers. For some days past we have been pretty certain that the enemy were going to move, by withdrawing their posts; ours were pushed forward and strengthened.

Yesterday the furthest in advance were near Merida, tomorrow the headquarters is intended to move to Llerena. The troops in the rear are ordered up; Henestrosa, who commands the first division, to proceed on, and the Duke Albuquerque to take the post of Fuente de Cantos. The further movements of the army must depend on that of the enemy, and the conjectures of what is their object; whether this movement of theirs proceeds from a fear that the English mean to co-operate with this army against them, or whether they mean with the whole or a part to unite with the other French corps to act against the English, is to be ascertained.

On the march of Genl. Wellesley and of Soult, of the probability of bringing him to action alone, you will be better informed than we are here. There seems no doubt, however, that the French are in motion everywhere, and that they intend to act with numbers against the English; and there is reason to believe also that circumstances will force them to act in this country with two or three corps at most. This will, of course, give the different parts not occupied by them an opportunity to rise. But self-preservation is the first object, and as the French have, from the best accounts, from a hundred to a hundred and twenty thousand men, they can certainly act first against the English offensively and take care of their remaining forces, if they adopt this resolution.

I examined a deserter last night, a German and soldier of ours in the Hanoverian Legion, who was taken at Benavente; he escaped two days ago, and robbed his master of much silver, jewels, and a horse and a mule. His master was young Cabarrus; they had robbed him before, he says, and it was but fair to retaliate. He says that the French told him that he would soon see his countrymen, the English. Their whole army consists of five and twenty thousand men. The garrison of Merida is of fifteen hundred with fortifications. Medellin they had also begun to fortify. He gives much the same account as the Spaniards of the last battle, but with the exception that they lost few men.

Among the officers here I cannot but take notice of Genl. O'Donoghue (*sic*), who is fortunately the chief person about Cuesta; he is by far the best-informed military man I have met with in Spain, indeed in any country.

The force of the whole army is considered at thirty thousand. But I believe they have near twenty thousand infantry pretty well disciplined, and six thousand cavalry. The aggregate number twenty-three thousand infantry and eight thousand cavalry. But they are very active in getting the people on with their exercise, and some of the corps are well clothed.

Pray present my best respects to Lady Holland, and
    Believe me always,
        My dear Lord,
           Faithfully,

                      MacDuff.

No. 2

                    Monasterio, Monday, 15th May.

My Dear Lord,—I have only time to add a few lines to what I wrote you last night. The whole plan of the march of the army is changed from the information received of the French genl., Cuesta seems determined to follow them as fast as possible. We hear that they have taken the direction of Alcantara; Genl. Victor in the van, with the artillery, carts, &c. On the 12th, a part of them were near Alcantara; four hundred men have been left at Merida, fortified in a convent, with four pieces of cannon. Yesterday our advance must have been there. It has been ordered to proceed on Monasterio also, with the first division of cavalry. Troops are marching to strengthen them. Merida, if not taken at first, is ordered to be blockaded. The *cuartel general* is to be tomorrow at Medina de las torres: the main body of the army in the towns near. The whole army is to advance on the great road.

The French must sacrifice also a great part of their artillery, which is at Truxillo.

I shall proceed before and try to overtake Henestrosa. I wish Genl. Mackenzie, who is at Abrantes, and Genl. Mayne at Alcantara, may have got timely information of the movements of the French.

I remain.

> My dear Lord,
>> Faithfully,

>>>> MacDuff.

No. 3

Headquarters, Venta de Almaraz,
June 28th; 1809.

My Dear Lord,—Since I received your letter from Cadiz, little or nothing passed worthy of notice, till our march in pursuit of Victor's army. I was perfectly certain this would take place that I did not judge it necessary to give you a detailed account of positions which I conceived any hour might be changed. We have been here four days; the bridge of pontoons being too small, it was obliged to be turned into a flying bridge. The passing of the troops was stopped one day from information that the French were concentrating, but it was only to their further retreat.

His army is composed of five divisions of infantry and two of cavalry, besides the rear-guard and the reserve. The whole amounting to near thirty-eight thousand men. One division of infantry and two thousand cavalry have passed the Tagus at the Arzobispo. On the 26th, in the evening, the French began their retreat from Oropesa, and formed behind Calera. The 27th, the vanguard of cavalry from the Arzobispo entered Oropesa, commanded by the Prince Anglona, the Duke of Albuquerque being ill. The French halted at Gamonal, 3½ leagues from thence. The 5th division of infantry was to enter Calera on the 27th, in the evening.

Victor's force is in full retreat, so is Sebastiani's. The vanguard of Venegas, was on the 22nd at Villarta. We do not know whether Victor means to join near Toledo, or continue his retreat. The vanguard of this army is now in the rear of the 5th division of infantry and 2nd of cavalry, besides another division of infantry sent to strengthen them. It passed the river on the 27th, made a reconnaissance and occupied the position opposite here to cover the passing of the army

169

yesterday. We contrived to get made a foot bridge near the old bridge of Almaraz, which wants one arch; on this the whole infantry of the army passed yesterday. The cavalry, for the most part, has also passed; but the artillery, carts, &c., will take some time on a bridge which can only contain eight men and horses at a time   20 minutes in passing and repassing. This morning the vanguard proceeded forward, and we expect the general to follow every hour.

You will be surprised to hear that in such a retreat that our army took neither provisions nor baggage, but the fault was not the general's. That the French might be induced to keep their position, all the attacks by the vanguard on Merida, &c., were disapproved, and strict orders were given that the army not only should avoid fighting but not provoke the enemy. I was with the vanguard in the several attacks made on Merida, and near it, and was convinced that, from the manner of the French, they intended to retreat, and thought right to give my opinion to Genl. Cuesta, who exactly thought the same. But the French, as usual, before they retreat, made three great reconnaissances, which induced most people to believe that they intended to attack before the English came.

The division near Medellin was augmented to 12,000 men, and the opinions of most were that the general ought to hazard nothing before the arrival of the English. The general gave orders to the Medellin force to follow the enemy and attack them. The same to the vanguard at Calmonte, the 1st division of cavalry at Almendralejo. All the divisions at Villafranca and Aceuchal and all the villages where troops were quartered, to move on as fast as possible to support one another. We found that the reconnaissances near Merida and Medellin were only to carry off the 300 men in the convent, and that the French had been taking measures for some time before for their retreat. The general followed; came to Merida the first day, Miajadas the 2nd, and Truxillo the 3rd—21 leagues, when to his great disappointment he found the orders given had been delayed a whole day, and the troops were all together, with the exception of the vanguard which was in presence of the French rear.

They followed them to the Puerto of Miravete, and in the night the French retired across the river, destroyed the bridge, and were found next morning in front of our present position with five batteries. At Miravete the French advanced a body of infantry to relieve their rear-guard of cavalry, which gave them the advantage in this country where cavalry cannot account. The van of course unsupported could not attack them. The general hearing these things, after one day's halt at Truxillo, came to the Casas of Miravete, reconnoitred the enemy, and although of opinion that a passage might be forced, delayed. The next day occupied in observing the batteries, which constantly kept firing. The night the French retreated the general came immediately from the Casas of Miravete to this place, which is an inn close to the road, expecting to be able to pass in one night, when again, to our disappointment, the pontoons, 14 in number, were only found half sufficient.

After many experiments and consultations the mode I have explained was adopted. In short you will find that a concurrence of circumstances have happened to foil and disappoint our worthy old general. Of the English we have no certain accounts of their march. They are to come by Plasencia. But if the French continue their retreat, and we our pursuit in the same manner, they will not see an enemy for a long time. We expect they left Abrantes the 23rd, so that on the 3rd of next month they may reach Plasencia. They are always tardy and late. I shall not close my letter till I see the general, from whom I may hear something new.

I remain, my dear Lord,

Very faithfully yours,

MacDuff.

Since writing in the morning, information has come that José Napoleon arrived at Toledo on the 23rd, and left it the 24th with the division of Leval, and went to Mora. What this means is yet to be learnt; whether they intend to attack Venegas, or continue their retreat. The troops in advance have retired from Oropesa. The party of guerrillas near Calera killed ten Frenchmen, took three, and one escaped. Thus none joined the rear of the enemy, and also returned and burnt the town. Bassecourt, hearing this, retired, and so did the division of cavalry. No news of the English, which is astonishing. We understand too that a division of Victor's army was near Plasencia, and passed by it the 21st, and, we imagine, is now at Talavera. They have broken down the bridge at Talavera. Genl. Cuesta seems now a little unconvinced about pushing on, from the very extraordinary motions of the enemy. It is reported also here that Ney and Soult have invaded Portugal, which is extraordinary. No news yet of the English. I trust they do not mean to give us the slip. I trust you will be able to read this scrawl. We have nothing here to eat, to write on, or to sleep on, and the pen I write with I have had this fortnight in use.

The force of Victor, *on the 1st of May,* from a return I have seen was 29 thousand fit for duty, and ten thousand sick.

No. 4

Venta de Almaraz; June 29th, 1809.

My Dear Lord,—Since I wrote you yesterday we have received accounts that José Napl. returned to Toledo on the 26th, and was advancing towards Talavera with his whole force. It became necessary to think seriously of our situation, as this army was placed in the most disadvantageous position, with no regular bridge, and half the cannon, baggage, &c., on this side. Letters also from Wellesley, that be intended to begin his march on the 27th, and requesting Genl. Cuesta to hazard nothing till he arrived. He intended to be at Zarza on the 2nd or 3rd, and not to halt till he arrived at Plasencia. The intentions of the French being too evident that they intended to attack us, and the general not having given over his desire of pursuing, Genl. Whittingham, Roche, and myself went to him and represented the extreme danger and the importance of keeping that army entire till the arrival of the English. That if any accident happened they would not advance, that the campaign would be lost, as on the fate of this army everything depended, and that it was better to forego the precarious chance of some advantage in pursuing the enemy than hazard its existence in such a critical time and against such numbers.

Whittingham spoke to him very properly, and he listened with much attention, and answered us with great sincerity and satisfaction. Genl. O'Donoghue, a most worthy man and of great talents, persuaded him, after talking the whole subject over, to give immediate directions that the advance parties should retire, and that the whole troops should repass the road and take up our position and wait for events and for the English. The divisions of Portago, Bassecourt, with the cavalry under the Prince of Anglona are to repass at the Arzobispo. The remainder of the army at the bridge here. Fortunately the pontoons arrived (I mean the remainder of them) today. With the orders which have been given and the directions for the defence of the Arzobispo and the batteries leaving, I trust, if it is the intention of the enemy to attack us, that the army will repass without loss. We shall be, for the present, in security, which is the great object, and by drawing on the enemy, will give us a better chance to strike a decisive blow when the English come up.

I cannot conclude without observing that Genl. Cuesta, who is represented as sullen to all his officers, and particularly to foreigners, has, in this critical situation, acted with the greatest candour and deference to the opinions of others. Indeed, during the whole time I have been with him, he has behaved to me, on all occasions, rather as an equal and friend, than as one who is only here from curiosity. On all occasions open, friendly, and kind.

Last night the advanced guerrillas were two miles from the village of Calera, the French two thousand horse two miles further, and behind them four regts. of infantry. Brigadier Zayas with the advance guard was today at Calzada; the whole will retire, I hope, tonight.

We are obliged to Whittingham, not only for the good Spanish he speaks, but for the manner he expressed himself.

At twelve o'clock last night the positions of the advanced corps were as follows:—

Puente de Arzobispo.—Major-Genl. Bassecourt: 6000 infantry, 500 cavalry, 8 pieces cann.

Azutan.—Marquis Portago, Lt.-General: 5000 infantry.

Alcola del Tajo.—Prince of Anglona, Brigr.-General: 1500 cavalry, 200 It. infantry, 6 pieces cann.

Advanced posts to Oropesa, and near to Calera.

Br. Zayas (the vanguard of the enemy).—Calzada: 1948 cavalry, 2 113 infantry, 6 pieces cann.

Marquis de Zayas, Major Genl.—Naval Moral: 4268 infantry, 2 pieces cann.

Main body between Naval Moral and Puente de Almaraz.

Whittingham informs us that most of the French officers spoke at Oropesa of their marching back to France. But one of the generals said that they intended to fight a great battle, and then it would be seen what they would do afterwards.

Appendix F

Letters from Sir Charles Vaughan to Lord and Lady Holland

No. 1

Coruña; Sunday; August 14th; 1808.

Dear Lord Holland,—No event of importance has occurred since the date of my last. The rumours of this place you will collect from the *Diarios*, which accompany this letter. It has been reported that the army of Estremadura, which consists of 24 thousand infantry and

173

about 9 thousand cavalry under General Galluzzo, had cut in pieces a detachment from Junot of 7 thousand French troops, near Evora in Portugal Two days have passed without any confirmation of this report, which was brought in a Portuguese vessel to Coruña, and also in a letter from Salamanca. The French forces were, it is said, attempting to make their way to Burgos. Perhaps it may turn out that the garrison of Elvas has been checked in some movement to join Junot upon the Tagus. We have been amused also with another report of the escape of Ferdinand to Madrid, and of the Duke de Infantado to the army of Cuesta. The last is still in some measure credited, and was at first circulated in so authentic a manner that I undertook to be the bearer of some communication between him and Stuart.

The approaching assembly of the Cortes of the North at Lugo, made it appear advisable to sound the dispositions of the Duke de Infantado and to engage him to co-operate heartily in the defence of his country; and at the same time we might have put an end to the dissention that has arisen between Cuesta and Blake and the growing dislike of the *Junta* of Coruña to the former. Cuesta is a zealous patriot, but he has been an imprudent officer. He brought on the battle of Rio Seco. He was at the head of a small division of cavalry and about 10 thousand Castilian peasants, and formed the advanced part of Blake's army.

The latter had taken a strong position and had no intention of engaging the French, when Cuesta advanced and brought on the action of Rio Seco, and the troops under Blake, consisting of the garrisons of Galicia, in vain hastened to his support. The Castilian peasants were dispersed, Cuesta retreated with his cavalry towards Ciudad Rodrigo, separating himself from Blake, and the latter retreated to Manzanal midway between Astorga and Ponferrada. Blake is now advancing a second time, and by the last accounts his army of 23 thousand infantry, regular regiments filled up with new levies, was at Astorga. From what I hear this army is in great want of cavalry, and but ill supplied with artillery. The mules and small oxen, which are the draft cattle of the country, are not equal to the removal of parks of artillery in a mountainous district.

The mountains of the Asturias are defended by 18 thousand peasants under the Generals Miranda and Ponti.

The French have retreated from Madrid upon Burgos (their outposts extend to Palencia), where they are entrenching themselves. They are said to have abandoned a considerable quantity of ammunition upon quitting the Buen Retiro. We hear nothing here of their numbers, but in a *Diario* you will see some attempt to calculate the original force and its losses.

The patriot army of Estremadura under General Galluzzo, said to consist of 24 thousand infantry, and cavalry that has increased from 4000 (the original number) to 9000, has been of great service, though with the exception of the affair of Evora (should it prove true) they have not been engaged with the enemy. By taking up a position at Almaraz, upon the Tagus, which you will find in the map north in a direct line of Truxillo, they interrupted the communication between Madrid and Lisbon and kept open the district between Blake and Castaños.

Since the defeat of Dupont, a letter has appeared in the Santiago *Gazette* from General Castaños to General O'Farril. He makes O'Farril responsible for the people of Madrid, and it is written in rather a ludicrous as well as threatening manner; but if it is to be believed, it tells us that he has under his command 120 thousand men, in which he includes the armies of Estremadura and other provinces of the South, an immense park of artillery, and moreover he declares that he has in his possession 27 thousand French prisoners, amongst whom he numbers 12 generals and 7000 cavalry. Castaños is marching with all the forces of the South towards Madrid.

Valencia, as we have long since heard, was attacked in the latter end of the month of June by Moncey. I yesterday saw a private letter from that city, which states that *sixty* pieces of cannon are mounted upon the walls, and that the only entrance into the city is by the Puerta del Mar, on account of the ditches dug round the walls. A French battery upon the Torre Santa Catalina nearly destroyed the Convento del Socorro. The French bombarded the town in vain and retreated by way of Albacete. The letter says nothing of subsequent actions. The son of Captain-General Caro commanded. I mention the particulars, judging from my own feelings about Valencia that they may be interesting to you and Lady H.

It would be too much to expect perfect unanimity during this success of the patriots. So many provincial govts., with their armies under distinct commanders, must have many difficulties to overcome before they can legislate for the whole Peninsula. The first attempt to establish a Cortes originates in Galicia. They have persuaded the *Junta* of Leon to meet them at Lugo in this province, and they do not appear to have any doubt but that the *Junta* of the Asturias will also join them. As soon as they assemble at Lugo it is their intention to invite Estremadura, the Castiles, and the Southern provinces to co-operate in forming a Cortes. The outline of this plan is simple and rational, but you, who know how wedded the Spaniards are to precedent and how variously the provinces used to be represented, will foresee much discussion and division about the numbers of deputies to be sent from each province. Galicia has already procured the assent of Leon to seven deputies. The *Junta* sitting at Coruña asked for eleven. You know how insignificant the influence of Galicia used to be in a Cortes. The 20th of this month has been appointed the day for the assembly at Lugo of the deputies of Leon and this provinces. Orders have long since been dispatched for houses to be prepared for them, but I cannot venture to hope that they will meet for many weeks.

The people of Coruña dislike the departure of their *Junta*, and it is thought that they may assemble to prevent it. The *Junta* here is composed of seven persons. The most intelligent man amongst them is the Bishop of Orense, whose letters about the French have appeared in the English newspapers. His countenance does not betray that religious gloom sometimes visible in the Spanish priest, but has in it a good deal of fun and more cunning. I have been at one of their meetings and everything was very *regulár*. At a table in a long room sat their secretary, and opposite to him the members of the *Junta* under a portrait of the King Ferdinand, over which there was a large crimson canopy. They work very hard, but I am afraid that they will become idle as the cause advances, and daily show a greater disposition to jobbing. Don Freire, their deputy to London, was a lieutenant in the Navy, and they have given him a ship for the success of his negotiation.

Nothing can be more creditable to the Spanish character than the conduct of the people of this district during their revolution. The only person killed was the Capt.-General of Ferrol, Filanghieri, who disgusted them by his coldness and indisposition to their cause. Soon after the arrival of the prisoners from England, there was a popular tumult in which the French houses were assaulted; but it ended only in the arrest of the Consul and some individuals who are now on board a hulk in the harbour. A saddler of the place, who has a good deal of the Andalusian in his person and character, is the *Capitan del Pueblo*. He has shown that he has more influence over them than any other person, being a clever, daring fellow, and the *Junta* very wisely have put a silver badge upon his arm, and thereby obtained a control over him. He presented me with his card, styling himself, 'Sinforiano

Lopez, *Defensor de la Patria*.'

The kindest feeling towards the English prevails everywhere. The government have made an excellent choice in Stuart. In the harbour we have the *Tonnant*, Admiral de Courcy, and the *Defiance*, Capt. Hotham, both officers of the most amiable and conciliatory manners. I am happy to say that we have no drunken riots, or anything which can disturb the harmony between the two nations.

I understand that Galicia has received a million of dollars from England, and Leon and the Asturias half a million each. Blake has earnestly entreated the English Government to send him two thousand cavalry. I wish that it may be done promptly. Cuesta's separation from him is unfortunate. I must entreat you not to suppose from anything that I may have said about the differences between these generals, or the difficulties in forming a Cortes, that anything, *has yet*, or *seems* ever *likely* to occur that can have a fatal influence on the general welfare of the nation.

Depend upon it that the cause of the patriots is in the hands of the people; it borrows no fancied importance from any illustrious leaders, and woe be to those who shall be weak enough to expose to them their quarrels and dissentions. It is natural that the priesthood should have greater influence over the people than the *noblesse*. I hope that in the formation of the Cortes they may not predominate. The Archbishop of Santiago de Compostella is suspected of being very unfriendly to the *Junta* of Galicia. He remains near the shrine of his Saint and is too wise to be troublesome. It is curious to know that the Spaniards here have not yet seen the correspondence between the French and the Pope. It should be translated and sent out to them immediately.

Stuart has given me a room in his house, which is called *el palacio* from being certainly the best house in Coruña. Mr. Walpole is with Stuart, rather as a friend than a secretary.

We have a comedy in a small temporary theatre, a fire having consumed a very good one. The *bolero* and *fandango* are tolerably well danced, but they succeed better in the dance called the *farongo*, which is new to me. The *tertulias* after the play are sometimes in wretched garrets, sometimes in very decent houses. But I have not yet formed an high opinion of the *Gallego* nobility. Spain is more interesting to me and more dear to me than ever. It was my intention to have set out for Blake's army this week, but the approaching assembly of the Cortes tempts me to defer it, and to visit Santiago on my road to Lugo. If the Cortes do not meet, I shall set out for Blake and the

Asturias. Mr. Arguelles gave me two letters for the Asturias, and if the deputies should assemble from the province at Lugo I shall be well off for introductions.

I have extended this letter to an unusual length, and send you very little to satisfy your curiosity about Spain. I wish that I could deal less in reports and speak more from actual observation.

Present my kindest remembrances to Lady Holland and believe me to be

> Yr. obliged and Faithful Servt.,
>
> Chas. R. Vaughan.

P.S.—Colonel Doyle and Capts. Kennedy and Cawel, who came over with the Spanish prisoners, have been promoted by the Spaniards, the first to the rank of brigadier-general in their service, and the latter to lt.-colonelcies. They are not attached to any divisions of the army. Capt. Kennedy remains at Coruña, and Doyle and the other officers are with Blake. I hope they will not make the latter give battle to the French.

No. 2

Lugo, Galicia, Sept 1st; 1808.

Dear Lord Holland,—I arrived here with Stuart on the 29th ult., the day appointed for the assembly of the *Juntas* of Old Castile, Leon, Galicia, and the Asturias at this place. For reasons at present unknown, the Asturias have not kept their promise. Six deputies assembled from each of the other provinces, and amongst those of Leon, I found your friend Valdes. I gave him your letter, and I was much pleased with his manner of receiving it.

Stuart has this moment received an official document from the assembly of the deputies, announcing their immediate departure from Lugo, to join a general assembly of deputies from every *Junta* in Spain at Ocaña. They state that probably a royal *sitio* will afterwards be agreed upon as the place of meeting; and I conclude that they allude to Aranjuez, which you know is within two leagues of Ocaña. From what I can learn, there is a difficulty in assembling at Madrid, on account of the Council of Castile, which has lost the confidence of many of the Northern provinces by having continued in the capital while it was in possession of Bonaparte.

The assembly of Ocaña is to be composed of two members deputed from each *Junta*. Valdes is amongst those of Leon; and it is officially announced that the *Junta* of Valencia has deputed the Conde de Contamina and the Prince Pio; and that of Murcia, Florida Blanca, and the Viscount del Villar. Although the assembly at Lugo mention only the names of deputies from Valencia and Murcia besides those of their own body, yet the general tenor of their communication indicates that an assembly of deputies from every *Junta* in Spain, at some central place, is now *universally* agreed upon.

The people of the Asturias seem to be less capable of laying aside their provincial prejudices than any other Spaniards. The English Government has, I think, been too lavish of supplies to that province. It ought to be remembered that nothing passes those mountains that once finds its way into them, and that arms and ammunition which must have been intended for the service of Spain in general have been exclusively appropriated by the Asturias to themselves.

The settlement of the future government of this country is of course a topic of conversation, and a favourite scheme is the Regency of the Princess of the Brazils. The names universally mentioned to form part of a Council of Regency are those of Florida Blanca, the Duke de Infantado Jovellanos, and Saavedra.

I wish that I could confirm the report I sent you of General Cuesta being ready to rejoin Blake. I fear their quarrel is more violent than ever, and I shall not be surprised to bear that Cuesta fell a sacrifice to his obstinate refusal to restore the cavalry to Blake's army.

The evacuation of Aragon is confirmed, and there are no other military movements worth noticing. It is supposed that an attempt is about to be made to cut off the retreat of the French.

On my way to Lugo I staid two days at Santiago. The wealthy priests of that shrine were very civil to us. Stuart and his party were received with enthusiasm by the people and lodged and fed at the expense of the municipality.

It is my present intention to proceed with the deputies to Ocaña in the suite of my good friend Stuart, unless any particular circumstance should arise to render such a scheme impracticable.

General Broderick arrived here today on his way to Blake's army. Scarcely a vessel arrives from England without a military or a civil mission.

With best and kindest remembrances to Lady Holland, I am,

> Yr. much obliged and faithful Servt.,
>
> > > Chas. R. Vaughan.

As I have left Coruña I have no newspapers to send you, and as the *Junta* has left it they have lost some sources of intelligence.

Madrid, Sept. 17th, 1808.

Dear Lady H.,—Your note, dated Hinckley, overtook me at Valladolid. I thank you for your letter to Mrs. Hunter, and I have no doubt but that I shall profit by it before I leave Spain. Your commissions shall be executed with all due dispatch.

My last letter to Lord H. from Lugo, will have informed you of my intention of accompanying my friend Stuart to Madrid, on his way to the Central *Junta* now forming at Ocaña. Many deputies are already arrived there, but the place for their future deliberations is not finally agreed upon. Aranjuez or the Pardo near Madrid are talked of.

It is impossible to describe to you the manner in which the people in every town through which we have passed have expressed their opinion of the English. We have been feasted by the upper classes of society, and we have been literally hugged and carried in the arms of the mob. It is singular that in every class and in every district, the same anxious wish has been repeatedly expressed that the Royal family of England should give a wife to Ferdinand VII. The outrage of seizing their frigates is now considered as the miraculous interposition of Providence, which placed in the hands of the English a treasure which would certainly have fallen into the hands of the French, and which treasure is now given back to them by the English when the nation is most in need of it.

The revolution seems to have changed the Spanish character in many respects. They are incessant talkers. In every town thro' which you pass the people collect together anxiously enquiring the news, and the post no sooner arrives than the *Gazette* is read aloud to the multitude by some fellow mounted upon a chair. We have had no reason to complain of bad police on our journey, though as usual we have heard from time to time that in some distant district we must expect to meet with robbers. Agricultural and commerce wear as little appearance of war as you can well imagine.

At Segovia we passed through what may be called the left wing of the Spanish Army, advancing against the French stationed upon the Ebro. We found there General Cuesta and about 8 thousand infantry, principally battalions of newly raised peasantry. Eight hundred of his cavalry were at St. Ildefonso and, according to the officers, the horses were sadly out of condition. The whole of his cavalry is said to amount to 15 hundred.

Yesterday I saw a part of Reding's corps file off through Madrid for Soria, to join the centre of the Spanish Army. Twelve thousand men had arrived some days since in the environs of that place, and the forces of Castaños amounting to 30 thousand men continue daily to collect upon that point.

The right wing of this army will be composed of 18 thousand effective men under Palafox, who is already on his march upon the Ebro.

The French have a few hundred cavalry in Burgos and the rest of their force is in cantonments upon the Ebro, to facilitate the supplying them with provisions. It is understood that they have not a single magazine. Their most advanced post upon the Ebro is Milagro.

Blake is at Reinosa in the mountains of Montana, ready to fall upon the flank or rear of the French in co-operation with the corps advancing from the South.

These military movements I am sorry to say have been much impeded by the provincial *Juntas*. The *Junta* of Seville refused to advance any supplies to Castaños if he quitted Andalusia, but they were more peremptory with him about not quitting Madrid. Under these circumstances General Doyle drew for as many thousand dollars as would put him in motion, and since that the *Junta* have altered their conduct and have been very liberal. Galicia also does not like its army being carried so far from the frontier of their own province.

All these circumstances prove to you the necessity of immediately forming one central government. The deputies have been appointed from their respective *Juntas*, but their meeting does not appear to me to be so certain or so simple a business as one should at first suppose. I have before told you of the quarrel between Cuesta and Blake. The latter has been made Captain-General of Galicia, and the command of the army of that province has been given to him, and which army consists of the regular troops of the several garrisons of Ferrol, Coruña, &c., &c. Cuesta, who is Captain-General of Castile and Leon, had only an army of peasantry and a respectable body of cavalry, acting with the forces from Galicia, which were at first under the command of Filanghieri, who resigned and was afterwards murdered by his soldiers.

Upon this event happening, Cuesta as an old general expected to be appointed his successor, but to his great mortification Blake, an officer of very inferior rank, was appointed to the command of the forces of Galicia by the *Junta* at Coruña, and immediately after the battle of Rio Seco, Cuesta separated himself from him with the levies of Leon and Castile. From this moment there has been great difference of opinion between the provinces under the control of Cuesta and Galicia. As soon as we had passed the frontier of the latter kingdom we heard of nothing but Cuesta and his great merits, as far as this city, where he does not seem to be a favourite. He is, I understand, a man of great pride, harsh manners, cool and determined courage, and though considerably advanced in age, strong and active. His quarrel with Blake has just given rise to a circumstance which, if true, will impede for some time the meeting of the Central Government. It was yesterday reported on the authority of a letter from a cousin of Don Antonio Valdes (the friend of Ld. Holland) that Cuesta had arrested Valdes on his way to Ocaña at Tordesillas, and carried him to the tower of Segovia.

The Duke de Infantado and the best informed people of Madrid believe the report, inasmuch as Cuesta threatened so to do upon hearing that Valdes, as President of the *Junta* at Leon, had joined the assembly of deputies at Lugo in Galicia. Valdes was not far behind us on our way to this city; we passed him on the frontier of Galicia and at Segovia. Stuart had a long interview with Cuesta on the 14th when he talked with the utmost frankness and spared nobody, but said nothing of his intention of arresting Valdes. We shall soon have the confirmation of this news.

We have heard much complaint upon our road about the formation of *Juntas*; sometimes because the members were not natives of the province for which they were named. The assembly at Lugo also has given great offence in Leon, Castile, and even Madrid by a pompous kind of treaty that they made upon assembling together. For my part I see nothing offensive in it but the form. It was right that they should declare on what grounds they met, but a formal treaty as between three powers was an odd form for a Declaration.

I have had the pleasure of being in company with the Duke de Infantado and General Castaños. They both look worn with fatigue, and the latter is become so old in looks since I saw him at Algesiras in 1802 that I should not have known him again.

General Doyle is just returned from Saragossa and speaks of the defence of that place as being the most singular event that has happened. The Portuguese and French deserters and prisoners make the loss of the French amount to 8 thousand killed, and only 2 thousand wounded. Palafox is said to be very like Sir Sidney Smith in person and manner.

I have sent Ld. Holland a very curious and interesting pamphlet by Cevallos, and another, *The Justification of the Council of Castile*. I hope that they will arrive as soon as this letter. Admiral de Courcy at Coruña will forward them to Admiral Young at Plymouth, and thence they are to be forwarded according to their address. I send you two or three Madrid *Gazettes* also.

It is wished that the army of Romana should debark at Santona near Santander, where Blake can cover the landing.

Throughout Spain there is a singular anxiety about the arrival of a detachment of English cavalry to act with Blake or the other armies upon the Ebro. A mistake of the *Junta* of Coruña induced everyone to believe that such a detachment was on the way to Galicia, and it has been a hard work wherever we have been to explain away this mistake. Certainly applications for cavalry have been made to the British Govert. I believe first through Sir T. Dyer. Perhaps the time that has elapsed would not justify any complaints against the British Government for delay, if they have the intention of sending it.

I do not know how far it might be advisable to meet the wishes of the Spaniards on this subject, or what difficulties we may have to encounter in finding an English general to act under a Spanish one. But this I know, that the Spaniards are in great want of cavalry and that their operations must be confined owing to that circumstance. It is said that they have a large body of horse in Estremadura, but that General Galluzzo will not move from before Elvas till he has had the honour of its surrendering to him. Elvas must fall to the first British officer who can secure the safety of the French.

Believe me to be with the highest respect and esteem.

Your much obliged and obedient Servt,

C. R. V.

We are lodged at Madrid in the House of the *Inquisitor General*. The brutality and dirty pilfering of the French in every place thro' which we passed is astonishing. Particularly Valladolid and Rio Seco.

No. 3

Aranjuez, Sept 28th; 1808.

Dear Lord H.,—Your letter of the 12th of September and one without a date, inclosing a letter to the Duke de Infantado, both reached me last night, by couriers from Gijon and Coruña. The arrival of the duke at this *sitio* upon business with the *Junta*, gave me an opportunity of putting your letter into his hands this day, and tomorrow I shall carry your letters to Count Florida Blanca and Jovellanos. I am much obliged to you for the kind manner in which you have chosen to recommend me to them. I have had several opportunities of being in company with the Duke de Infantado. You know how attractive his manners are, and the revolution has made him one of the most interesting characters in Madrid.

I hope to profit by your introduction and to become better known to him. He tells me that he has received your book and speaks of it, as every other Spaniard does who is acquainted with it, in terms that you would think it vile flattery in me to repeat. The Spanish also of your letters is highly thought of.

I despair of seeing much of the Count Florida Blanca and Jovellanos. The first has severe duties to fulfil for a man of his great age as the President of the Central *Junta*, at present scarcely formed, and the latter, I am told, is much broken by his long imprisonment and must devote also the greater part of his day to public business.

The *Junta* are assembled in the palace here, from 9 to 1 and from 7 to 9 in the evening. The *siesta* and visits occupy the few hours that they remain at home. But I shall have much to thank you for, if your letters should procure me only one interview with two such interesting characters.

The Central *Junta* met in due form, as I told you in my last, on the 25th inst. I enclose you a list of the members, with such observations upon them as I have been able to collect from conversation with different people. You will be surprised like myself not to find Saavedra amongst them. The truth is that the *Junta* of Seville was formed by the mob, who looked at their work and did not like it, until some one proposed to give respectability to the whole by placing at the head of it Saavedra. This provincial *Junta* is not abolished by the establishment of the Central one, at least at present, and the people who are accustomed to obey it acting under the name of Saavedra, would run riot if they found it abandoned to the *mauvais sujets* that they originally placed there. The absence of Saavedra is thus accounted for to me by natives of Seville.

I am afraid that the hasty formation of many of the provincial *Juntas* may be felt in the Central one. In some parts of Spain the *Juntas* were named by a Captain-General, in others selected in haste by a mob from the persons surrounding them, and in very few were the deputies the choice of the people. It is natural, therefore, that complaints should be heard against many persons sent to the Central *Junta*, sometimes for incapacity, sometimes want of character, and at others that they are not *natives* of the province that they represent. There has been likewise great liberality in admitting a larger proportion of members from one kingdom than another, which is not yet talked of as a grievance, though deputies have been sent back, as two from Cadiz and the same number from a *Junta* at Carthagena. I agree with you in your opinion that the popular assembly should be numerous, but I cannot find a Spaniard who does not think that the number of deputies in the Central *Junta* is already too large.

The members are as follows—those marked ★ were present on the 25th:—

SEVILLE.

El Señor administrador, el Arzobispo de Laodicea.★ He is appointed to officiate as Bishop at Seville by the Archbishop of Toledo and Seville. A good man, very timid and warmly attached to his patron. Perhaps I ought to add that the Archbishop of Toledo, &c., is a Bourbon, who was not acknowledged by the Court of Spain until the Prince of the Peace married his sister, when he was made an Archbishop, and subsequently a younger sister was proposed as a second wife for Ferdinand VII. The Princess of the Peace now goes by the name of Countess of Chinchon.

El Conde de Tilly,★ the other deputy, is a noted gambler, who was at the head of the populace at Seville, May 26th. A man of some wit, but very slender capacity. It is said that he cannot go to Madrid on account of a criminal process against him for stealing jewellery.

GRANADA.

Sr. Dn. Rodrigo Riquelme,★ a man of great talent and very likely to become a leader in the National *Junta*. A lawyer: bad heart, and suspected of dishonest intentions.

El Canonigo Luis Gineo Funes,★ an ecclesiastic who is not likely to take an active part in any business.

CORDOVA.

Marqués de la Puebla,★ a plain, good sort of man.
Dn. Juan de Diez Rabe.★

JAEN.

Dn. Sebastian Jocano.★
Dn. Francisco de Paula Castanedo.★

Estremadura.

El Intendente Dn. Martin Garay,★ a man of great talents, an high sense of honour, very likely to become a leader in the *Junta*, but deficient in discernment, and not unlikely to be misled by Riquelme.

El Tesorero Felix Ovalle,★ a man of excellent understanding, great acquired knowledge but ill-digested. Not likely to take an active part in public life. Subservient to his colleague Garay.

Asturias.

Sr. Dn. Gaspar Jovellanos.★ It would be impertinent to sketch his character, but it may be proper to add that the Spaniards believe that he will not develop his talents or take a lead, lest he should be suspected of being ambitious of holding altogether the reins of Government.

El Conde de Campo Sagrado.★

Leon.

El Señor Don Antonio Valdes. The Spaniards speak of his *esprit de corps*. Daniel, elected in his room by Cuesta, is not received.

El Visconde de Quintanilla.

Castilla La Vieja

El Sr. Dn. Lorenzo Bonifaz Quintano.★. I believe that he is the author of a sort of newspaper, and must not be mistaken for your friend.

Dn. Francisco Xavier Caro.

Valencia.

El Conde de Contamina.★

El Principe Pio. Two quiet members unless upon nobility. The latter is friendly to the Council of Castile.

Murcia

El Conde Florida Blanca.★

Marqués del Villar,★ good natural talents, without acquirements.

Catalonia.

Marqués de Villel.★

Baron de Sabazona,★ a good man, of considerable knowledge of books.

TOLEDO.

El vicario Dn, Pedro Ribero.★

El abogado Dn. José Manuel Garcia de la Torre,★ a lawyer of an intriguing disposition and mischievous temper.

ARAGON.

Dn. Francisco Palafox,★ brother of the general.

Sr. Dn. Lorenzo Calvo,★ said to be very clever and very cunning.

MALLORCA Y ISLAS BALEARES

Dn. Tomas de Veri,★ an officer in the militia of his island. A man of letters, timid, and unlikely that he will take an active part.

Marqués de Togoséz.★

GALICIA.

Conde de Gimonde, an honest patriot of plain understanding.

Sr. Avalle, who was a cipher in the *Junta* of Coruña.

Biscay, Navarre, and Madrid are wanting. Deputies are arrived at the army of Palafox from Navarre out of whom they are to be chosen, and the Count de Altamira is said to be one of those named for Madrid. I cannot account for other provinces wanting.

You will smile at the flippant manner in which I have attempted the characters of these worthy legislators. But it will serve to give you some idea of what is thought of them by the Spaniards. I do not speak of any of them from personal knowledge of them or acquaintance with them.

I understand that their first meetings were devoted to arranging the form of choosing a President, the duration of that office, &c., and dividing themselves into committees for the dispatch of business.

Florida Blanca, it is supposed, will continue President for two terms, and then that the President will be chosen by lot. Marqués del Villar is appointed to be their organ of communication with the British Envoy. They have been pressed upon the subject of military arrangements since the arrival of Ld. W. Bentinck, who is empowered to treat about the movements of our army and they talk of appointing immediately a Council of War.

The state of parties seems to be this. The Council of Castile and the people of Madrid talk of a Regency. The Central *Junta* declare that they shall exercise the power of the Sovereign and they have proposed to the Council of Castile an oath of allegiance, at which they begin to revolt. You know the constitutional powers of this Council:—that all edicts of the king, to have effect, must be promulgated by the Council of Castile; that they have the right to remonstrate with the Crown and to refuse to publish its edicts; and that in the absence of the Cortes they are the barrier between the power of the Crown and the people. You also know that these 30 councillors are appointed by the king and exist only during his pleasure, wherefore little practical good has been derived by the people from this constitutional check upon the Crown. Inasmuch as the acts of the Court have of late years been more than usually disgraceful, it was necessary that the Council of Castile should be composed of persons not likely to revolt at any proposal from the King's Minister. It is said, therefore, that the present members of that council are persons unworthy of their trust and creatures of the Prince of the Peace.

However little they may merit such harsh language, it is certain that the people of the provinces detest them, for having issued the edicts of the King Father on his resumption of his crown at Bayonne and of the Bonapartes, with the same tame submission as those of Ferdinand. The host of writers, and others employed by them at Madrid, give them there a strong party in their favour, and those noblemen whose views are inclined to the Regency think well of them. The *Junta*, however, are alive to the feelings of the people, and they have assembled at a distance from the Council of Castile; but I apprehend that they will issue their edicts thro' this constitutional organ, though the people consider it as impure. If so, we must expect a good deal of discussion. The edict of the *Junta* will not pass without observation, and the people exercising the power of the Crown would not surely destroy the only check upon that power which is to be restored to their king by removing counsellors who give them advice.

Had the Duke de Infantado been a man of talent and ambition he must have been at the head of the government. A council of Regency has been a favourite idea amongst the people, but it never will be so with the *Junta*. The duke, should such a council be formed, must be a leading character in it. He is popular; he has been the friend and fellow-sufferer with Ferdinand, has been once named by him Regent. I allude to the period when the King Charles IV disinherited Ferdinand, and the latter appointed the Duke Regent, in the event of his being prevented ascending the throne on the death of his father. It was the commission to the duke that was the cause of the arrest at the Escorial. I cannot help thinking that the Council of Castile have the ear of the D. de I., and that they wish to put him forward. But on his part we hear of nothing but joining the armies.

The Central *Junta* are sometimes, I observe, spoken of with contempt; and I know not whether to attribute it to the bad characters of some members, or to a jealousy of the growing influence of the people. It is something represented as ridiculous the people exercising the power of the Crown, and the slowness of their proceedings is complained of. I do not think that the nobility of this country have much claim upon the people. They were slow to take up arms and they would have formed the *levée* of Bonaparte, as they had formed that of the Prince of the Peace, had not the just indignation and noble efforts of the most virtuous people in the world driven them to defend their country.

But however it is yet too early to speak of the characters of the several orders in this country. The enemy is still at their gate, and I am sorry to say that much time has been lost in appointing a chief of their armies. It would be well if they could do without one. But such men as Cuesta should be controlled.

Since my last, Blake seems to have made a good movement. He advanced from Reinosa to Frias, and the French outposts were in consequence of it obliged to fall back upon Pancorvo. In the meantime Blake pushed a division of 5000 men to Bilbao, and the French garrison of that place consisting of 12 hundred men escaped only by 3 hours. The Spaniards put to death 70 Frenchmen they found there, and were in pursuit and likely to cut off the retreat of the twelve hundred. This movement of Blake's has put in motion the Asturias, who have received about half a million sterling from England without one soldier passing their mountains. In the Montaña 4000 men have got arms, and about double that number in Biscay.

Blake at present has his left at Ona, centre at Frias, and the right extends to Orduña. His headquarters are at Trapaderno and he has not the least apprehension of the French daring to attack his position. He cannot descend into the plains of Alava for want of cavalry.

Sept 29th, 1808.

I have just heard that the Central *Junta* have resolved to appoint Don Juan Ruiz de Apodaca, who is already in London, their minister at the British Court and to recall immediately all other deputies.

It is said that the cavalry of Estremadura and a regiment from Granada are ordered by forced marches to join the army assembling in front of the French. I rather suspect that everything is arranged for our army joining the Spanish forces upon the frontier.

No. 4

Aranjuez, Oct. 24th, 1808.

Dear Lord H.,—The *Junta* are still at Aranjuez, and their adjourning to Madrid is postponed to some distant day. They named the Ministers of State last night. They are as follows: *Cevallos*, Foreign Affairs; *Hermida*, Home Department or *Secretario de la Gracia y Justicia*; *Cornel*, War Department; *Escaño*, Minister of Marine; *Saavedra*, the Department of the *Hacienda* or Finance. The deputy *Garay* is named Secretary of the *Junta*, permanently.

I hear that the deputies have resolved that Florida Blanca is to remain their President with a salary of 25 thousand dollars per ann.; that he is to reside at Madrid in the palace; to have the title of Highness, and to be escorted by guards when he appears in public. They have voted the inviolability of their persons and they are to wear the costume of Counsellors of State, with the addition of a rich crimson velvet mantle on gala days; moreover, every deputy is to have an annual salary of 5 thousand dollars.

Today, the birthday of Ferdinand VII, the *Junta*, after chapel, held a Court in the palace. I am just returned from making my bow to them. The President surrounded by the deputies received a few people who are at the *sitio*, and the ceremony was merely advancing, making a bow, and immediately retiring. I accompanied Stuart, who is the only Minister who has taken any notice of them. The *chargés d'affaires* of Austria and America, and the Russian Ambassador, Count Strogonoff, are the only ones remaining at Madrid of the Diplomatic corps.

I hear that orders have arrived at Lisbon for 20,000 of our troops to advance immediately into Spain, and that they are to be joined by 10,000 under Baird expected at Coruña. The Marquis de Romana has experienced bad weather off the coast of Spain, and I do not hear that he is yet arrived. I saw his brother this morning, who left him at Gottenburg.

My next letter will be dated from Palafox's headquarters. I leave Aranjuez tonight, and set out tomorrow evening with Colonel Doyle and Mr. Cavendish for Saragossa. Thence I mean to advance with Palafox towards the French and return shortly to Madrid by way of the centre of the Spanish Army. All that I know of their positions at present is that they are advancing. Since the alarm of the French reinforcements, the utmost activity has prevailed in drawing together troops from all quarters. By the way, the French have not received their reinforcements, but by an intercepted letter they are promised them by the 20th Nov.

The *Junta* will lose no time in appointing Ambassadors to the Courts of Vienna and Petersburg. The Council of Castile is very submissive, and the *Junta* is popular at Madrid.

I cannot thank you too often for your letter to Jovellanos. He is one of the most modest men in his manners, and of the most amiable disposition I have yet seen. It is impossible to see anything of Florida Blanca, and indeed it is very seldom that I have an opportunity of speaking to Jovellanos. He has never seen your book.

Count Tilly gave us a dinner the other day. I presume that it was in celebration of his person being declared inviolable. All the deputies are now arrived. Cuesta and Valdes are before the *Junta*.

The quarrel with Cuesta is the only unpleasant circumstance that has yet occurred. Otherwise the most perfect harmony and unison now prevails in all classes of the Govert. and of the people.

Remember me kindly to Lady H. and Mr. A. I do not send you the *Semanario*, as Stuart informs me that he received a packet for you from Quintana of them, and forwarded it, as well as a pamphlet by Capmany, *dedicated to you*. The *Semanario* is very much sought after.

P.S.—The Bishop of Orense is appointed Inquisitor General. You will observe that not one of the ministers has been taken from the *Junta*.

Since writing the above I learn that Romana's forces have landed at Santander. The French have abandoned the line of the Ebro and their force is divided between Bilbao and the posts of Olite, Estella, and Pampeluna.

No. 5

Saragossa, Nov. 8th, 1808.

I have just heard of your embarking on board the *Amazon* frigate for Spain, and I expect that this letter will find you at Coruña. I regret that I did not read your intention of setting out immediately in your enquiries about roads. I ought to have told you of the great difficulty of procuring money for bills upon England; Coruña is a better place for discounting bills than Madrid, and I would recommend you to negotiate your business with M. Barrié, a most respectable merchant, who has been unfortunately persecuted on account of his French origin. He has correspondents in all parts of the world, and may be very useful to you. There cannot be a worse man of business at Coruña than the English Vice-Consul, Magniac. I hope that you have not any French servant in your suite, as he will certainly be discovered and occasion you great uneasiness. Coruña is a bad place to move from with carriages, as I remember that there was but one miserable *tiro* of mules in the place.

If Ferrol and the surrounding district has been swept of mules to carry the baggage of the English Army, you would do well to send in to Leon, the country of *margatos* (*sic*), and purchase *tiros*, which you would dispose of afterwards to advantage at Madrid. You need have no fear of the road over the Galician mountains; it is excellent. I cannot give you any information respecting inns, as I travelled post to Astorga, and thence to Madrid rapidly with relays of mules. Before you receive this letter you will know as much of Coruña as myself. The *Gallego noblesse* are not very well lodged, nor are their *tertulias* the most brilliant. If Mr. Allen is with you tell him that he will find a very good library in the *Consulado*.

I am just returned from the army of Aragon on the frontier of Navarre and the headquarters of the Central Army at Tudela. I accompanied Doyle and Palafox. In Exea 12 leagues from Saragossa and in Sadava 4 leagues beyond Exea, we found a division of 4960 effective men, of which number about 500 cavalry, under the command of General St. Marc, a native of Flanders with the vivacity of a Frenchman, and who has the reputation of being an excellent executive officer. The state of the division did him credit. His men well cloathed, particularly the Valencian regts., owing to the exertions of the *Junta* of Valencia. At Sos, 6 leagues from Sadava, and a very strong position in the mountains, we found a small detachment of infantry.

General O'Neil who commands the army of Aragon in the absence of Palafox had established headquarters at Sanguesa, 2 leagues from Sos. His division, according to the returns on the 1st of Nov., amounted to 9368 effective men, of whom about 200 cavalry armed with lances. The advanced posts of this division at Aybar and Lumbier. In Sanguesa were stationed the men most in need of cloathing, and I was sorry to see many soldiers of advanced guards turned out to their general almost naked. But enthusiasm and a spirit of obedience prevailed everywhere notwithstanding the most severe wants. The divisions of St. Marc and O'Neil have since been reinforced by 4000 Murcians infantry and 120 cavalry, well cloathed and organized. The position of these divisions ought by this time to be as follows: *O'Neil* at Sanguesa, Aybar, and Lumbier. *Gen. Villaba* at Sos, Caseda, and Gallifienso. *Gen. St. Marc* at Sadava.

It is the intention to move up to Exea 2000 infantry from Saragossa and 2000 new levies with 100 dragoons from Calatayud, leaving in Saragossa about 2000 men to do the garrison duty and guard 1500 French prisoners. Thus the whole effective force of what may be called the army of Aragon, which forms the right of the Spanish line, amounts to 24,548 men, of which number the cavalry are about 1500. It must be remembered that about 6000 men under the Marqués de Lazan, the brother of Palafox, marched from Aragon to the relief of Catalonia, soon after the siege of Saragossa. There will be no difficulty in adding 30,000 recruits to this army whenever musquets can be found for them. Eight thousand English musquets are daily expected here from Tortosa, which will immediately give as many soldiers to the army, and the people of this province are the best formed for soldiers that I have met with. The utmost effort is made here to cloath, to arm, and to organise a force.

In the midst of the siege the gunpowder failed and the inhabitants immediately set about making it. They have now established a manufactory of it in the city which produces from 10 to 12 *anobas* pr. day. The earth in the neighbourhood furnishes saltpetre; the sulphur is drawn from Teruel and other places, and the charcoal is made from the stalks of the hemp which grows to an immense size. Several hundred monks are daily employed in a large church making cartridges. Since the siege, extensive works have been constructed for the defence of the city, and they have established magazines for cloathing their armies, and I hope that very shortly they will have completed uniforms for the troops already in the field. The active spirit of the chief pervades every department and is well seconded by the people.

At Tudela, the headquarters of the Central Army, there are about 10,000 men under Gen. Castaños. On the left his line extends to Nalda where he has 2000; at Ansejo 1000; at Calahorra, 6000; at Alfaro and Corella 13,000. The whole force about 29,000 men, of whom abt. 4000 cavalry. The Estremadura army has been ordered to Burgos to support the right of Blake, who has had a severe engagement with the French, and been obliged to retire to Valmaseda, where his letter was dated on the 3rd of Novr. The French General Lasalle has moved towards Burgos to check the Estremadura forces. Six thousand of Castaños' division still remain at Madrid.

The army of Castaños is well cloathed, but want shoes; and tolerably well appointed. He mingles his levies with his regulars. It has been proved again and again that armed masses of peasantry cannot resist in the field a regular force such as the French. The Battles of Cabezon, Rio Seco, and all the engagements in Aragon before the siege of Saragossa are proofs of it. But behind walls and in towns peasantry are quite as formidable as regular troops.

The French have received during the month of October and the first week of November a reinforcement of 24,681 infantry of the line, 3500 cavalry, 3662 light infantry. I have seen the regular returns, and many of the regts. are Dutch and others of the Confederation of the Rhine. Bonaparte was at Bayonne with Savary on the 3rd of this month, with about a thousand infty. and a proportion of *gendarmes*.

The deputies from the Spanish *Junta* held a Council of War while we were at Tudela, and it was agreed to make a combined attack upon Caparrosa. The French in Navarre, to the amount of about 28,000 men, are at Pampeluna, and thence extend to Estella, Falces and Peralta, Tafalla, Olita, and Caparrosa. Delay has taken place again in the movements of Castaños, and suspicions gain ground with those who would be active that he is under the influence of two people upon his staff, who were formerly *aides-de-camp* of the Prince of the Peace and allowed each of the military departments under their control to go to ruin. Their names are Navarro and St. Pierre. It is impossible to know with what justice their patriotism is suspected, but at the headquarters at Tudela I heard much of their talents.

Nov. 9th.

I have just heard that the enemy are in movement in Navarre; and we expect an attack upon the central and right wing. The attacks of the enemy at Logroño on the 25th of Oct., and the same day at Lerin, on the 29th at Calahorra, and the 24th at Sanguesa, look to me very like what the military people call attacks of reconnaissance and having ascertained the position of the Spaniards and their force, I shall not be surprised at an irruption into Aragon, dividing Castaños from the Aragon Army and beating both in detail before the English arrive.

What would I not sacrifice, my dear Lord, for the satisfaction of seeing you the Ambassador in Spain. Your regard for the Spaniards is well known in this country. You are the only foreigner of distinction who has made himself acquainted with their literature, and I so often hear your name mentioned with pleasure where I least expect it that I cannot but feel grieved that you are not the organ of my own Govert. in this country. It would not be right to canvass the character of the person who is sent to Madrid, but I must observe, that I never heard one individual in Spain ever mention his name.

I have witnessed the conduct of Stuart from living in the house with him, and in my opinion it has been very judicious. He is very diligent, and there is a frankness in his manners which pleases the Spaniards and he does not, like my countrymen in general, shun their society. Hitherto there has been no lack of missionaries in Spain: major-generals and their staff with every army, not one of whom has ever known enough of the language to obtain the confidence of those with whom they have been placed. This does not apply to Doyle, who is really beloved by the Spaniards, and I do not believe that Palafox receives a private note without submitting it to his perusal.

Nov. 10th.

Buonaparte at Vitoria on the 5th. The French seem to meditate an attack upon Castaños. They appear to be collecting a force to pass the Ebro at Logroño and Lodosa. The army of this province are ordered to descend the Aragon River, destroying all the bridges, and to support the centre.

I shall probably in the course of the next month shake you by the hand at Coruña on my way to England. Kindest remembrances to Lady H. and Mr. A.

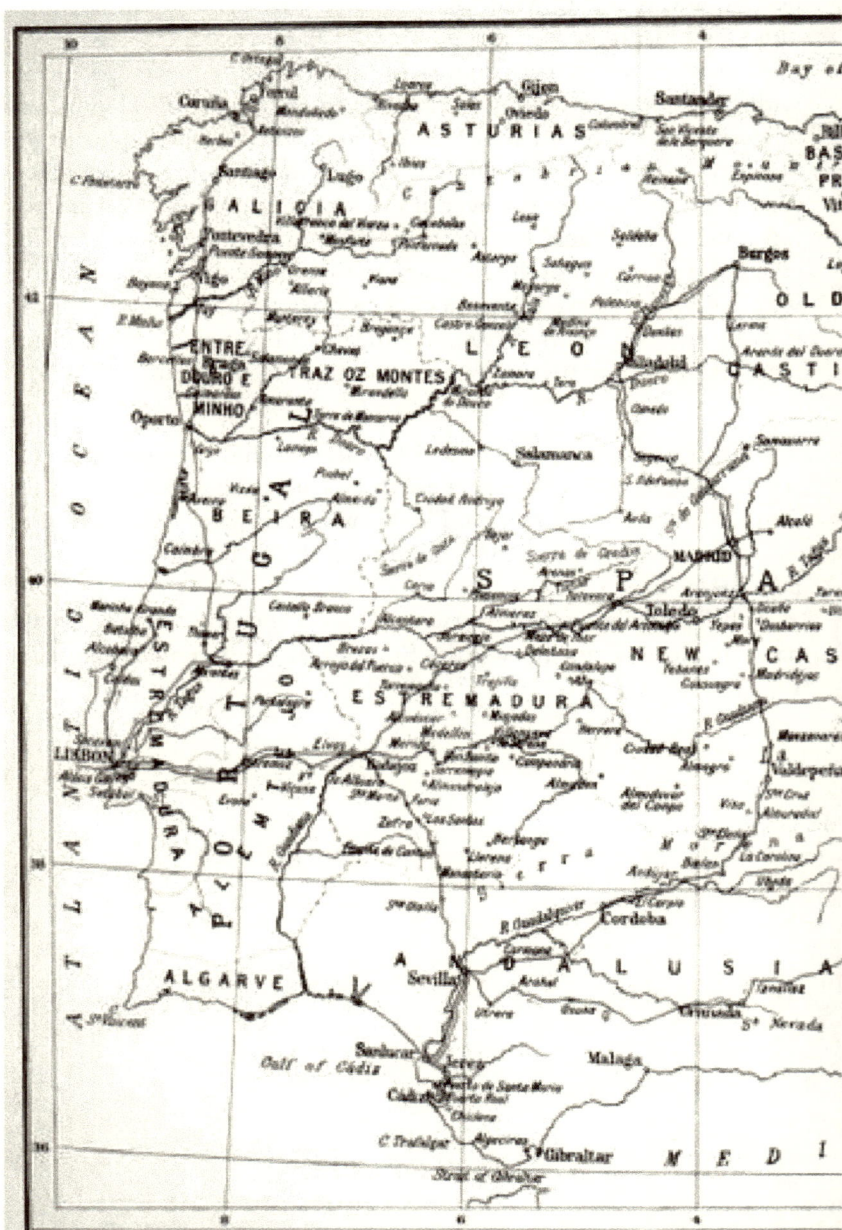

MAP OF

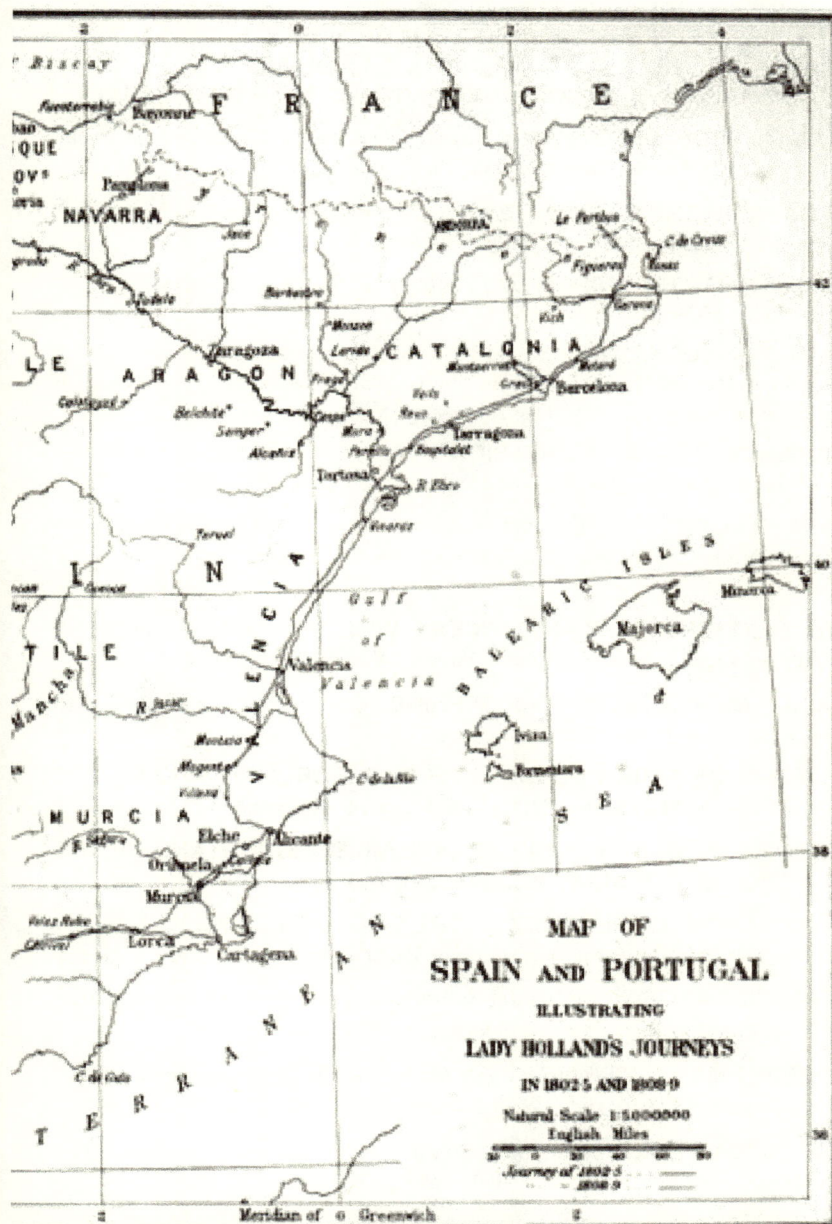

SPAIN AND PORTUGAL

ILLUSTRATING

LADY HOLLAND'S JOURNEYS

IN 1802-5 AND 1808-9

Natural Scale 1:5,000,000
English Miles

Journey of 1802-5
   "   1808-9

LEONAUR

ALSO FROM LEONAUR
AVAILABLE IN SOFTCOVER OR HARDCOVER WITH DUST JACKET

A DIARY FROM DIXIE *by Mary Boykin Chesnut*—A Lady's Account of the Confederacy During the American Civil War

FOLLOWING THE DRUM *by Teresa Griffin Vielé*—A U. S. Infantry Officer's Wife on the Texas frontier in the Early 1850's

FOLLOWING THE GUIDON *by Elizabeth B. Custer*—The Experiences of General Custer's Wife with the U. S. 7th Cavalry.

LADIES OF LUCKNOW *by G. Harris & Adelaide Case*—The Experiences of Two British Women During the Indian Mutiny 1857. A Lady's Diary of the Siege of Lucknow by G. Harris, Day by Day at Lucknow by Adelaide Case

MARIE-LOUISE AND THE INVASION OF 1814 *by Imbert de Saint-Amand*—The Empress and the Fall of the First Empire

SAPPER DOROTHY *by Dorothy Lawrence*—The only English Woman Soldier in the Royal Engineers 51st Division, 79th Tunnelling Co. during the First World War

ARMY LETTERS FROM AN OFFICER'S WIFE 1871-1888 *by Frances M. A. Roe*—Experiences On the Western Frontier With the United States Army

NAPOLEON'S LETTERS TO JOSEPHINE *by Henry Foljambe Hall*—Correspondence of War, Politics, Family and Love 1796-1814

MEMOIRS OF SARAH DUCHESS OF MARLBOROUGH, AND OF THE COURT OF QUEEN ANNE VOLUME 1 by A. T. Thomson

MEMOIRS OF SARAH DUCHESS OF MARLBOROUGH, AND OF THE COURT OF QUEEN ANNE VOLUME 2 by A. T. Thomson

MARY PORTER GAMEWELL AND THE SIEGE OF PEKING *by A. H. Tuttle*—An American Lady's Experiences of the Boxer Uprising, China 1900

VANISHING ARIZONA *by Martha Summerhayes*—A young wife of an officer of the U.S. 8th Infantry in Apacheria during the 1870's

THE RIFLEMAN'S WIFE *by Mrs. Fitz Maurice*—*The Experiences of an Officer's Wife and Chronicles of the Old 95th During the Napoleonic Wars*

THE OATMAN GIRLS *by Royal B. Stratton*—The Capture & Captivity of Two Young American Women in the 1850's by the Apache Indians